The voyage continues....

TREK
THE NEXT GENERATION

By James Van Hise

Books for the entertainment buyer

PIONEER

OTHER PIONEER BOOKS

•THE MAGICAL MICHAEL JACKSON
Edited by Hal Schuster. March, 1990. $9.95, ISBN#1-55698-235-6
•FISTS OF FURY: THE FILMS OF BRUCE LEE
Written by Edward Gross. March, 1990. $14.95, ISBN #1-55698-233-X
•WHO WAS THAT MASKED MAN?
Written by James Van Hise. March, 1990. $14.95, ISBN #1-55698-227-5
•PAUL MCCARTNEY: 20 YEARS ON HIS OWN
Written by Edward Gross. February, 1990. $9.95, ISBN #1-55698-263-1
•THE DARK SHADOWS TRIBUTE BOOK
Written by Edward Gross and James Van Hise. February, 1990. $14.95, ISBN#1-55698-234-8
•THE UNOFFICIAL TALE OF BEAUTY AND THE BEAST, 2nd Edition
Written by Edward Gross. $14.95, 164 pages, ISBN #1-55698-261-5
•TREK: THE LOST YEARS
Written by Edward Gross. $12.95, 128 pages, ISBN #1-55698-220-8
•THE TREK ENCYCLOPEDIA
Written by John Peel. $19.95, 368 pages, ISBN#1-55698-205-4
•HOW TO DRAW ART FOR COMIC BOOKS
Written by James Van Hise. $14.95, 160 pages, ISBN#1-55698-254-2
•THE TREK CREW BOOK
Written by James Van Hise. $9.95, 112 pages, ISBN#1-55698-256-9
•THE OFFICIAL PHANTOM SUNDAYS
Written by Lee Falk. $14.95, 128 pages, ISBN#1-55698-250-X
•BLONDIE & DAGWOOD: AMERICA'S FAVORITE FAMILY
Written by Dean Young. $6.95, 132 pages, ISBN#1-55698-222-4
•THE DOCTOR AND THE ENTERPRISE
Written by Jean Airey. $9.95, 136 pages, ISBN#1-55698-218-6
•THE MAKING OF THE NEXT GENERATION
Written by Edward Gross. $14.95, 128 pages, ISBN#1-55698-219-4
•THE MANDRAKE SUNDAYS
Written by Lee Falk. $12.95, 104 pages, ISBN#1-55698-216-X
•BATMANIA
Written by James Van Hise. $14.95, 176 pages, ISBN#1-55698-252-6
•GUNSMOKE
Written by John Peel. $14.95, 204 pages, ISBN#1-55698-221-6
•ELVIS-THE MOVIES: THE MAGIC LIVES ON
Written by Hal Schuster. $14.95, ISBN#1-55698-223-2
•STILL ODD AFTER ALL THESE YEARS: ODD COUPLE COMPANION.
Written by Edward Gross. $12.95, 132 pages, ISBN#1-55698-224-0
•SECRET FILE: THE UNOFFICIAL MAKING OF A WISEGUY
Written by Edward Gross. $14.95, 164 pages, ISBN#1-55698-261-5

Library of Congress Cataloging-in-Publication Data
James Van Hise, 1949—
       Trek: The Next Generation

       1.   Trek: The Next Generation (television)
I. Title

Published by Pioneer Books, Inc., 5715 N. Balsam Rd., Las Vegas, NV, 89130.

Fourth Printing, 1992

GENE RODDENBERRY (1921—1991)

It came as a surprise to many when Gene Roddenberry died of a heart attack on October 24, 1991. While the news that he had suffered a series of strokes during the year had leaked out, the full extent of his illness had not.

There had been rumors, though, when a gala 25th anniversary celebration for STAR TREK at Paramount was scaled down in September when he was too ill to attend. But a couple of actors from the original series have long been rumored to be in frail health, but no one ever thought Roddenberry would be the first to depart.

While some fear that with Roddenberry's passing the light of STAR TREK will die, it has been known for some time that he was all but retired, having stepped down from his on-line duties on THE NEXT GENERATION more and more as each year passed until for the last two he has been little more than a consultant. His involvement with the motion pictures has been minimal since the first one, the only one he worked full time on.

STAR TREK was a synthesis of many talents. While it was created by Roddenberry over 25 years ago, it was developed by such people as Gene Coon, Dorothy Fontana and others whose contributions added much to the legend. While Roddenberry had the original vision and steered the ship on a true course, he was not the only one to dream the dream as his biggest gift was to inspire others to join his creation. The many forms of STAR TREK over the years serves as living testimonial.

When people die they face the danger of being elevated to a role they never had in life or ever aspired to. So one should not suddenly elevate Roddenberry to godhood after he no longer walks among us. Gene was a man with the foibles of a man but he should never be forgotten for his many abilities and most of all for his dream, a dream he shared with so many of us. This dream will insure that Gene Roddenberry will never be forgotten.

    —James Van Hise,
    November 11, 1991

Designed and Edited by Hal Schuster
with assistance from David Lessnick

JAMES VAN HISE writes about film, television and comic book history. He has written numerous books on these subjects, including BATMANIA, HORROR IN THE 80S, THE TREK CREW BOOK, STEPHEN KING & CLIVE BARKER: THE ILLUSTRATED GUIDE TO THE MASTERS OF THE MACABRE and HOW TO DRAW ART FOR COMIC BOOKS: LESSONS FROM THE MASTERS. He is the publisher of MIDNIGHT GRAFFITI, in which he has run previously unpublished stories by Stephen King and Harlan Ellison. Van Hise resides in San Diego along with his wife, horses and various other animals.

A NEW GENERATION

In the Fall of 1987 when *Star Trek: The Next Generation* premiered, it was greeted with a mixture of applause and skepticism. Even William Shatner criticized the notion of a new *Star Trek* television series for fear the public would be so saturated with Star Trek that the feature film business would drop off. Perhaps this was one of the reasons that *Star Trek V* did not perform up to expectations, although I think that would be a simplistic estimation of a more complicated set of circumstances. In fact, *The Next Generation* has actually brought new fans to *Star Trek* who had not previously followed the series in any form. With the end of the fourth season, *The Next Generation* has actually outlasted the original *Star Trek* series by a full season and has passed its 100th episode, a milestone for *any* television series. And while *The Next Generation* had its expected birth pangs, its weak first season has given way to three much stronger seasons, producing scripts more complicated and challenging than most of those written for the original Star *Trek* . Clearly the styles of these two series have proven themselves to be much more different. Picard is not just Capt. Kirk with another name, nor is Riker. The stories deal with suspense and mystery as well as imagination on levels seldom attempted in Trek Classics. Much of this has to do with the fact that television was very different in the sixties, and the old *Star Trek* had more network interference to contend with than The *Next Generation* does. On the other hand, the dramatic conflicts on *The Next Generation* all involve guest stars and *never* take place among the main characters. While it was not unusual to see Kirk and McCoy or McCoy and Spock to have personality conflicts, this just never happens on *The Next Generation*.

If mankind had not overcome its basic hostilities up to the time of the original *Star Trek,* the next 75 years (which is the acknowledged time span between Trek Classic and *The Next Generation*), would surely not have found the magic genetic solution. This remains the one continuing failing of *The Next Generation,* and thereby blunts its drama by shifting it to supporting characters and guest stars. While we've been shown that Picard and Riker have a temper, it has never been directed at any of the people they most come into contact with. The only regular to display a more realistic temperament is Worf, an alien, who acts more human than any of his shipmates under any given situation.

As the series enters its fifth season, hopefully it will not just cover the same ground already well explored in its first one hundred episodes but journey into new and exciting territories.

—James Van Hise, 1991

TREK: THE NEXT GENERATION

THE ENTERPRISE NCC 1701-D

The Enterprise NCC 1701-D is the fifth starship to bear that name. This new vessel is twice the length of the ship that Captain Kirk was familiar with 78 years before and has nearly eight times the interior area to house the crew. The basic structure is the same even though the vessel looks more sleek and cohesive.

While the first starships to bear the name Enterprise were designed to represent the Federation in matters both political and military, the 1701-D is designed for exploration, de-emphasizing the importance of being a battle cruiser. This Enterprise has been designed to be the home of 1,012 people, which is two and a half times the ship's complement of the Enterprise 1701-A. This is the result of a century of technological evolution emphasizing human interaction with the hardware they use. This technological progress as been dubbed "Technology Unchained". What this means is that technical improvement has gone beyond developing things which are merely smaller, faster or more powerful but has become centered on improving the quality of life of the people the hardware was designed for.

The reason this is of particular importance aboard the new Enterprise is that the crew consists of many families. Thus, service in Starfleet no longer means that families are separated for many long months but can stay together on this, the first starfleet vessel of this class. As the first captain on this bold new experiment in human exploration, Picard is uncomfortable with the idea of dealing with families. He's accustomed to a crew of professional, Starfleet-trained men and women who know their duty and understand their jobs thoroughly. The concept of children and other non-Starfleet personnel running around unnerves him even though he understands that it contributes to the morale of those hardy men and women who will be called on to labor aboard this starship for many long months. Non-crew spouses and children are rarely seen in the command and duty areas of the ship. In "The Last Outpost" Riker enters the lounge behind the bridge and encounters three young children whom he escorts out, kindly reminding them that they are not to be in that area.

The sophistication of the new Enterprise includes a variety of single and group family modules, various levels of schools, study facilities and other features designed so that children and spouses can live lives as normal as possible aboard what is practically a colony ship. recreation has always been a facet not neglected on starships but now this role has been expanded with the presence of children. There is a large selection of entertainment, sports and other recreational forms, but the most elaborate by far is the holodeck. The Holodeck, as seen in "Encounter At Farpoint," can simulate almost any landscape or sea world complete with winds, tides, rain or whatever is needed to make the illusion convincing to the tactile senses. They achieve an amazing sense of reality and are employed in both education and recreation, as studies of other worlds can be richly enhanced by a holographic simulation of the society or climate in question. The special reality of the holodeck helps prevent the crew from feeling a sense of confinement from their prolonged voyage on board the starship. The holodeck can also be used for purposes of exercise as an opponent can be conjured up who is capable of responding to various modes of self-defense, as shown in the episode "Code of Honor."

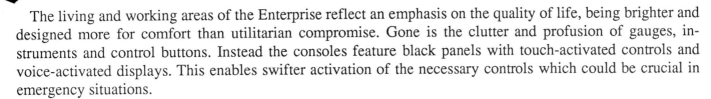

The living and working areas of the Enterprise reflect an emphasis on the quality of life, being brighter and designed more for comfort than utilitarian compromise. Gone is the clutter and profusion of gauges, instruments and control buttons. Instead the consoles feature black panels with touch-activated controls and voice-activated displays. This enables swifter activation of the necessary controls which could be crucial in emergency situations.

There is nowhere on the Enterprise where this is more crucial than on the bridge. The new bridge is much larger, reflecting the increase in the volume of the vessel and thus allowing for more functions to be more efficiently accomplished there. The new bridge combines the features of ship control, briefing room, information retrieval area and officers' ward room. Much the same kinds of things happen here as on the old bridge but with less emphasis on the mechanics of steering the starship. It is a place where the starship officers can meet, check information, make plans or just catch up on what has been happening.

The control of the starship is handled by two bridge duty officers assigned to the tasks designated *command* and *control*. These are designated as CON (command and vessel control, including helm and navigation) and OPS (vessel operations, including some duties formerly performed in Engineering.)

The center of the bridge consists of the Command Area, which is the focal point of all bridge activities. The Captain, his Number One and close advisors are located here. Just in front of this area are the two previously designated OPS and CON. Geordi La Forge and Data are in charge of these duty stations when on duty and when not assigned to an Away Team. Their backups, who assume these duties when either Data or La Forge are unavailable, are simply referred to by the designations of their duties: OPS and CON.

At the rear of the bridge is a raised semi-circular area which is separated from the Command Area by a railing, behind which is another set of console stations. This is the Tactical Control and those on duty here are responsible for the functions of the weaponry, defensive devices (such as the shields) as well as the internal security of the Enterprise.

On the rear wall of the bridge are the Aft Consoles. These five stations are generally unsupervised functions unless specifically needed at any given time. Viewing them from left to right, they are as follows:

Emergency Manual Override: In the event of main computer failure, many of the ship's primary functions can be operated from this station.

Environment: This can adjust the Life Support systems and related environmental engineering functions anywhere on the ship. A similar system was employed against the bridge crew in Kirk's time in "Space Seed" as well as against Khan's cronies during the same encounter. No doubt this is to prevent the vessel from being used as a weapon against it inhabitants.

Propulsion Systems: This is a backup system to OPS and CON which ties in directly to Engineering and the control of the warp drive and impulse engines.

Sciences: This is essentially a research station generally unmanned except for research purposes. It is used by the Science Officer and various mission specialists and can also be accessed by the Chief Medical Officer.

Sciences II: This is a second console identical to the Science station next to it so that more than one researcher at a time can access information and interact.

The stage-left side of the bridge has two turbo-lifts and next to these is another door, but that one leads to the Captain's Office (also called the Captain's Ready Room). This has an auxiliary turbolift as well as the Captain's private head and washroom. This Ready Room can serve both as the Captain's office, as it is often so designated, as well as a room where he can have private conversations out of earshot of other bridge personnel.

On the right side of the bridge is a door leading to the bridge head and washroom, something they didn't seem to have on the original starship. A running joke at the time of Captain Kirk was that the Klingon's didn't have a head anywhere on their ships, which is what made them so mean.

Continuing the overview of the bridge, the forward section contains a huge wall-sized holographic viewscreen. This viewer is almost always activated and dominates the bridge, giving the impression of a window into space even though it is only reproducing what the Enterprise's viewing sensors are seeing. The viewscreen has magnifying capabilities and in some cases can lock into equipment on another vessel and send back an image of the other vessel's bridge.

Behind the bridge, but not immediately visible from inside the bridge proper, is a room filled with comfortable furnishings and lined with actual windows facing to the rear of the vessel. This affords an awesome view of the aft portion of the Enterprise saucer section as well as of the nacelles of the starship. This lounge is completely equipped as an observation deck and contains food units and often serves as a retreat from the pressures of duty by bridge officers. Access to it is a privilege.

The Transporter Room is more colorful than the plain battleship grey of the old Enterprise. Although people to be beamed out usually go to stand on the transporter pad, site-to-site transportation is also possible, and people can be beamed directly to the bridge or elsewhere in the ship. Communicators, now a part of the gold plated chest insignia, can be locked in on by the transporter when needed. The transporter beam has a range of 16,000 kilometers (roughly 10,000 miles). The Transporter is also designed to filter out viruses, bacteria and other alien matter which might be picked up on the surface of a planet. It can also be used to detect and, if necessary, deactivate weapons.

A special feature of the new Enterprise is the ability of the saucer section of the vessel to separate from the main hull in emergency situations. The only drawback to this escape procedure is that the warp engines are located in the main hull while the saucer section contains only Impulse Power from an engine located at the rear of the saucer. Earlier versions of the Enterprise also contained this feature but it was never employed in any of the stories chronicled before "Encounter At Farpoint."

There are also shuttlecraft aboard the Enterprise which are used when the transporter is malfunctioning or should the starship become disabled and evacuation in deep space become a necessity. One must assume that there are enough shuttlecraft the hold all aboard the Enterprise, lest the tragedy of the legendary Titanic be repeated.

This new Enterprise 1701-D is the most amazing yet in a proud heritage of ships bearing that title.

CAPTAIN JEAN-LUC PICARD

At the time of the voyages chronicled in *Star Trek: The Next Generation,* Captain Picard has already become legendary in Starfleet, as legendary as the name Enterprise, which his new vessel has been christened.

Picard has recently completed a 22 year mission as captain of the deep space charting starship Stargazer. With only 11% of the known galaxy charted, the Stargazer contributed important information to these chronicles. Tragedy was no stranger during those two decades of exploration, as it was near the end of the mission that Jack Crusher was killed saving the life of Picard. Jean-Luc accompanied the body when it was returned to the family, thereby meeting Jack's wife, Dr. Beverly Crusher, and the very young Wesley Crusher. Beverly requested posting with Picard on the Enterprise, even though she subliminally blamed him for her husband's death, but has since learned to trust and admire him. (The true depth of her feelings for the Captain have been hinted at but never fully revealed.) Picard feels some guilt himself, and in the episode "Justice" found himself having to weigh the Prime Directive against the life of Wesley Crusher when the boy violated the inflexible laws of a planet. Picard would have been troubled with any crew member thus endangered, but the dilemma took on added weight when the person in question was the son of the man who saved his life. The inherent unfairness of the situation led Picard to confront the entities responsible, thus saving Wesley, whose progress since then has been watched by Picard with growing pride.

Picard was born on Earth, in Paris, France. In the 24th Century, ethnic accents are uncommon due to advanced forms of language instruction, and Picard betrays his Gallic background only in times of deep emotional stress. He uses French on rare occasions, as when he bid farewell to Dr. McCoy in "Encounter At Farpoint", or when he visited his ancestral home in "Family."

The young Picard was a far cry from the disciplined commander of the Enterprise, losing his original heart when stabbed from behind in an ill-advised brawl, a secret he revealed to Wesley in "Samaritan Snare." Still, his career has been an exemplary one; a young and awestruck Lieutenant Picard was in attendance at the wedding of the legendary Spock, an incident referred to in "Sarek" and which, according to rumor, may be the final scene in *Star Trek VI.*

Captain Picard can be very tough and pragmatic but he is also a 'romantic' who believes sincerely in honor and duty. He also has very human traits such as being uncomfortable around children. After being on a 22 year long mission in which he rarely had contact with human children, the concept of commanding a vessel which carries entire families does not sit easily with him. His initial reaction to Wesley Crusher was, of course, one of extreme annoyance.

Picard is also a philosophical man with a keen interest in history and archaeology. He still accesses information in the old-fashioned way, from books, and is especially fond of Shakespeare and 1940s hard-boiled detective fiction. The past, to him, is as vast a storehouse of knowledge as the future, and must not be

disregarded or forgotten. His gift to Data, the complete plays of Shakespeare, is a fitting guide to the various aspects of humanity, and is much cherished by the android officer.

Although baldness had been cured generations before the 24th century, the men of this time find the natural look appealing, and Picard is content to remain so. He is not vain, and has no interest in cosmetic surgery or other artificial enhancements of his external appearance. On the other hand, he was very secretive when he had to have a new cardiac implant ("Samaritan Snare"), fearing, although incorrectly, that the knowledge would lessen his crew's respect of his leadership. With the advance medicine and extended life spans of his time, Picard in his fifties is just entering his prime and would be comparable to a man of 30 in the 20th century. Active duty Starfleet males and females are in prime physical condition through their seventies.

While still relatively young by 24th century standards, Picard remains content with a 'starship love,' a personality attribute accented by his 22 year duty on the Stargazer. But on the Enterprise 1701-D, with its ship's complement of over a thousand crewpersons and family members, Picard is facing new challenges to his skills, experience and intellect, learning along the way that life is more complex than he ever imagined.

PATRICK STEWART

Patrick Stewart reveals that he was "compelled" to become an actor, "as a result of an argument."

At age 15, Stewart left school and landed a job on a local newspaper. He also happened to be an energetic amateur actor, which wasn't unusual since the English town of Mirfield (population 11,000) supported a dozen dramatic clubs. but he two vocations didn't mix.

"I was always faced with either covering an assignment or attending an important rehearsal or performance," he explains. "I used to get my colleagues to cover for me, but often I would just make up reports. Finally, of course, I was found out. I had a terrific row with the editor who said, 'Either you decide to be a journalist, in which case you give up all of this acting nonsense, or you get off my paper.' I left his office, packed up my typewriter and walk out."

There followed two years of selling furniture. "I was better at selling furniture than I was at journalism," Stewart observes good natured. He also enrolled in drama school at the Bristol Old Vic to bring his skills up to the level of his enthusiasm.

The actor used to see his roles as a way of exploring other personalities and characteristics, but nowadays it has become more of a means of self-expression.

"When I was younger, I used to think in terms of how I could disguise myself in roles. Now I want my work to say something about me, contain more of my experience of the world.'

Patrick Stewart has become a highly regarded actor in Great Britain from his roles in such BBC productions as "I, Claudius," "Smiley's People," and "Tinker, Tailor, Soldier, Spy," all of which have aired in America, thus making

his work familiar to American audiences as well. His face is also known to American filmgoers from roles in a variety of motion pictures. In the David Lynch adaptation of *Dune*, he played Gurney Halek, one of the more prominent roles in the film. In *Excalibur*, he played Leondegrance, while more recently he was seen in the strange science fiction film *Lifeforce* as the character Dr. Armstrong. On stage, he starred in London is a production of "Who's Afraid of Virginia Woolf?" which garnered him the prestigious London Fringe Best Actor Award. As an associate artist of the Royal Shakespeare Company, Stewart is considered one of the leading talents of the British stage. His impressive list of stage credits include Shylock, Henry IV, Leontes, King John, Titus Andronicus and many others. In 1986, he played the title role in Peter Shaffer's play "Yonadab" at the National Theatre of Great Britain.

After Supervising Producer Robert Justman saw Stewart on stage at UCLA, the actor was cast as Captain Picard. "A friend of mine, an English professor, was lecturing and I was part of the stage presentation," he recalls. A few days later he was called to audition for *Star Trek: The Next Generation*. Since then, he has become a well-known face, although occasionally fans get confused. One woman accosted him at a party and racked her brains until she recognized him. "You fly the Endeavor," she told him triumphantly, when her memory finally clicked, "and you play William Shatner!"

COMMANDER WILLIAM RIKER

Not since the first starship Enterprise 1701 was under the command of Captain Christopher Pike has the executive officer been called "Number One." William Riker has been given this honor by his commander, Captain Picard, to whom he is responsible for vastly important duties. When a landing team, or "Away Team", is assembled, Riker is generally in charge of the team. Although it is not strictly prohibited for the starship Captain to head up the team, Riker correctly recognizes that too much depends on the Captain remaining safe to guide and protect his vessel. Sending the most experience officer down into an unknown situation is deemed too dangerous by Number One until he checks out the status of the planet and its culture for himself. Picard isn't entirely happy being forced to remain behind after so many years of taking charge of everything himself, but he understands and respects his executive officer's viewpoint. If he didn't respect Riker's talents, Picard wouldn't have approved him as Number One.

Riker is also in charge of overseeing the condition of the vessel and the crew. When a Federation propulsion expert came aboard in "Where No One Has Gone Before," Riker would not allow him to run tests on the system until they had been fully outlined to him and approved by the ship's chief engineer.

"Number One" is an expression whose meaning has not appreciably altered since Earth's seventeenth century when the second-in-command of a sailing ship was generally known as a "First Lieutenant" (hence "Number One" is used in the sense of "First"). The term also implies executive officer and captain-in-training.

In those bygone days, the executive officer was also generally in command of shore parties for the same reason Riker takes such tasks upon himself now—the life of a ship's captain is not considered to be expendable. But even though Number One is in charge of the Away Team on the ground, Captain Picard retains final authority over their actions.

William Riker joined the Enterprise crew when it picked him up at the Farpoint Station, which is where he also met some other crew members for the first time, including Beverly and Wesley Crusher, and Geordi La Forge.

Riker regards his Captain with a mixture of awe and affection, but is also privy to Picard's self-doubts, such as the commander's annoyance at having to deal with children and families in a starship setting. As time passes, Riker has seen the Captain adjust to this new situation.

While Riker has a lively interest in women, he considers it a point of honor never to let it come between himself and his duty. He is intellectually committed to sexual equality and tries to live up to that. this was put to the test in "Justice" in which the people in Edo proved to be extremely affectionate and greeted the opposite sex with deep hugs and kisses instead of a bow or a handshake. The whole truth is that, at thirty, Riker

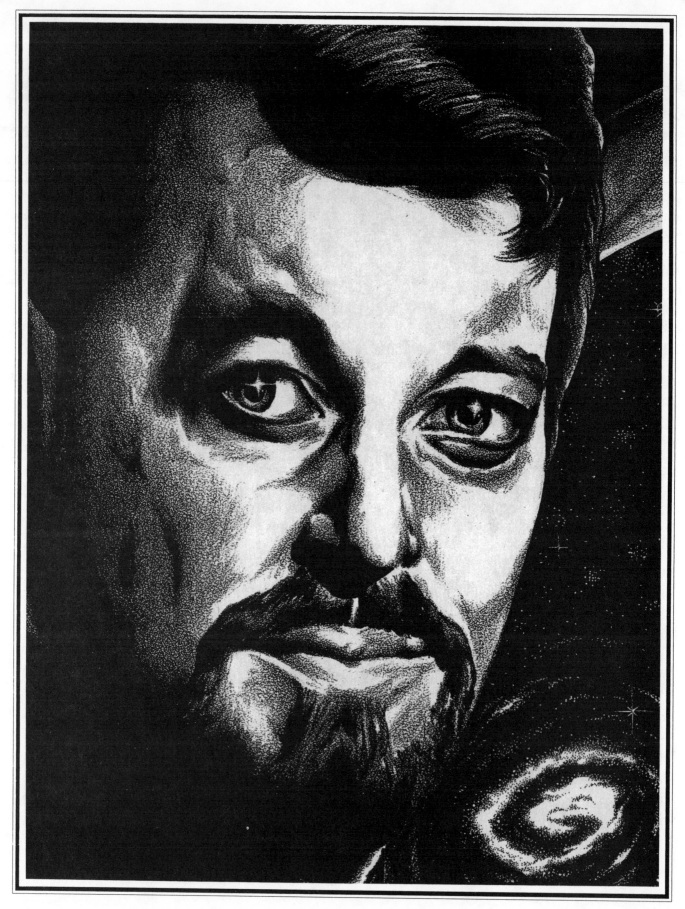

is still young and hasn't learned yet how completely different the two sexes can be. He's not fully aware that human females have needs of their own, such as the power of a woman's need to be needed.

Number One was surprised to meet Deanna Troi after beaming aboard the Enterprise as he had met her before. They had a strong attraction for one another but it was never consummated. Riker is slightly uncomfortable thrown into a situation where he deals with Troi every day, but each treats the other with respect and they seem to have put their past flirtation behind them. They have prevented it from interfering with their working relationship.

While Riker can accept Troi, and even the Klingon Worf, Lt. Commander Data posed some problems at first, but Riker has come to accept the android as a equal. He agonized when he was obliged to act as prosecutor in "The Measure Of A Man," but carried out his duty, perhaps too well for his conscience. Data helped him cope with this by pointing out that if he had declined to fulfill that duty, the judge would have made a summary judgement which would have gone against Data, but the full hearing gave Picard a chance to mount his most persuasive arguments.

While Riker is called Number One by the Captain and crew alike, this distinction is reserved for starship personnel and not for people who are not a part of the ship's complement.

JONATHAN FRAKES

"I knew this was a real part, a big one," says Jonathan Frakes regarding the six weeks of auditions he went through for the role, "and I had to get it."

The actor credits Gene Roddenberry with giving him the needed insight into the character that eventually became his.

"Gene is so very non-Hollywood and really quite paternal. One of the things he said to me was, 'You have a Machiavellan glint in your eye. Life is a bowl of cherries.' I think Gene feels that way, which is why he writes the way he does. He's very positive and Commander Riker will reflect that," states Frakes.

The actor sees Riker, the executive officer and second in command of the Enterprise as, "strong, centered, honorable and somewhat driven. His job is to provide Captain Picard with the most efficiently run ship and the best prepared crew he can. Because of this he seems to maintain a more military bearing than the other characters in behavior, despite the fact that salutes and other military protocol no longer exist in the 24th Century."

While Frakes cannot help but regard this role as "a real step up in my career," he's had recurring roles on other series such as *Falcon Crest, Paper Dolls* and *Bare Essence*. For a year he was even a regular on the daytime drama *The Doctors*. Other television appearances include a role in the made-for-TV movie *The Nutcracker* and critically praised roles in the miniseries *Dream West* and both parts of the extended miniseries *North & South*. The actor has also appeared both on and off-Broadway and in regional theatre productions.

Born and raised in Pennsylvania, Frakes did undergraduate work at Penn State before going to Harvard. He also spent several seasons with the Loeb Drama Center and then moved to New York.

"I gave myself a five year limit," he reveals. "If I wasn't making a living at acting in five years, I would find something else to do. After a year and a half of being the worst waiter in New York and screwing up my back as a furniture mover I got a role in 'Shenandoah' on Broadway and then landed a part in *The Doctors*." Then his career was off and running.

Frakes spent the next five years in New York City and then moved to Los Angeles in 1979, at the suggestion of his agent. there he landed work immediately in episodic television.

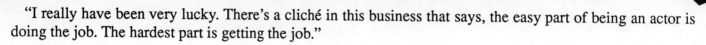

"I really have been very lucky. There's a cliché in this business that says, the easy part of being an actor is doing the job. The hardest part is getting the job."

Jonathan Frakes resides in Los Angeles and is married to actress Genie Davis, who appears on *The Days of Our Lives*.

LIEUTENANT COMMANDER DATA

Data is an android so perfectly fabricated that he can pass for human. At first it was thought that he was the product of some advanced alien technology until the discovery of an earlier model, Lore, revealed him to be the work of Dr. Noonian Soong, a human cyberneticist believed to be dead. ("Datalore") Much of the information given by Lore may be false, as is learned in "Brothers", when a homing signal brings Data face to face with his creator, who in fact created both of his androids quite literally in his own image, with his own face.

When tested by Starfleet upon his application for admission to Starfleet Academy, Data tested out as being alive. The only clues to his true origin are his peculiar yellow eyes, pale skin and encyclopedic memory which is comparable to that of a Vulcan, but is actually more extensive. It takes a skilled biologist to detect that Data is composed of artificial tissues instead of real flesh and blood. Although he only uses it in extreme circumstances, Data also possesses superhuman strength.

Data was discovered by a Starfleet Away team investigating the disappearance of an Earth colony. The colony was completely destroyed but the android was near the site, deactivated, and programmed with all the knowledge and memories of the lost colonists— except for the memory of what eradicated them so utterly. All this was rediscovered later, when Lore was reassembled. At the time of his discovery, Data had no memories of his own, and was impressed by the humans who rescued him. He chose to emulate them, hoping to become more human in the process. His remarkable abilities do not give him a superiority complex. In fact, he seems to feel a bit less than human, as he cannot feel emotions, but he seems to somehow overlook the truth that his loyalty and actions towards others would actually qualify him as an exemplary human being.

He excelled in the Starfleet Academy entry tests and has never received a mark against his performance. Data benefitted from the Starfleet regulation which prevents the rejection of a candidate so long as it tests out to be a sentient life form which doesn't stain the furniture or leave a slimy trail where it walks. This was later put to the test by Commander Bruce Maddox, whose efforts to classify the android as a possession of Starfleet were thwarted by Jean-Luc Picard. Picard's spirited defense of his colleague also served to strengthen Data's rights and liberties.

Data was created in the male gender, is fully functional (see "The Naked Now"!), and seems incapable of falsehood. While he speaks a more formal brand of English, and does not use contractions, he tends to ramble on a bit because of his vast knowledge. He does learn and adapt, however, and discontinued calculating times to the exact second because he learned that this often annoyed humans. He has difficulty understanding humor and idiomatic language, although he can learn vast glossaries of slang, such as that of the 1940s ("The Big Goodbye"), when he deems it relevant to the situation at hand. He also involves himself in amateur acting. Picard has shared his interest in Shakespeare with him, and Data's researches in theatrical history have

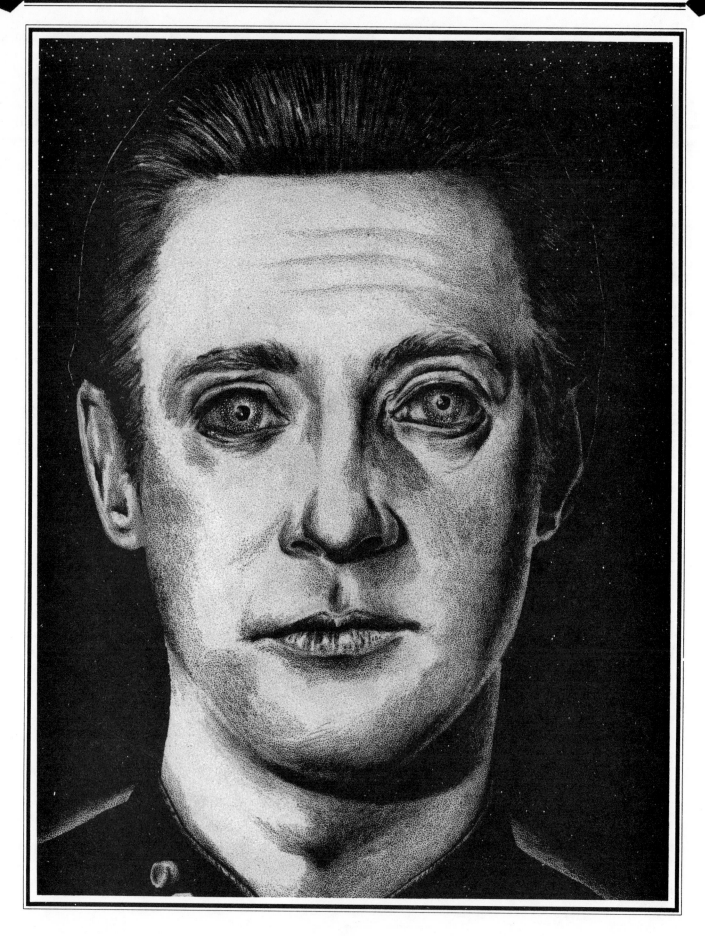

led him to become an adherent of Stanislavsky's Method approach to acting, although his reasons are peculiar. The Method is rooted in drawing on deep emotions to bring characters to life; Data hopes to reach emotional depths through creating characters on stage, in essence reversing the original Method concept.]

While Data appears to be an adult in his late twenties, he has probably existed a much shorter time than that, as he entered Starfleet soon after being found and basically entered life as an adult. Because Data was never a child, he seems particularly interested by children such as Wesley Crusher as they mark an aspect of existence which he has never experienced and represent another example of his goal of being human.

In fact, his older 'brother' Lore was given basic emotions, but Dr. Soong had overreached himself in this attempt and did not try to give emotions to Data after they went seriously awry in Lore. Years later Soong developed circuitry to remedy this, but was fooled by the jealous Lore, who obtained the implant himself. Soong died soon afterward, leaving Data the same. What affect this inappropriate technology will have on Data's "evil twin" remains to be seen, but Data, despite his misgivings, continues to learn and grow as a sentient, and certainly very human, being.

BRENT SPINER

"I'm one of those people who believes that mankind will find all the answers out in space," says Spiner, "but the first step is to get off this planet. The sun is going to burn out eventually and we better be somewhere else as a race of people by the time that happens. I think that's why everybody digs Star Trek because they know its a part of all of our futures and represents a vision of home."

The character played by Spiner is not human, but he is not an alien. Data is an android who can pass for human and even graduated from Starfleet Academy with top honors.

"As the series opens we don't know much about Data, only that he was constructed by beings on a planet which no longer exists. He's the only thing left. His creators programmed him with a world of knowledge— he's virtually an encyclopedia— but only in terms of information, not behavior. He's totally innocent. However, he does possess a sense of question and wonder that allows him to evolve. His objective is to be as human as possible."

Brent Spiner was born and raised in Houston where he saw an average of three movies a day between the ages of 11 and 15.

"At fifteen I was already a major film buff. I could quote lines from movies, tell you who was in it and in what year it was made. I always fantasized about being an actor. I was also lucky enough to have a brilliant teacher in high school named Cecil Pickett, who was capable of seeing potential, nurturing it and making me aware of it."

Spiner did a lot of "gritty, ugly plays" off-Broadway after college. "The one that finally pushed me over into the serious actor category was a public theatre production of 'The Seagull' for Joseph Papp." The actor went on to roles in the Broadway musical productions of 'Sunday In The Park With George,' 'The Three Musketeers,' and 'Big River,' based on Mark Twain's *Huckleberry Finn.*

Since moving to Los Angeles in 1984, he's appeared in such plays as 'Little Shop of Horrors' at the Westwood Playhouse. His feature film credits include the Woody Allen film Stardust Memories. On television he has appeared on such series as *The Twilight Zone, Hill Street Blues, Cheers* and *Night Court.*

One could say that he was very well prepared for his role as Data by his belief in extraterrestrials. "Obviously I'm from another planet," he laughs, but adds that he seriously does believe in beings from other planets and will continue to do so until such things are disproven.

LIEUTENANT WORF

The prediction made by the Organians nearly a century before has come to pass. The Klingon Empire and the Federation are at peace. Even so, Worf is unique as the only Klingon officer of a Starfleet ship. When his family was destroyed in a treacherous Romulan attack on a Klingon outpost, Worf was rescued and raised by humans of Slavic extraction, who did their best to keep their adopted son in touch with his Klingon roots. He joined Starfleet, and is treated with the same courtesy and respect shown any other bridge officer—possibly even more, since the Klingons still have a remarkable reputation for violence.

Although Worf is still very aggressive by nature, he is able to control his anger even when he feels he has been provoked. As a bridge officer, and the third in the line of command after Picard and Riker, Worf takes his duties very seriously. In combat situations, when the Enterprise or its crew are threatened, Worf wants to instinctively respond in kind and confront the menace head on. When a crew member is killed by a device left by a long-dead race, Worf is frustrated because there is no one to take revenge against, and, while he obeys the orders of his superiors, he is not entirely at ease with the nonviolent solutions often dictated by Starfleet policy. The Klingon Empire does not stress cool deliberations as the preferred method for problem solving.

Worf rarely talks about himself and his culture, but in "Justice" Riker inadvertently got Worf to talk about Klingon sexual attitudes. When Riker wonders why Worf is not enjoying the pleasures offered by the sybaritic Edo, Worf explains, quite casually, that only Klingon women could survive sex with a Klingon male. When Riker wonders if this is simply bragging, Worf is confused. He was merely stating a simple fact of Klingon life.

Eventually, Worf did renew a long-unconsummated relationship with the half-human K'Ehleyr, who came back into his life as a Federation emissary. Their encounter in "The Emissary" produced a son, but unfortunately K'Ehleyr was murdered in "Reunion", a crime that provoked Worf to a bloody and time-honored Klingon revenge. His son now lives with his Earth parents, since Worf's status in the Klingon Empire has become a precarious one.

Years after Worf's rescue, the Klingons captured a Romulan ship whose records revealed the identity of the Klingon who betrayed the outpost. This Klingon was a member of a very powerful family, and his son was an important Klingon, so the Klingon High Council decided to avoid societal disruption by altering the records and blaming Worf's father for the crime.

They did not believe that Worf still kept the Klingon ways, or that he would even learn of this dishonor, but they were unaware that he had a younger brother who had been secretly raised by another family. Worf's brother contacted Worf, drawing him into the Machiavellian intrigues of Klingon power politics. Ultimately, Worf underwent discommendation rather than let his brother be killed, in essence corroborating his father's

guilt to outside eyes, but this also gives him time to set matters aright. He has already scored one hollow victory, for his enemy in this matter was also the killer of his mate, but his death at Worf's hands does not restore Worf's family honor.

It seems that Worf may turn out to be a key factor in Klingon/ Federation relations. Klingons as a rule do not feel comfortable with humans, often holding them in contempt, and there may be a faction (see "The Drumhead") which favors improved relations with the Romulans; even though Klingons have a deeply ingrained hatred of Romulans, they understand them better than humans, whose manners and motivations often must seem strange to the warrior Klingons. Worf occupies a unique position between these two cultures, and may provide the key to future developments between them.

MICHAEL DORN

As a longtime *Star Trek* fan, Dorn says that this role "was a dream come true. First, because I'm a Trekkie and second, I'm playing a Klingon, a character so totally different from the nice-guy roles I'd done in the past. Worf is the only Klingon aboard the Enterprise. That still makes him an outsider, but that's okay by me because Worf knows he's superior to these weak humans. But he never lets the other crew members see that because he's a soldier first and second."

The actor gives enthusiastic praise to series creator Gene Roddenberry for having the "genius and vision" to depict an optimistic future in which a peaceful alliance could be struck between Earth and the Klingon Empire. "Gene believes there is good in everybody— even Klingons!"

But the actor enjoys playing very different kinds of characters, and knows what its like to appear in a series after playing a regular on *CHIPS* for three years. "I love doing cop roles, and as a highway patrolman I got to drive fast and I never got hurt."

Dorn hails from Liling, Texas, but he was raised in Pasadena, California, just minutes away from Hollywood. He performed in a rock band during high school and college and in 1973 moved away to San Francisco where he worked at a variety of jobs. When he returned to L.A., he continued playing in rock bands until a friend's father, an assistant director of *The Mary Tyler Moore Show,* suggested the young man try his hand at acting. Dorn can be seen in the background, as a newswriter, in episodes from that classic comedy's last two seasons.

"I had done a little modelling by this time and had studied drama and TV producing in college. Once I started, I caught the bug."

His first acting role was a guest spot on the series *WEB,* a show based on the satirical film *Network.* Dorn was introduced to an agent by the producer of the show and began studying with Charles Conrad. Six months later Dorn was cast in *CHIPS.* Following that series, Dorn resumed acting classes. "I worked very hard; the jobs started coming and the roles got meatier."

Dorn has made guest appearances on nearly every major series, most notably *Hotel, Knots Landing* and *Falcon Crest.* He has also had recurring roles on *Days Of Our Lives* and *Capitol.* His feature film credits include *Demon Seed, Rocky* and *The Jagged Edge.*

Dorn hopes eventually to direct, but for now, "I want to take one step at a time and do the best work I can do." He's still interested in rock music, plays in a band, does studio work as a bass player and writes music in his spare time.

DR. BEVERLY CRUSHER, CHIEF MEDICAL OFFICER

Beverly Crusher worked long and hard to secure her posting aboard the Enterprise, where she is stationed along with her brilliant son, Wesley. Beverly's husband, Jack Crusher, was killed while serving under Captain Picard aboard the U.S.S. Stargazer. Jack Crusher died saving Picard's life, and to show his respect for the man, Picard accompanied the body back to Earth when it was returned for the funeral. While Beverly knows that is is not logical to blame Picard, she associated him with her loss and was not, at first, certain how she would react to working with Picard. When Picard offered to have her transferred if she so desired, she declined, since she wouldn't have been there if she hadn't requested the position. Any initial misgivings have given way to mutual respect and understanding.

Dr. Crusher chose to sign aboard the starship commanded by Picard because she has an enviable Starfleet record which has earned her this prestigious assignment. As demonstrated by the position held by Dr. McCoy on the Enterprise commanded by James T. Kirk, a starship's Chief Medical Officer is in no way regarded as a rank inferior to that of Captain. In fact, outside of a court martial, the CMO is the only force capable of removing a starship captain from his or her post

Beverly is an intelligent and strong-willed diagnostician. She has a profound sense of medicine, the kind of skill that takes years to develop. Often she uses her diagnostic skills to confirm what she has already seen, smelled and sensed about a patient's condition. First and foremost she is a brilliant ship's doctor.

In "The Naked Now" there were many truths revealed about various crew members. In Crusher's case it revealed that she is interested in Picard, and certainly no longer harbors the suspicion and resentment she feared might affect her job performance. Being in her late thirties to early forties, the attractive Dr. Crusher has not escaped the notice of Captain Picard, but it is doubtful that this could develop into anything as any good officer knows that complications arise when key personnel become involved.

Dr. Crusher's most difficult moments on the Enterprise generally involve Wesley, as in "Justice" when Wesley was sentenced to death for an inadvertent crime, only to be saved by Picard's intervention. She has also been trapped in a false reality inside a static warp field, which she narrowly escaped from, and recently found romance only to have it shattered by the bizarre secrets of the alien humanoid she'd fallen for.

GATES McFADDEN

Dr. Crusher is the first regular role in a television series for actress Gates McFadden. Her character is presented with more background than most of the others as she is the mother of Wesley Crusher, and the widow of the man who died while saving Picard's life on an earlier mission.

Gates trained to be a dancer when quite young, while growing up in Cuyahoga Falls, Ohio. "I had extraordinary teachers: one was primarily a ballerina and the other had been in a circus. I grew up thinking most ballerinas knew how to ride the unicycle, tap dance and do handsprings. Consequently, I was an oddball to other dancers."

Her interest in acting was sparked by community theatre and a touring Shakespeare company. "When I was ten, my brother and I attended back-to-back Shakespeare for eight days in a musty, nearly empty theatre. There were twelve actors who played all the parts. I couldn't get over it— the same people in costumes every day, but playing new characters. It was like visiting somewhere but never wanting to leave."

She earned her Bachelor of Arts in Theatre from Brandeis University while continuing to study acting, dance and mime. Just prior to graduation she met Jack LeCoq and credits the experience with changing her life.

"I attended his first workshop in the United States. His theatrical vision and the breadth of its scope were astonishing. I left for Paris as soon as possible to continue to study acting with LeCoq at his school. we worked constantly in juxtapositions. One explored immobility in order to better understand movement. One explored silence in order to better understand sound and language. It was theatrical research involving many mediums. Just living in a foreign country where you have to speak and think in another language cracks your head open. It was both terrifying and freeing. Suddenly I was taking more risks in my acting."

McFadden lives in New York City where she has been involved in film and theatre both as an actress and director-choreographer. Her acting credits include leads in the New York productions of Michael Brady's "To Gillian On Her 37th Birthday," Mary Gallagher's "How To Say Goodbye," Caryl Churchill's "Cloud 9" and, in California, in the La Jolla Playhouse production of "The Matchmaker" with Linda Hunt.

Gates was the director of choreography and puppet movement for the late Jim Henson's *Labyrinth* and assisted Gavin Milar in the staging of the fantasy sequences for *Dreamchild*. "Those films were my baptism by fire into the world of special effects and computerized props," Gates reveals.

Following the first season of *Next Generation*, Gates was inexplicably dropped from the cast and just as inexplicably returned in the third season, after her role as ship's doctor had been played for one season by Diana Muldaur. During her absence from the series, among other work Gates had a small role in *The Hunt For Red October* as the wife of the main character. Due to the demands of being back on the series, it is unlikely that she will repeat this role in *Patriot Games,* the second film to feature the Jack Ryan character and based on another of the novels of author Tom Clancy.

LT. COMMANDER DEANNA TROI, SHIP'S COUNSELLOR

Deanna Troi holds the position of counsellor, a position that didn't exist during the time of the voyages of the first starship Enterprise 78 years before. In the 24th century it has been realized that the success of a starship's mission depends as much on efficiently functioning human relationships as it does on the vessel staying in one piece and having fully functional warp drive. Counsellor Troi is fully trained in human and alien psychology. When a starship encounters alien life forms, the counsellor's role is second only to that of the Captain and Number One is making decisions on how to deal with the other life forms.

The world has changed much in the future and the crew of a starship actually welcomes the insights of a ship's Counsellor, even when it deals with an individual's own behavior and level of performance. While 20th century psychiatry and psychology is considered to be more of an art than an empirical science, in the 24th century solid evidence and medical research have radically changed things. Psychiatry has become a field of applied science in which hard evidence has replaced guesswork, supposition and mere practiced insight. Command ranks aboard starships both respect and actively make use of the skills of the Counsellor in much the same way that they solicit advice from the medical officers, chief engineer and other shipboard specialists. With the commissioning of the Galaxy Class starships, with the added complexities of families and the presence of children, the Counsellor is in even more demand.

A Starfleet graduate, Deanna is half human and half Betazoid. Her father was a Starfleet officer who lived on Betazed with one of that world's humanoid females. Her mother Lwaxana is an aristocratic eccentric who provides Deanna with acute embarrassment whenever she appears on board the Enterprise, since she seems insistent on pursuing Captain Picard (she thinks he has great legs), or whatever other male she sets her eyes on.

While Lwaxana and all other full Betazoids are fully telepathic, Deanna has telepathic abilities limited to the emotional range; she can "read" feelings and sensations, but not coherent thoughts. Another extreme example of Betazoid ability is the hyper-sensitive Tam Elbrun, who vanished with the spacefaring being dubbed "Tin Man" by the Federation. While most Betazoids develop their full telepathic abilities during adolescence, Elbrun was born with them fully functional, which led to extreme problems for him, leading him to seek the solitude of space. He was, in fact, Deanna's patient at one time, but she was not able to do much for him.

Due to her particular training and inherent abilities, Counsellor Troi is often selected as an Away Team member as she can provide important insights into the motives and feelings of the beings they must deal with.

(Some beings, notably the Ferengi, are impervious even to full telepaths. While some races may be able to intentionally block their minds, the Ferengi probably are resistant due to peculiarities of their brain struc-

ture.) Generally, when dealing with alien life, Deanna can sense something of the moods or attitudes that a being harbors toward the Federation representatives. In the case of the Traveller ("Where No Man Has Gone Before") she could detect nothing from him, as if he wasn't even there. With humans she is able to sense more when it is a person she has some sort of rapport or relationship with.

For instance, Troi was acquainted with William Riker before either was posted to the Enterprise. Neither knew the other had been assigned to this starship until they first encountered one another on board. While Troi had not become deeply involved with Riker, she did find their affair meaningful and pleasant. It has not progressed any further as each feels honor bound to maintain a disciplined and professional status while aboard ship.

MARINA SIRTIS

A British actress, Marina Sirtis had been working in various roles in England for years before she decided to give the colonies a try, but she landed the continuing role of Deanna Troi after being in America only six months. "It's taken me years to become an overnight success," she quips. "I had a six-month visa, which was quickly running out. In fact, I got the call telling me I had the part only hours before I was to leave for the airport to return home."

Marina enjoys the irony of being a British actress playing an alien on American television. But viewers won't notice a British accent coming out of an alien being as she's devised a combination of accents for the character to use.

"In the 24th Century, geographical or nationalistic barriers are not so evident. The Earth as a planet is your country, your nationality. I didn't want anyone to be able to pin down my accent to any particular country, and being good at accents, the producers trusted me to come up with something appropriate, Sirtis states.

Counsellor Troi is like an empath in that she can open her mind to the feelings and sensations of those around her, unlike a full Betazoid telepath.

Sirtis initially auditioned for the role of Security Chief Tasha Yar, rather than that of Deanna Troi.

"After my third audition for Tasha, I was literally walking out the door when they called me back to read for Deanna. While I was looking at the script, director Corey Allen came in and said, 'You have something personally that the character should have. . . an empathy, so use it.' I love being able to play someone who is so deep with that kind of insight into people, particularly since I usually get cast as the hard 1980s stereotype."

Born to Greek parents in North London, Marina demonstrated an inclination towards performing at an early age. "My mother tells me that when I was three, I used to stand up on the seat of the bus and sing to the other passengers." But her parents wanted their daughter to follow "more serious" pursuits, so after finishing high school, Marina had to secretly apply to the Guild Hall School of Music and Drama, where she was accepted. "My first job after graduating was as Ophelia in 'Hamlet' for the Worthing Repertory Company."

Following that, she worked for a few years in British television, musical theatre and in other repertory companies throughout England and Europe. She landed some supporting roles in features such as *The Wicked Lady* with Faye Dunaway and in *Deathwish III* opposite Charles Bronson.

She decided to stay on in the United States and has settled in Los Angeles where she watches "far too much MTV" and keeps track of her local soccer team in London, in which she owns a few shares. Her brother is a professional soccer player.

Marina has always been interested in the stars and space exploration and believes that she once saw a UFO. "I was working with a repertory company in Worthing, a seaside town in England. One night as I was walking down the street, I saw this huge orange thing in the sky. At first I thought it must be the moon, but it was very off color. It was very close, but too high to be a balloon. Apparently a lot of other people saw it, too."

LT. J.G. GEORDI LA FORGE, (CHIEF ENGINEER)

Geordi is both trained to work on the bridge ans is an away team regular whose unique prosthetic eyes allow him to perform some of the functions of a tricorder. His high-tech artificial eyes are actually a visor-like device worn on his head which can detect the entire spectrum of electromagnetic waves, all the way from raw heat to high-frequency ultraviolet. Other crewpersons seem blind by comparison, although Geordi often wishes he could see the way they do, since he has been blind since birth.

Although in his early twenties, Geordi has the maturity of a seasoned Starfleet graduate and has the highest respect for Captain Picard, hoping to emulate the Captain when he gets older. His best friend aboard the Enterprise is the android Data. Each aspires to be "fully human," because even though they have traits that make them superior in what they can achieve compared to their normal counterparts, neither asked to be different, nor wants to be. Perhaps Geordi needs an intensive therapy session with Counsellor Troi in order to accept himself for what he is so that he can more readily get on with his life.

LEVAR BURTON

Due to the longevity of the original series, the new crew has more than one actor who was a *Star Trek* fan before landing his role, and Levar Burton is one of them. He states that he has long "appreciated Gene Roddenberry's approach to science fiction. Gene's vision of the future has always included minorities—not just blacks, but Asians and Hispanics as well. He's saying that unless we learn to cooperate as a species, we won't be able to make it to the 24th Century. I think that by projecting that image, we're actually creating a reality for today."

Philosophy has long been an interest of Levar Burton. At 13 he entered a Catholic seminary, with the ultimate goal of becoming a priest. But after two years he discovered an interest in Existentialism and by 15 was reading Lao-Tzu, Kierkegaard and Nietzche.

"I began to wonder how I fit into the grand scheme of things. The more I thought about it, the less sense it made that the dogma of Catholicism was the end-all, be-all of the universe," Burton explains.

Following what Burton describes as his "pragmatic search," comparing the things he did well with the things that excited him about being a priest, he decided to pursue an acting career.

"What attracted me to the priesthood was the opportunity to move people, to provide something essential. I was drawn by the elements of history and magic. As a priest, you live beyond the boundaries of the normal existence. It's like joining an elite club. You see, it's not that different from acting, even the Mass is a play, combining these elements of mystery and spectacle."

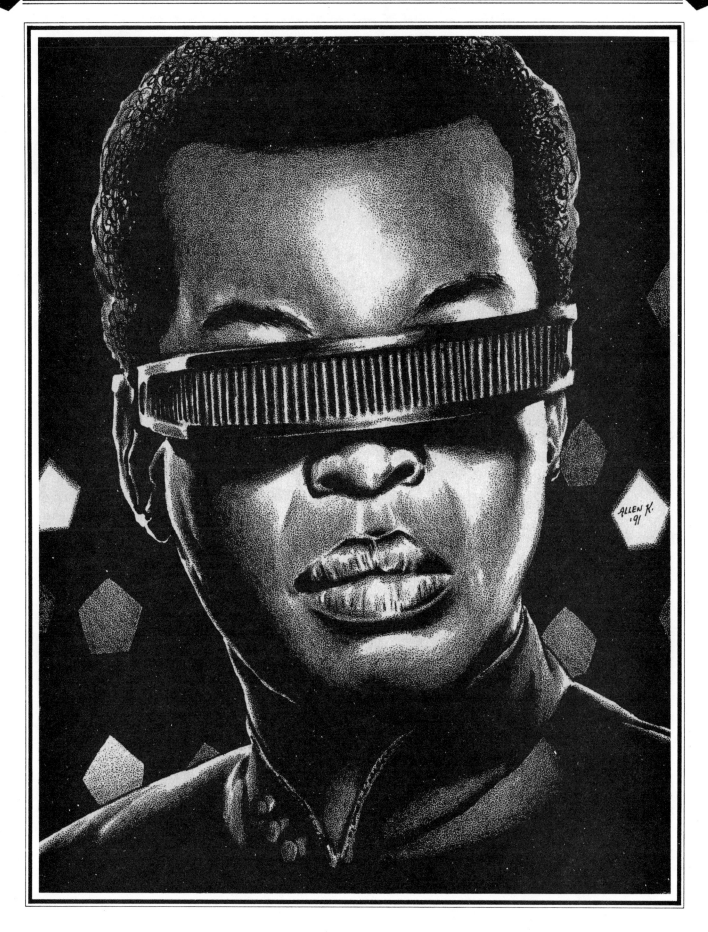

After he left the seminary, Burton won a scholarship to USC, where he began working toward a degree in drama and fine arts. But the contrast between the sedate, introspective life in a small town seminary and the USC campus, which he calls "Blond Central," was startling. "I'd never had so much freedom and it was difficult to concentrate the first year."

It was during his sophomore year at USC, while only 19, that he auditioned and landed the pivotal role of the young Kunta Kinte in the award-winning mini-series *Roots*.

"I think the producers had exhausted all the normal means of finding professional talent and were beating the bushes at the drama schools," the actor ventures. The role would win him an Emmy nomination and subsequent acting roles, which prevented his return to college.

Burton starred in a number of made-for-TV movies such as the Emmy-nominated *Dummy, One In A Million: The Ron LeFlore Story, Grambling's White Tiger, The Guyana Tragedy: The Story Of Jim Jones, Battered, Billy: Portrait of a Street Kid,* and the mini-series *Liberty.* The actor has also been the host of PBS' highly acclaimed children's series *Reading Rainbow* since its inception in 1983. Among his film credits are *Looking For Mr. Goodbar, The Hunter* (with Steve McQueen) and *The Supernaturals* (with Nichelle Nichols).

The actor was born in Landsthul, West Germany, where his father was a photographer in the Signal Corps, Third Armored Division. His mother was first and educator, then for years a social worker who is currently working in administration for the County of Sacramento Department of Mental Health. Burton is single and resides in Los Angeles with his German Shepherd, Mozart.

The character Burton plays, a blind engineer named Geordi LaForge, is supposedly named after a disabled *Star Trek* fan who passed away.

TASHA YAR, SECURITY CHIEF (FIRST SEASON)

T asha grew up on a failed Earth colony where law and order had broken down and the survival of the fittest became the order of the day. An orphan, she spent her nights and days foraging for food and fleeing the roving rape gangs. The colony broke down due to being comprised largely of renegades and other violent undesirables who were being given a second chance. Instead, order broke down and violence rules. A sample of what life was like there was briefly seen in "The Naked Now", while later developments were seen in the episode entitled "Legacy."

In her teens, Tasha escaped to Earth, leaving behind a sister who remained by choice, and discovered Starfleet. She worshipped the order and discipline of Starfleet because it is the exact opposite of the chaos she grew up fighting.

At the age of 28, she achieved the rank of Security Chief and was hand picked by Captain Picard. She was one of the few crew members who performed the same duties on and off the ship. When an Away Team was selected to investigate a landing site, whether for a possible shore leave or for a conference that Captain Picard is being called to attend, Yar, as Security Chief, was always a part of the initial contact team.

The young Security Chief satisfied her need for peace and order in her chosen occupation, and held the Starfleet officers embodying this quality of devotion to duty and decency in the highest possible regard. She came close to worshipping them. This is particularly true in her attitude toward the commanding officers of the Enterprise. In her youth, figures of authority had been brutal and deadly.

Captain Picard, having visited Tasha's homeworld, her "hell planet," understood what she went through and became her mentor. He taught her to apply the cushioning of history and philosophy to her almost obsessive need to protect the vessel and crew.

Natasha was of Ukrainian descent. This, combined with her own strict exercise regimen, gave her a quality of conditioned, subtle beauty that would have flabbergasted males from earlier centuries. With fire in her eyes and a muscularly well-toned and very female body, she was capable of pinning most crewmen. She was also an exciting sensual and intellectual challenge to men who enjoyed full equality between the genders. Neither Number One or Picard was blind to these qualities in Tasha, but she could never bring herself to view these "saints" as mere mortals.

In "The Naked Now," Tasha revealed a previously concealed interest in Data. She even went so far as to take him into her quarters and seduce him! When the judgement-inhibiting effects wore off, Tasha realized that she had completely violated her personal sense of decorum, and told the literal minded android that "It never happened." Since she didn't specify what "it" was, Data was a bit confused as to what, exactly, had never occurred.

Tasha's death at the hands of the creature Armus was a senseless tragedy which left her comrades stunned and bereaved. Oddly enough, it seems to be the emotionless Data who cherishes her memory the most; he keeps a holographic snapshot of her among his most cherished possessions.

The Enterprise crew later encountered Ishara Yar, Tasha's sister, when they went to rescue a Federation freighter's crew from captivity on Tasha's hellish home world. She reminded them of Tasha, but she was using them to get help for her political faction. Perhaps she was as capable of loyalty and friendship as Tasha, but Ishara's loyalties were bound up in the ongoing struggle of her world, and she lacked the courage to turn her back on the chaos and follow her sister's path.

In "Yesterday's Enterprise," a temporal anomaly gave Tasha a chance to die a meaningful death, sacrificing herself to go back to a certain doom in order to restore reality to its proper balance.

DENISE CROSBY

Denise Crosby described the character she played with this thumbnail sketch. "She comes from an incredibly violent and aggressive Earth colony where life was a constant battle for survival. She can fight and she knows her job, but she has no family, is emotionally insecure and somehow feels that she doesn't quite belong on this ship of seemingly perfect people."

As the granddaughter of the late legendary crooner Bing Crosby, Denise enjoyed the part and even related to it to some extent.

"My grandfather was a Hollywood legend. Growing up with that wasn't exactly normal or typical either, and I think that helps me understand Tasha's imbalance and insecurities," explained the actress in a first season interview.

Prior to getting involved in developing an acting career, Denise went through what she describes as her "European runway model thing. I hated modeling, but I was taken to Europe by three California designers who were trying to launch their fashions there. I loved London, so I just stayed on."

When she returned home for the Christmas holidays, she was almost tapped for an acting role. "Toni Howard was casting a movie called *Diary of a Teenage Hitchhiker* and had seen my picture in a magazine. I looked wild. My hair was about a quarter of an inch all the way around. I wore army fatigues and no makeup." While she didn't land that role, Toni Howard encouraged her to enroll in acting classes. The roles soon followed.

Her feature film credits include *48 Hours, Arizona Heat, The Eliminators, The Man Who Loved Women, Trail of the Pink Panther* and *Miracle Mile*.

The TV credits for Denise also include *L.A. Law, Days of Our Lives, The Flash,* and the made-for-TV movies *O'Hara, Stark, Malice In Wonderland* and *Cocaine: One Man's Poison*.

Denise has also appeared in some local Los Angeles theatre productions, including the critically well-received "Tamara", in which she had the lead, as well as the controversial one-act play "Stops Along The Way" directed by Richard Dreyfuss.

Needless to say, Denise Crosby reprised her role as Tasha Yar in "Yesterday's Enterprise," and will be returning to the show in its fifth season. The form this character will take is revealed in the final episode of the fourth season. A clue about this occurs in the episode "The Mind's Eye" in which Denise Crosby plays one of the Romulans on the ship which kidnaps Geordi.

GUINAN

The mysterious Guinan serves exotic drinks and meals in Ten Forward, but her most important role seems to be that of counsellor, as she is also a fount of wisdom, giving advice and support, sometimes unsolicited but always needed, to members of the Enterprise crew. She has Captain Picard's complete trust, as when she alone sensed that something was amiss when the timelines shifted in "Yesterday's Enterprise" and Picard believed her, but their shared background has never been revealed. In "The Best of Both Worlds," she says that she was "more than family and more than friend" to Picard, but elsewhere it is revealed that the two had never met before the Enterprise-D was commissioned.

What is known is that Guinan is thousands of years old, and that the Borg destroyed her homeworld and dispersed its people. She was not there at the time, however, and did not witness the destruction.

She is an old nemesis of Q, however, who obviously fears her. She undoubtedly possesses powers that have never been revealed. Her encounter with Q, two centuries ago, is another mystery, deepened by Q's revelation that she wore a different form at that time. Supposedly, her relationship with Q has something to do with her presence on the Enterprise, but, as usual, revelations about the character only deepen the mystery which surrounds her.

Still, to most crew members who encounter her, Guinan is the 24th Century equivalent of the classic bartender, who not only serves up just the right variety of Synthehol, but also lends a caring ear and freely gives a touch of humane wisdom wherever and whenever it is called for.

WHOOPI GOLDBERG

Whoopi Goldberg describes her character Guinan as "a cross between Yoda and William F. Buckley," but freely admits that she's put a lot of herself into the role as well. Growing up in New York, young Whoopi was inspired by the harmonious message of the original *Star Trek*, and especially by Nichelle Nichols. When Goldberg learned that her friend LeVar Burton would be on a new *Star Trek* series, she asked him to tell Gene Roddenberry that she wanted to be on the program, too—but the producers of *The Next Generation* thought he was joking. A year later, Goldberg took matters into her own hands and contacted Gene Roddenberry; the two worked together to create the mysterious alien bartender who runs Ten Forward, a popular gathering place for the crew of the Enterprise.

Although Whoopi's first showbiz experience took place at the age of eight, there was a large gap in her career, as she raised a child and, at one time, contended with a heroin problem. She worked at a variety of jobs, including one in a funeral parlor whose owner had a curious sense of humor, and 'initiated' his employees by hiding in a body bin and playing "zombie," scaring them witless in the process. Whoopi was not amused.

By the time the 1980's rolled around, however, she was active in theatre and comedy, working in Southern California with the San Diego Repertory Theatre and putting on a number of one-woman shows. (She also washed dishes at the Big Kitchen restaurant, where the menu still carries a special named after her.) In 1985 she got her big break, in Steven Spielberg's film of *The Color Purple*, in a role which earned her an Oscar nomination and the Golden Globe Award. Since then she has starred in *Jumpin' Jack Flash, Burglar, Fatal Beauty, Clara's Heart* and *Homer and Eddie.*

Her role as psychic Oda Mae in *Ghost* netted her the Oscar for Best Supporting Actress, and she continues to work in such films as *The Long Walk Home* (with Sissy Spacek) and *Soapdish.*

She has also won an Emmy for her 1986 guest appearance on *Moonlighting*, and starred in the CBS sitcom *Bagdad Cafe* with Jean Stapleton.

She is concerned with the plight of our nation's homeless, and has, with Robin Williams and Billy Crystal, been a prime force behind the annual *Comic Relief* benefit concerts. In 1989, her various charity projects resulted in her being granted the Starlight Foundation's Humanitarian of the Year.

Still active on stage, Goldberg has performed in *Moms, The Spook Show*, and *Living On The Edge of Chaos*, as well as returning to the San Diego Repertory Theatre, a.k.a. The Rep, to take part in fund raising performances (along with Patrick Stewart) for that organization.

Goldberg continues to reveal new aspects of Guinan as *The Next Generation* continues its voyages, but, as always, each new revelation only raises more questions than it answers—and that's the way Whoopi Goldberg likes it.

SEASON ONE

INTRODUCTION

While the average television series sets up a format in the first episode and almost never varies from it thereafter, *Star Trek: The Next Generation* has not been like that. While it started out with some very weak early episodes, it learned from its mistakes. Initially the large cast was downright unwieldy as the stories searched in vain for a focal point and tried to spin too many subplots out at once.

There was also the problem of episodes like "The Naked Now," a bland sequel to "The Naked Time," as well as the character of Q who is an annoying clone of Trelane from "Squire of Gothos." Roddenberry was for some reason so taken with this character that an interesting script by D.C. Fontana, "Encounter At Farpoint," was all but crippled by his addition of the Q subplot. Watching the episode, it's quite evident that the sequences with Q are totally independent of the rest of the story and bear no relation to the real action.

The early scripts are so universally bad that by the time "The Big Goodbye" comes along, one has stopped expecting anything good. The cleverness and invention in this story are so far above what had come before in the series, it was a shock. But was it a flash in the pan? "Datalore" (the obligatory "evil twin" episode) and "Angel One" sunk back into mediocrity but "11001001" demonstrated invention again, as well as how good a story could be when it dealt with just one plot at once rather than several. The scripts that followed were inconsistent, but when they were good, they were very good. And there were more and more of these, such as "Conspiracy" and "Heart Of Glory" to name only two. The season finale, "The Neutral Zone," ended on a weak note only because it didn't have a final act—the story just stopped as though it were cutting away to a commercial only to vanish without even a passing nod at a resolution. If this was their idea of a cliff-hanger, they should have given it more thought.

All things considered, the first season showed remarkable improvement overall, journeying from mediocrity to winning a Peabody Award, which nonetheless makes for quite a rocky voyage.

EPISODES ONE AND TWO: "ENCOUNTER AT FARPOINT"

(Two hours)

Written by D.C. Fontana and Gene Roddenberry

Directed by Corey Allen

Guest Cast: John deLancie, Michael Bell, DeForest Kelley, Colm Meaney, Cary Hiroyuki, Timothy Dang, David Erskine, Evelyn Guerrero, Chuck Hicks

Captain Picard has recently been posted to the new Enterprise (NCC 1701-D). He doesn't even have a first officer yet, but is taking the ship to Farpoint Station to pick him up.

Suddenly, Deanna Troi, an empath, senses a powerful mind scanning them and ahead they detect a strange grid in space. A being appears who calls himself "Q". He states, "You are notified that your kind has infiltrated the galaxy too far already. You are directed to return to your own solar system immediately."

When a crewman draws his phaser in an attempt to subdue Q, the being freezes the crewman solid. Picard points out that the weapons had been set on stun, to which Q responds that he would not want to be captured in a helpless state by humans.

Q demonstrates his knowledge of human history, but Picard points out that everything Q has described is centuries out of date. Humans are far different now, and Picard doesn't fear the facts. This gives Q an idea and he departs to make preparations. As soon as he leaves, Picard orders the Enterprise to maximum warp. He and other bridge crew members descend to the battle bridge so that a saucer separation can take place, which sends the part of the ship with families off in another direction.

As expected, Q catches up with them and Picard surrenders to be taken before Q for judgement. Picard, Tasha, Troi and Data are taken they know not where, but it appears to be a trial chamber from the pre-holocaust period. They fence with words and Q impetuously freezes Troi and Tasha, but finally unfreezes them when Data plays back Q's assurance that the prisoners would not be harmed. Finally Q decides to submit the Enterprise crew to a test and chooses their destination of Farpoint station as the perfect examination of their merits. Q returns the four to the Enterprise.

On Farpoint, Riker is meeting with the Administrator Zorn, and has a curious encounter when he mentions that he wishes he had an apple and suddenly finds a bowl full on the counter when he could have sworn they weren't there a moment before. When Riker leaves the office, Zorn seems to be speaking to empty air when he threatens to punish someone if they ever do anything like that again.

Riker encounters Dr. Crusher and her son Wesley, who are also awaiting the arrival of the Enterprise. They have a similar experience when she is looking for a certain style of cloth which appears where a moment before a different style had been hanging.

While walking around, Riker encounters Geordi and Markham, who have also been posted to the Enterprise.

The stardrive section of the Enterprise arrives in orbit around Farpoint. Riker is beamed aboard to meet Picard. There he is briefed on what has just happened. The saucer section arrives about an hour later and Riker oversees the rejoining.

Elsewhere on the Enterprise, Data is escorting an admiral to the shuttle bay because he refuses to use the transporter. It is Dr. McCoy, now 147, who has been overseeing the medical lay-out. He is impressed with the new Enterprise and tells Data, "You treat her like a lady. She'll always bring you home.'

Picard meets with Dr. Crusher and expresses concern that she might not have wanted to be posted there. She states otherwise. Picard thought she might harbor a grudge because her husband died while under Picard's command.

Later, Picard is sending a farewell message to Admiral McCoy when Q appears on the bridge and states that they are taking too long and have only 24 hours to solve the mystery of Farpoint. Q vanishes; Picard states that he will not act any more quickly that usual. He won't be rushed into making a rash decision.

Picard, Riker and Troi beam down and go to Zorn's office. There Troi reveals that she is detecting great pain, loneliness and terrible despair. Zorn is offended by this, particularly when Picard doesn't believe Zorn when he states that he has no idea what Troi could be encountering, or why.

Wesley talks his mother into letting him accompany her to the bridge, where he peers out from the turbolift. At first Picard is annoyed to see him, but when he learns that the boy is Dr. Crusher's son he allows him to come on to the bridge.

Down at Farpoint, Riker, Data, Troi, Tasha and Geordi do some exploring to try to learn what's going on. They find underground passageways and Troi feels that she is very close to the source of the pain.

Just then an unknown spacecraft approaches the planet and begins firing on it. The blast hits the Bandi city but not Farpoint station itself. The ground team beams back to the Enterprise. Then Q reappears, mocking Picard and his efforts, coaxing him to blast the intruding ship.

Riker and Data have stayed behind and make their way to Zorn's office. He pleads for help but insists he doesn't know what's happening, or why. Suddenly he vanishes before their eyes in a transport beam. He has been taken aboard the other vessel.

Picard guesses what must have happened and he orders Farpoint evacuated and then an energy beam sent down to the planet. Farpoint was actually a gigantic alien being which had been wounded and landed on the planet. The Bandi captured it and enslaved its transformation powers, but now its mate has found it. Energized by the Enterprise, the enslaved being can now free itself, and it leaves with the other creature, which frees Zorn.

Q is disappointed that the humans passed the test and didn't use brute force against what they didn't understand, but the being promises that there will be other times and other places. Picard orders Q off his ship, stating that the only one proven guilty of savagery here is Q himself.

EPISODE THREE: "THE NAKED NOW"

Teleplay by J. Michael Bingham

Story by John D.F. Black and J. Michael Bingham

Directed by Paul Lynch

Guest Cast: Benjamin W.S. Lum, Michael Rider, David Renan, Skip Stellrecht, Kenny Koch

The Enterprise is operating at warp 7 on its way to rendezvous with the S.S. Tsiolkovsky, a science research vessel monitoring the collapse of a red supergiant into a white dwarf star. The Enterprise has gone to encounter the other ship because communications from it are indicating that something is wrong.

The last message they receive is from a woman who sounds stoned and who remarks that they're going to have a real blowout. There's the sound of encouraging voices followed by what sounds like a blast, and the transmission ends. Data observes that he believes that the explosion they heard was an emergency hatch being blown open in deep space.

Upon arrival, Riker assembles an Away Team consisting of himself, Tasha, Data and Geordi LaForge. They beam over to the Tsiolkovsky to investigate even though sensors indicate that there's no one aboard the other ship who is still alive. They split up and search the ship, finding scenes of carnage including a viewer showing the bridge, with its open emergency hatch.

Geordi finds a room where everyone is frozen, and when he checks a shower stall the ice covered body of a woman falls out into his arms. This has happened in regions of the ship where the environmental controls have been tampered with, allowing heat to bleed off into space. Riker reports to Picard, confirming that all 80 crewmen aboard the ship are dead, some having been blown out into space.

The Away Team beams back aboard the Enterprise. Dr. Crusher examines them and finds that they are all fine, except for Geordi, who is sweating and behaving oddly. She decides to run further tests on him.

The incident with people frozen to death and someone found in the shower fully clothed jogs Riker's memory as he recalls reading of a similar case but can't recall where. Data begins searching the ship's records for such a reference.

Geordi slips out of Sickbay and isn't caught until he has encountered Wesley, who is working on a small version of the ship's tractor beam. He's even come up with a device that can synthesize Captain Picard's voice. Geordi puts a friendly arm around Wesley's shoulder to congratulate him and then leaves Crusher's rooms. Next he encounters Tasha Yar. Geordi doesn't realize that he's infected with whatever drove the crew of the S.S. Tsiolkovsky mad, but he does know that something is wrong and begs Tasha to help him. She supports him and takes him back to Sickbay while Geordi talks about wishing he had normal human eyes.

Riker remembers that the reference he'd read was in the history of the Enterprise and Data tracks it to the Constitution class Enterprise commanded by James T. Kirk. The record even includes the cure synthesized by Leonard McCoy 87 years before.

The ailment is spreading through the crew. Tasha Yar wants Deanna Troi to show her how she can be more feminine and later uses her own unleashed sexual yearnings to successfully seduce Data.

The collapsing star begins hurling material into space, but Data assures the Captain that the Enterprise can outrun any danger from that. But then Picard hears his own voice over the P.A. system handing control of the Enterprise over to Wesley Crusher in Engineering. Wesley uses his new beam to create an impenetrable force field while he sits in Engineering with the assistant Chief Engineer, who is pulling control chips from the computer control panel.

The original antidote discovered by McCoy is ineffective against this strain of the toxin and so Crusher keeps working to find a cure.

They finally get back into Engineering, but the control chips are all over the floor and would take hours to replace in their proper slots. Wes remarks that Data could do it much more quickly. The challenge of this game intrigues Data, particularly since he has only 14 minutes to accomplish it. A piece of the star is hurtling in their direction and unless the Enterprise can regain motion control, the starship will be smashed by the huge chunk of the blazing star.

Dr. Crusher completes an antidote but the Enterprise still needs to maneuver from the path of the hurtling star matter.

Wesley tells the Chief Engineer how the tractor beam could be reversed into a repulsor beam; this enables the Enterprise to get a push away from the Tsiolovsky, which briefly blocks the star stuff by colliding with it first. This gives the Enterprise precious time to allow Data to finish, whereupon the starship blasts out of orbit and away from the deadly region.

Picard acknowledges the important help rendered by Wesley even though the stricken boy was also partially responsible for the ship being endangered to begin with.

EPISODE FOUR: "CODE OF HONOR"

Teleplay by Kathryn Powers and Michael Baron

Directed by Russ Mayberry

Guest Cast: Jessie Lawrence Ferguson, Karole Selmon, James Louis Watkins, Michael Rider

The Enterprise is in orbit around the planet Ligon II. They are there to pick up a rare vaccine needed to battle a plague on Styris IV. Picard has been instructed to open friendly negotiations with Ligon II in order to acquire the vaccine.

The Ligonian legation beams aboard to greet Captain Picard. He is accompanied by Riker, Troi and Tasha Yar. First four burly guards arrive. They are followed by the assistant to the leader, Hagon, who bears a small box as a gift. Then a carpet is unrolled and Lutan, the leader, appears.

When Hagon tries to present the box, which Lutan explains is a sample of the vaccine, to Picard, Tasha intercepts him, explaining that her duty is to examine it first. Annoyed, Hagon tries to brush her aside but instead is flipped on his back. Lutan is amused that a woman could do such a thing.

Lutan is taken on a tour of the ship and is suitably impressed. The monarch offers to open friendly relations with the Federation so long as the customs of his people are respected. Picard assures him that the Federation will honor the customs of his people.

When Riker explains that it is commonplace for women to hold positions of authority on a starship, Lutan remarks that among his people the duty of women is only to own the land while the men protect and rule it.

In the holodeck Lutan asks for a demonstration of Tasha Yar's skills. She agrees, and Tasha successfully defeats a hologram. Lutan reaches out to congratulate her while at the same time touching a jewel in his collar, and the two immediately vanish in a transporter beam. Picard immediately puts the ship on full alert and sends a message down to Lutan demanding that he release Yar, but there is no response. Since Data indicates that Ligonian culture respects patience, Picard chooses that route for the time being.

When questioned about what she detected among the Legation, Troi indicates that while all the males were attracted to Yar, Lutan's emotions were more along the lines of ambition or avarice, as though she represented something to him.

As another day passes without word from Lutan, Dr. Crusher reports that something must be done because the vaccine cannot be replicated in the lab. It must be obtained from Ligon II. After an analysis of Ligonian society, Data reports that they live by a strict code of honor. and by Lutan's standards what he did is considered extremely heroic in that he risked everything to kidnap her in the face of the Federation's superior power.

Finally, Lutan contacts Picard and states that if he beams down to the planet she will be returned. Riker is against the Captain beaming down but Data explains that by his reckoning things will go better if he does. Picard beams down and Lutan presents himself along with his primary wife, his "First One." Lutan promises that Yar will be returned at a banquet planned for that evening, after first showing that she is unharmed.

At the banquet Lutan congratulates Picard on his response to the situation, but then explains that he doesn't want to return Yar after all, but wants her to become his First One. Yareena, Lutan's present First One, challenges Yar to combat, as is her right: a fight to the death.

Yar accepts the challenge in order to obtain the vaccine, as the plague on Styris IV has reached serious proportions. Lutan reveals that if Yareena is killed, Lutan inherits all her land. If Yar is killed, he will be no worse off than before. The weapons that Yar can fight with can be one of a variety of different types. Those with blades are coated with a fast-acting poison.

Meanwhile, on board the Enterprise, Riker is trying to have the ship's sensors detect Yar so that she can be beamed up if the combat goes against her. Yareena is determined to fight Yar as she cannot believe that Tasha would not be attracted to a man like Lutan.

The field of combat is a small area of bars and poles surrounded by a force field. Yareena is more familiar with this style of combat, and the weapons used, but Tasha is still a trained warrior, which gives her a necessary edge. Once the battle starts they seem evenly matched, but the more Tasha becomes accustomed to the style of combat, the better she gets, and she defeats Yareena by scratching the woman's shoulder with her weapon. At the moment Yareena falls, they beam out of sight, back to the Enterprise. Lutan is upset, because Yar is supposed to become his First One now. Picard says that he won't stop her, should she choose to claim the honor

When the vaccine is beamed aboard the Enterprise, Lutan and Hagon beam back with Picard. There Lutan is shocked to find Yareena alive and claims to have been tricked. But Yareena did die, only to be revived by Dr. Crusher. Since their mating agreement ended with death, Yareena is free of Lutan, and turns her attentions to Hagon. Lutan, without Yareena's lands, is powerless, and Hagon, who asks Yareena to be his First One, inherits Lutan's title.

Negotiations completed, the Ligonians return to their planet and the Enterprise warps out with the vaccine for Styris IV.

EPISODE FIVE: "THE LAST OUTPOST"

Teleplay by Herbert Wright

Story by Richard Krzemian

Directed by Richard Colla

Guest Cast: Darryl Henriques, Mike Gomez, Armin Shimerman, Jake Dengal, Tracey Walter

The Enterprise is in pursuit of a Ferengi spacecraft which stole a T-9 Energy Converter from Gamma Tari IV. The Ferengi have never been seen before and the Federation wants to make contact with them. The Ferengi ship drops to subwarp and the Enterprise follows, and both go into orbit around a nearby planet.

The Ferengi ship fires on the Enterprise, but the shields hold. The Enterprise prepares to return fire when their power begins dropping. Shields and weapons systems fail. It seems that the Ferengi have some new, unknown but powerful weapon which puts them at a deadly advantage over the Enterprise.

Picard tries to contact Engineering but can't get a reply. Geordi leaves the bridge to go there himself to get a status report.

Troi tries to get an impression of the Ferengi but they can block out their thoughts and emotions so that she cannot get a reading from them.

Riker asks Data what he has on the Ferengi and is told that all that is really known about them is that they are ruthless businessmen representing the worst extremes of the capitalistic system

Since they seem to be at their foe's mercy, Worf wants the Enterprise to attack rather than sit and wait to be attacked. Picard tries a different strategy and contacts the Ferengi, demanding that they return the T-9 Energy Converter. There is no reply.

Data reports that some force is reading all of the information in the ship's memory banks. Troi suggests that they may be overlooking the obvious and points out that the planet they are orbiting could somehow be responsible. Picard contacts the Ferengi again and offers to open negotiations for an unconditional surrender. The response of the Ferengi indicates that they think that Picard wants them to surrender. This clinches the theory that the planet is somehow responsible for what is happening.

Scans of the planet detect no lifeforms and records indicate it to be part of the old T'Kan Empire which was destroyed by a supernova six hundred years before.

Picard offers the Ferengi an alliance against whatever force has captured their ships. The Ferengi reluctantly agree, but are angry at Picard for first suggesting that he was responsible for the capture of the Ferengi ship. The allies agree to meet at predesignated coordinates on the planet below.

Riker, Data, Geordi and Worf beam down together but arrive separately. The surface of the planet is covered by a sky which is grey and filled with raging storms. Riker finds Data nearby and they soon happen upon Geordi, who arrived upside down. But before they can lower him, the Ferengi appear and attack, using whips which shoot out energy lashes, one of which knocks Geordi to the ground. The Ferengi have already stunned and captured Worf, and after knocking out the humans they toss Worf alongside them.

Aboard the Enterprise the power continues to fail as the temperature drops. If it gets much colder, all aboard the starship will die. Back on the planet surface, Worf comes to and attacks the Ferengi, who are actually not very difficult to defeat in hand to hand combat since they are about two feet shorter than humans. A real free for all ensues until Tasha arrives and points a phaser at the Ferengi, which halts the conflict. The Ferengi and the humans stand off but when they try to attack each other with their weapons, their energy beams are drawn into nearby crystalline structures which are actually huge energy collectors. Geordi realizes that the entire planet is a power accumulator. There are peals of thunder, which bother the large, sensitive ears of the Ferengi, and the guardian of the planet appears, a being who calls himself Portal. Portal was apparently in suspended animation for hundreds of centuries until the appearance of the two starships awakened him. He still believes that the T'Kan Empire exists, even though Data explains what has happened. The Ferengi try to convince Portal that the Federation crew is there to loot the empire. Finally, Portal tells Riker that he will put him to a test: "He will triumph who knows when to fight and when not to fight." Riker demonstrates his wisdom and Portal realizes who the civilized ones are as he can read Riker's thoughts, while the Ferengi shield theirs. Portal returns the power to the Enterprise, just in time to save everyone aboard. He had observed the two starships seemingly bent on combat, and his first impulse had been to destroy them both. But when he observed them cooperating, Portal decided to wait and see. Portal even offers to destroy the Ferengi, but Riker points out that they would then learn nothing from the experience. Riker states that the Ferengi remind him of how humans were hundreds of years ago, but notes that with their advanced technology they are a present danger. Portal chooses to go back to sleep until needed again, and the two parties return to their respective ships.

As a parting gesture to the Ferengi, Riker suggests that they beam them over a box of Data's Chinese finger puzzles. Picard smiles and agrees.

EPISODE SIX: "WHERE NO ONE HAS GONE BEFORE"

Written by Diane Duane and Michael Reaves

Directed by Rob Bowman

Guest Cast: Biff Yeager, Charles Dayton, Victoria Dillard, Stanley Kamel, Eric Menyuk, Herta Ware

The Enterprise has a rendezvous with the USS Fearless. A Federation propulsion expert and his assistant are beamed over to conduct tests with new equations for the warp speed and intermix formulas. Riker questions the value of this since the Enterprise 1701-D is a brand new ship employing the latest in engine technology. Also, the formulae sent on ahead by Mr. Koszinski show no effect when run in computer simulations.

Koszinski is very arrogant about his formula. He is accompanied by his assistant, a humanoid alien from Tau Alpha-C. The alien does not give a name, stating that it is unpronounceable in the languages of humans.

Troi has been sent along to scan the two men. She states that Koszinski is exactly as he seems, arrogant and self-important, but that she cannot read anything from his assistant, almost as though the man weren't even there.

Koszinski is annoyed at having to explain his system, but Riker makes it clear that it will not be tested until it is approved by himself and the chief engineer. Eventually, Koszinski is allowed to proceed, and the alien lays in the basic formula at a speed faster than normal humans could. The alien allows Wesley Crusher to observe him and even responds when the boy makes suggestions about how the energy pulses are reading on the screen. The alien seems strangely open to reinterpreting Koszinski's theories. The warp drive test run is begun, but during the test, something goes wrong. The velocity achieved goes off the scale and Wesley observes the alien momentarily phase, as though parts of him are disappearing.

Picard has the vessel brought to a stop only to find that they are in a new system near a new star. The instruments calibrate their position to be on the far side of M-33, two million, seven hundred light years from their previous position. Geordi points out that it would take the Enterprise 300 years to return to Federation space even at maximum warp. They have traversed an impossible distance in mere moments. Koszinski admits that he made mistakes, but that he's certain he can easily get them back to where they started. The propulsion expert takes full credit for what has happened and states that they'll all be famous for breaking the warp barrier. Only Wesley notices that the alien is very tired.

Based on what he saw of the formula, Wesley asks if it wasn't based on the concept that space and time and thought are not as different as everyone believes them to be. The alien is startled by this observation and asks Wesley never to repeat it.

While preparing to repeat the propulsion maneuver, Wesley attempts to tell Riker that he doesn't think

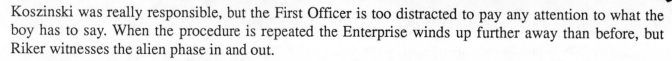

Koszinski was really responsible, but the First Officer is too distracted to pay any attention to what the boy has to say. When the procedure is repeated the Enterprise winds up further away than before, but Riker witnesses the alien phase in and out.

In this new region, space and thought are linked, and people can materialize things deep from within their minds. Tasha imagines herself back at the colony where she grew up, fleeing a rape gang, while Picard encounters his long dead mother. Realizing what is happening, Picard warns the crew to be careful what they think about, as it could be dangerous. The Captain is desperate to get the Enterprise out of the strange region before it becomes impossible to distinguish reality from fantasy.

The alien collapses and is taken to Sick Bay, but Picard insists that Dr. Crusher give it a stimulant, as it is the only one who can return the Enterprise to its proper place.

The being reveals that he is a traveller, but is vague about where he actually comes from. He states that he is capable of acting as a lens to focus thought and turn it into power. That is how the starship travelled millions of light years in moments. Alone with Picard, the Traveller reveals that Wesley has rare gifts and is capable of creativity, not unlike the Traveller himself. He admonishes Picard to keep this knowledge a secret, so that Wesley can develop normally.

The propulsion procedure is attempted again. The Traveller has Koszinski assist him in entering the formula while Picard instructs the crew to concentrate on giving strength to the Traveller. They succeed, but in the process, the Traveller fades out completely.

Back in familiar space, Picard invites Wesley to the bridge, justifying his presence there by making him an acting ensign. To top this off, he decides to sponsor Wesley's application to Starfleet Academy, which makes the new ensign extremely happy.

EPISODE SEVEN: "LONELY AMONG US"

Script by D.C. Fontana

Story by Michael Halperin

Directed by Cliff Bole

Guest Cast: Colm Meaney, Kavi Raz, John Durbin

The Enterprise is on its way to the planet Parliament, the site of a peace conference between two warring non-human races. Representatives of each race have been picked up and are being quartered on the ship, although each has a violent hatred of the other.

While passing near a strange energy cloud, the Enterprise brushes against it, and a bit of energy is transferred into the Enterprise. It manifests itself by flowing into Worf, who is shocked unconscious. The Klingon is taken to sickbay, and the energy transfers to Dr. Crusher She goes to the bridge and makes an excuse to use one of the science stations, whereupon the energy transfers into the ship's systems. Controls start to malfunction, but they are easily repaired. This annoys Picard, as a ship as new as the Enterprise should not be experiencing such systems breakdowns. He demands that an answer be found as soon as possible, if not sooner.

Meanwhile, one of the alien delegations is found with weapons, which are confiscated. They are given a stern warning not to cause further trouble.

Warp suddenly fades, along with subspace communications, but then it is restored, although not before Mr. Singh, the Assistant Chief Engineer, receives the same strange shock and is killed. This event is witnessed by Worf. Dr. Crusher realizes that she's suffering from a memory lapse just as Worf is, and asks Deanna to hypnotize them in order to get to the truth. Under hypnosis, each reveals that for a time they were under the control of another entity. Finally, the force emerges from the ship's systems and enters Picard, who immediately orders the Enterprise to double back to the mysterious cloud. Dr. Crusher and Riker determine that something is wrong with Picard and confront him in order to force him to take psychiatric exams. Picard deftly turns the situation around. Finally he admits to Crusher that he is an alien entity which has joined with Picard, and that he plans to take Picard with him into the cloud. Using strange powers, the Captain temporarily disables the bridge crew and the transporter chief and as the starship arrives back at the cloud, beams himself into it as pure energy.

Troi detects the presence of Picard in the cloud as energy disconnected from the energy— they could not stay united in the cloud as the entity had thought they could. Picard's energy enters the ship and Data surmises that it will know how to enter the transporter system. Since Picard was the last person to beam out, and since he did not reform outside, his pattern is still recorded in the transporter. Activating it, there are some tense moments until Picard reforms. He doesn't remember what happened to him when he was just energy although he does have some memory of when the entity was controlling him. Tired, he decides to let Riker handle the current crisis with the delegation: one side seems to have slain one of the others, and is preparing to cook and eat him.

EPISODE EIGHT: "JUSTICE"

Teleplay by Worley Thorne

Story by Ralph Willis and Worley Thorne

Directed by James L. Conway

Guest Cast: Josh Clark, David Q. Combs, Richard Lavin, Judith Jones, Eric Matthew, Brad Zerbst, David Michael Graves

While establishing a colony, the Enterprise discovers a new Class M planet. The people of the planet are not just friendly but very affectionate and display this affection with little provocation. Initial interviews and surveys deem the world safe and Captain Picard decides to grant the crew shore leave following a more detailed survey by an Away Team consisting of Riker, Tasha, Troi, Wesley and others.

Upon beaming down, the landing team is greeted by the Edo who embrace and kiss them. Wesley is a bit embarrassed by this although they only hug him. The Edo send Wesley off with some Edo teenagers of his own age.

Aboard the Enterprise, Data detects something off the bow which doesn't appear on the screens. At first it is regarded as a glitch but Data doesn't think so. Finally he tries broadcasting a communication beam asking whatever is there to identify itself, and something appears. It looks like a huge space station of some type but it is at a juncture which straddles more than one dimension, allowing the entities therein to be in many different places at once.

A small transparent globe shoots out of the craft and enters the Enterprise. It confronts Picard and projects a rather loud query: "State the purpose of your visit here." Picard explains what they are doing and the device ends its verbal communication by saying, "Do not interfere with my children below." The device then confronts Data and attaches itself to him in order to learn what he knows and what the people on the Enterprise are like.Down on the planet, Worf and Tasha are conversing with two of the Edo when they ask about laws and crime and the Edo casually admit that no one breaks any law because no one wants to risk execution. Tasha is astonished and immediately contacts Riker; they summon the rest of the landing team members to confer on this. But they can't immediately locate Wesley.

Wes is playing ball with the Edo teenagers and inadvertently blunders into a small greenhouse arrangement. The Mediators appear and attempt to execute the death sentence. Riker and the others arrive in time to use force and stop them. This creates great consternation among the Edo as no one is above the law, not even outsiders.

Picard is notified and he beams down. A hearing is held and the Edo explain their system of laws to Picard while the Captain, in turns, explains that his culture no longer practices capital punishment. It becomes clear to the Edo that Picard regards them as being a primitive culture, and become somewhat defensive over this. Picard then tries to calm things by stating that their own Prime Directive contains a non-interference clause, which insists that Federation personnel not interfere with alien cultures and must abide by their rules. Thus Wesley should be sacrificed to uphold this rule. The Edo state that the punishment of the boy can only be delayed until sundown.

Picard wants to know more about the entities in orbit nearby and beams up to the Enterprise with one of the Edo women. He takes her to the observation chamber and she reverently tells him that what they are seeing is "God." She knows this because "God" has appeared to them before.

Suddenly the alien craft starts moving towards the Enterprise, demanding that their "child" be returned to the planet below. Picard acts quickly and has the woman beamed down directly from the observation chamber.

Data states that the entities know all that he knows about the Federation, which would include the Prime Directive.

When Dr. Crusher asks Picard what he's going to do, he states that, no matter what the cost, he will not allow Wesley to be executed. The two beam down to confront the Edo once again.

Wes is brought out from confinement and Picard informs the Edo that he cannot allow the boy to be punished for a crime he wasn't even aware he was committing, particularly since no one came to any harm as the result of his actions.

EPISODE NINE: "THE BATTLE"

Teleplay by Herbert Wright

Story by Larry Forester

Directed by Rob Bowman

Guest Cast: Frank Corsentino, Doug Warhit, Robert Towers

The Enterprise is at the predetermined coordinates for a rendezvous with a Ferengi ship. The meeting is at the request of the Ferengi. Although the Ferengi vessel is there, it does not reply to the Enterprise's attempts to communicate for three whole days. Then Bock, the commander of the Ferengi vessel, states that he wants to meet with Picard alone. Picard invites the Ferengi to meet him aboard his vessel.

Ever since arriving at the meeting point, Picard has been suffering from increasingly severe headaches. Since this is an uncommon ailment in the 24th Century, Dr. Crusher is concerned, but can find no physical reason for the affliction.

As the Ferengi are preparing to beam over, Wesley Crusher arrives on the bridge to announce that he has detected the approach of a Constellation class starship on the long range scanners. The Ferengi beam aboard, and Bock announces that this vessel is a gift to Picard, with no strings attached and no asking price. Bock's comrades are shocked at this un-Ferengi display of foolish, unprofitable generosity.

Picard is just as shocked, but for a different reason. This Federation starship is the Stargazer, Picard's old vessel. He and the crew had to abandon it nine years earlier after they were attacked by an unidentified vessel (since revealed to be Ferengi) and only barely destroyed their attacker before having to flee in shuttlecraft. Picard had believed the Ferengi to be lost in space. The Ferengi express innocence and claim that they found it adrift on the far side of the galaxy.

This prompts a discussion of the Battle of Maxia, as Picard's engagement with the Ferengi is known. It introduced a new method of warfare involving the use of warp drive over a short distance so that a vessel would appear to be in two places at once, thereby confusing the enemy. Bock seems particularly sensitive about the Battle of Maxia, a name the Ferengi have applied to this encounter.

Picard's headache worsens and Bock casually asks if the Captain's conscience is bothering him, but no one picks up on the significance of the remark.

Tasha Yar, Geordi and Worf beam aboard the Stargazer to investigate the ship and find it in remarkably good condition. Picard soon follows and is amazed. When he abandoned the ship, it was on fire. Picard goes to his old stateroom on the vessel and packs some things which had been left behind nine years before.

Aboard the Ferengi vessel, Bock gloats over how he intends to destroy Picard with his secret device.

While a Federation tug is arranged to rendezvous with the ships and pick up the stargazer, Picard lies in his bunk and dreams of the Battle of Maxia.

Meanwhile, Geordi and the others find the old personal log of Captain Picard's aboard the Stargazer. It indicates a different chronology to the Battle of Maxia than the official report submitted by Picard. But Data soon proves that the log is a clever forgery. Someone is trying to discredit Picard.

Wes reveals that he has detected low intensity transmissions from the Ferengi vessel which match the strange wave patterns in Picard's brain scan.

But before the Captain can be contacted, it's discovered that he has beamed aboard the Stargazer and activated the shields.

Bock confronts Picard and reveals that it was his son who was in command of the Ferengi vessel that Picard destroyed. Bock has spent the accumulated wealth of a lifetime to acquire the forbidden and dangerous devices he is using against Picard. Bock beams back to his ship and leaves a brainwashed Picard thinking that he is back at the Battle of Maxia, and that he is under attack by a strange spacecraft which is in actuality his own ship, the Enterprise.

The Ferengi vessel contacts the Enterprise and reveals that Bock has been relieved of command because of his unprofitable quest for vengeance. Riker shows the Ferengi a device found in Picard's cabin on board the Enterprise and is informed that it is a forbidden mind control device.

Picard uses the warp drive maneuver against the Enterprise but is caught by the vessel's tractor beam. Riker then manages to get a message through, and convinces Picard of what is happening. Jean-Luc destroys the mind control sphere on the bridge of the Stargazer and is freed from its influence.

EPISODE TEN: "HIDE AND Q"

Teleplay by C.J. Holland and Gene Roddenberry

Story by C.J. Holland

Directed by Cliff Bole

Guest Cast: John de Lancie, Elaine Nalee, William A. Wallace

The Enterprise is on its way to Quadra Sigma III to assist in rescue efforts on an underground disaster at the colony there.

Suddenly a barrier appears in front of the starship, halting its progress, and a strange alien lifeform appears on the bridge. It says that it has the realization of impossible dreams to offer. The alien then chooses a form that the crew might more easily identify with, that of the alien Q.

Q insists that it wants to involve the crew in some deadly games and vanishes, taking Riker, Worf, Data, LaForge and Tasha Yar along to a barren planet surface.

Back on the Enterprise, Picard finds himself alone on the bridge, unable to contact any other part of the ship and even unable to leave the bridge.

On the planet, Q appears dressed in the uniform of an American Revolutionary War commander and invites Riker to drink with him. Riker accepts but Worf refuses, turning the offered drink upside down.

When they ask what the rules of this game will be, Q states that it will be completely unfair. When Tasha objects she is sent to the "penalty box." Q states that the next person to break a rule will also be sent to the penalty box, thus causing Tasha Yar's instant demise.

The penalty box that Yar is sent to is actually the bridge of the Enterprise, which is still trapped behind the barrier. Q appears to Picard and reveals that the one he's really interested in is Riker. Q plans to offer Number One something that he can not refuse. Picard says that he will lose. Q agrees that if he does he'll leave humans alone for ever after.

Worf goes on reconnaissance and sees brutal looking aliens dressed as Revolutionary War soldiers. The aliens approach, bent on attack.

Q appears to Riker and states that he has given Number One the power of Q to use as he will. Riker sends the other crewmen back safely to the enterprise. They find that the Enterprise is not only back on course, but was apparently never behind any barrier. Q had just suspended time.

On the planet, Q and Riker converse, as Riker wants to know what Q wants from humans. Q explains that he's fascinated by the human race's ability for growth and wants Riker to become one of the Q so that they can learn more about this facet of humankind. Riker turns Q down.

Suddenly the entire bridge crew is back on the planet, along with Picard and Wesley Crusher. The alien warriors attack and Worf and Wesley are killed, but Riker uses his new power to return them all to the Enterprise, along with restoring Worf and Wesley to perfect health. Riker still has the power of Q, which includes the power over life and death.

On the Enterprise, Picard tells Riker that the only way he can not give in to Q is by refusing to use his power. The more Riker uses his power, the more he will want to use it, so he must not give in to the temptation. Riker promises the Captain that he won't use the power.

The Enterprise arrives at Quadra Sigma II and the Away Team beams down on the rescue mission. They find many already dead, and as they 're removing the rubble, they discover the body of a child.

Riker doesn't use his power to revive her because he has promised Picard that he would not. Riker is angry at having to keep his word, and tells Picard.

Riker summons the bridge crew, including Wesley, to discuss his situation. Picard points out that Riker is already being corrupted by the power as he's started calling the Captain by his first name, making it clear that he no longer feels inferior to the Captain.

Q appears on the bridge as a monk in order to observe the proceedings.

Riker wants to use his power to give his friends what they've always wanted— to grant each of them their fondest wish. He makes Wesley ten years older.

Data refuses to be made human. He doesn't want to get his wish that way. Geordi is given human eyes, but has Riker make him the way he was. He, too, does not want to have his dream fulfilled like this.

Worf is given a mate, a savage Klingon woman who he fights with and subdues as part of the courtship rite. He suddenly realizes that he can't continue, as this part of Klingon reality is no longer part of his life. He has Riker remove her.

Wesley too asks Riker to take back his gift.

Riker rejects the power at last. Q has therefore failed. The other entities of the Q Continuum summon Q back to explain his failure, and the troublesome being disappears screaming.

EPISODE ELEVEN: "HAVEN"

Teleplay by Tracy Torme

Story by Tracy Torme and Lian Okun

Directed by Richard Compton

Guest Cast: Danzita Kingsley, Carel Struycken, Anna Katrina, Raye Birk, Michael Rider, Majel Barrett, Rob Knepper, Nan Martin, Robert Ellenstein

The Enterprise arrives at the planet Haven for some rest and recreation. Riker is on a holodeck when he's summoned to the transporter room. An object beams up which announces to Deanna Troi that the marriage party, consisting of the Miller family, will be arriving soon. Deanna is crestfallen at the news.

Troi had been promised in marriage as child and had believed it would never really come to pass. She knows that she and her husband would not be staying with the ship. Deanna tells Riker that she knows that he cares about her.

The Miller wedding party, consisting of the mother, father and their adult son Wyatt, beam aboard. Wyatt is a handsome young man who has become a doctor. The Millers are taken to their quarters so that Deanna's mother will beam aboard, the first sign of problems between them.

Deanna warns Picard that her mother is eccentric, as well as a full Betazoid with telepathic powers. The woman is loud and obnoxious, and even though she has a seven foot tall servant with her, she asks Picard to carry her bag, which is extremely heavy.

In her quarters, Deanna's mother, Lwaxana Troi, complains about her daughter not using her mental powers all the time, and that she has become lazy living among mere humans. Deanna explains that she has doubts about her wedding vows but will uphold them. Lwaxana states that she understands and had all but forgotten about the arranged marriage herself until the Millers tracked her down and confronted her with the old promise.

While this is happening, Haven detects an unidentified ship approaching. It contacts the Enterprise as Haven has a defense treaty with the Federation. The vessel is still too far off to be identified.

Deanna visits Wyatt to learn more about him and discovers that besides being a doctor, he's also an artist. His art has repeated images of a beautiful woman whom he has never met but has seen often in his dreams. Until that day he believed the woman to be Deanna Troi.

The Enterprise has the unknown ship on its screen and identifies it as a Terellian plague ship, even though the last known such ship had been believed destroyed seven years before. The Terellians had waged war on a planetary scale and one side had unleashed a plague which infected the world. The ship carries the last survivors of the contagion. Haven is in a panic over the ship's existence and demands that the Enterprise prevent the vessel from approaching.

A party is held for the bride-and-groom-to-be. An argument erupts over which type of wedding to have, Betazoid or Earth style. Picard finally declares all arguments resolved by his authority as Captain of the Enterprise.

Deanna finally explodes over the petty bickering and storms out.

Data asks, "Could you continue the petty bickering? I find it most intriguing."

Deanna visits Riker in the holodeck. He's unhappy over the impending marriage. Wyatt enters and Riker decides to leave. Wyatt asks Deanna if she really wants to marry him. They kiss.

Haven pleads with Picard to destroy the Terellian ship as it approaches transporter range. The Enterprise traps the vessel in a tractor beam.

The Terellians contact the Enterprise on the viewscreen and Deanna recognizes one of its passengers, Arianna, as the same woman who appears in Wyatt's drawings. They ask for Wyatt and when he comes to the bridge he is amazed by what he sees. The Terellians explain that there are only eight of them left alive. All they crave is a remote area of Haven where they can be alone to die.

Wyatt prepares medical supplies to be beamed over to the Terellians. He says good-bye to his parents and Deanna, but they don't realize what he's planning.

Wyatt goes to the transporter room, knocks out the technician and has himself beamed over to the Terellian ship before the transporter beam can be overridden. He joins Arianna, who had also dreamed about him but was never completely sure whether he was real.

Wyatt communicates with his parents, explaining that he'll try to cure the Terellians, who have chosen to remain aboard their ship and continue on their journey through space, away from Haven.

EPISODE TWELVE: "THE BIG GOODBYE"

Written by Tracy Torme

Directed by Joseph L. Scanlan

Guest Cast: Mike Genovese, Dick Miller, Carolyn Alport, Rhonda Aldrich, Eric Cord, Lawrence Tierney, Harvey Jason, William Boyett, David Selburg, Gary Armagnal

The Enterprise is en route to contact a reclusive alien insect race. The Harada are very fastidious about their language, and when the previous Federation representative mispronounced a word during the last contact, twenty years before, the aliens were so offended that they refused further contact with the Federation until now. As Captain of the Enterprise, Picard must memorize the alien greeting and deliver it flawlessly in their strange language.

Picard has been working hard to memorize the greeting, and Deanna Troi suggests that he take a break in the holodeck. Picard agrees and calls up the 1941 Dixon Hill program, based on the exploits of a fictional pulp magazine detective.

Still wearing his normal uniform, Picard enters the holodeck and walks into the office of dixon Hill, which is the role he has adopted for himself in this fictional holodeck simulation. A woman is waiting in his office, who wants to hire Dixon Hill to keep her from being killed. She gives him a C-note (century note: a hundred-dollar bill) retained and tells him to wear a suit the next time.

Picard looks around "Hill's" office, calls out "Exit" and then leaves, even though someone is knocking at his normal office door. He tells them to come back later. But even after Picard leaves the holodeck, the program keeps running and the person enters the office only to look around in confusion because he knows that he just heard Dixon Hill in the office.

At a meeting in the conference room, Picard can't contain his excitement over the holodeck and how real it all seems. It was so real that Dr. Crusher leans over and wipes some lipstick off Picard's face that he'd retained as a reminder of the enthusiasm of his grateful client.

Picard dresses appropriately in clothes fitting the time period of Dixon hill and has Mr. Whelan, an expert on 20th Century culture, accompany him. But Data has just scanned the computer and absorbed all the information on Dixon Hill, and so he, too, has dressed up in 1940s garb and requested to accompany them. Picard has no objection.

They enter the holodeck and emerge on a street outside the building housing Dixon Hill's office. At a newspaper stand, Picard reads a newspaper which has a picture of the woman who'd hired him as "Dixon Hill." She's been murdered. When a police detective sees Picard, he is taken in for questioning. The dead woman had one of his business cards on her.

Meanwhile, the Harada sends out a long-range probe which sweeps over the Enterprise, and they announce that they want to hear from Captain Picard immediately. When Lt. Riker tries to speak to the aliens, they angrily terminate their communications.

Dr. Crusher puts on a 1940s style dress and enters the holodeck to find Picard. She enters the police station and learn that he's being interrogated by the police. Crusher is very excited by this adventure.

Geordi attempts to contact Picard on the holodeck, but the communication link fails, and the Holodeck doors won't open. When the Harada probe swept the ship, it apparently disrupted some of the Holodeck mechanisms.

Riker and Wesley go down to investigate the Holodeck problems. Wesley is familiar with the holodeck mechanisms, and is concerned because his mother is trapped inside.

In the holodeck, Picard is released from police custody. He's given a cigarette by a police detective friend, but finds that he doesn't know how to smoke. The cop is a friend of "Dixon Hill" and invites Picard over to dinner with his family

When Picard enters the lobby of the police station, he's surprised to see Beverly Crusher, and is particularly impressed by how she looks in her costume. Picard now seems to feel restrained by having Data and Mr. Whelan along.

When the four return to Dixon Hill's office, a ferret-faced little man named Felix Leach is waiting there. None of them take hkm seriously because, after all, he's merely a hologram of a stereotyped pulp character. When Felix loses his composure and shoots Mr. Whelan, the historian is seriously wounded by the gunshot.

Picard disarms and strikes Leach, recalling Humphrey Bogart and Peter Lorre in a similar situation, and Leach flees. Picard calls for the exit but it fails to appear. Dr. Crusher tells him that Whelan is badly hurt and may die if he is not taken to sick bay immediately.

Cyrus Redblock (the Sydney Greenstreet of the piece) enters with his bodyguards, Felix Leach in tow. They hold Picard and the others at gunpoint, demanding to know where "the item" is. When Picard claims ignorance, Redblock allows Leach to strike him, in revenge for Picard having hit him.

The police detective arrives and is taken prisoner as well.

Picard confesses that they're from another world and that he's not really Dixon Hill. Data even tells Cyrus Redblock that he is not real, which does not go over well with the now-dangerous hologram. Redblock plans to test how real he is by killing one of Picard's people.

Picard appeals to Redblock's greed by telling the man that he has "the item" in his world. He convinces Redblock of this when the holodeck momentarily flickers, replacing 1941 San Francisco with an arctic blizzard.

The exit finally opens in the Holodeck and Picard lures Leach and Redblock through it. Once they leave the holodeck, they vanish, much to their own consternation. The Captain and friends then over-power the thugs remaining in the holodeck, and take Whelan to sick bay.

Picard says farewell to his friend the police detective, who wonders if he'll exist after Picard leaves. The Captain admits that he honestly doesn't know. As Picard departs, the holodeck goes dark.

Picard then goes to the bridge, still dressed as Dixon Hill, Private Eye, and flawlessly delivers the Federation's greeting to the Harada.

EPISODE THIRTEEN: "DATALORE"

Teleplay by Robert Lewin and Gene Roddenberry

Story by Robert Lewin and Maurice Hurley

Directed by Rob Bowman

Guest Cast: Biff Yeager

The Enterprise enters the Omicron Theta star system with plans to stop over at Data's home planet. Data holds the complete recorded knowledge and experiences of the 411 members of the Earth colony that once existed there but disappeared shortly before Data was found, in a nonfunctional state. No life exists there now.

Upon achieving orbit, the Enterprise sends an Away Team down, and Data shows them where he was found.

Geordi's artificially enhanced sight detects a false wall of rock which conceals a cave, not apparent to the unaided normal human eye. He finds a way in and they discover a fully functional laboratory— the lab where Data was created. They also find something odd— children's drawings of a weird configuration in the sky.

Data suddenly remebers that Dr. Noonian Soong was his creator. Soong was Earth's foremost cybernetic scientist until he tried to make Asimov's dream of a positronic brain come true. When his attempts to do this failed, he disappeared from Earth.

The Away Team locates Data's patterns and an epidermal mold, as well as parts for another Data. They return to the Enterprise with them and assemble the second android.

The android is activated and says that its name is Lore. It looks exactly like Data, but has a facial tic and an attitude that set it apart from its 'brother', whom Lore claims is an imperfect version of himself. Soon, Lore manages to replace Data, disabling the real Data amd triggering a tic like his own. Lore is also able to halt his own twitch, and replaces Data on the bridge.

Lore contacts a strange space creature which feeds on life and summons it toward the Enterprise. This is the same creature depicted in the children's drawings on the planet in the Omicron Theta system, and the force which destroyed the colony.

Wesley Crusher is suspicious of Data and senses the truth of his identity. They try to revive the unconscious android in Data's quarters, but without success.

The gigantic crystalline creature attacks the Enterprise but Lore warns it off. He offers to go over to it and goes to the transporter room. Wesley protests but Riker belittles him. Wesley complains that people would listen to him if he were older.

Worf follows Lore and is suddenly cut off and cornered in the turbolift. Lore attacks him, demonstrating that his strength and fighting skill can defeat even a Klingon warrior.

Wesley and Dr. Crusher revive Data and together they confront Lore in the transporter room. Lore grabs a phaser and threatens Wes, forcing Dr. Crusher to leave. As a parting gesture, he shoots the doctor in the arm.

Data atacks Lore. During their struggle, Lore is maneuvered into the transporter and Wesley beams him out. Without Lore to communicate with it, the huge crystal creature leaves.

EPISODE FOURTEEN: "ANGEL ONE"

Teleplay by Patrick Berry

Directed by Michael Rhodes

Guest Cast: Karen Montgomery, Sam Hennings, Leonard John Crowfoot, Patricia McPherson

The Enterprise encounters a derelict ship which turns out to be the freighter Odin, a vessel reported lost seven years earlier. Three escape pods are missing, so the Enterprise visits the nearest planet, Angel One, to search for possible survivors.

Angel One is similar to mid-20th Century Earth in technology but it is a matriarchical society in which men are the meek servitors of women. The last time that a Federation ship visited the planet was 62 years before. When the Enterprise ask permission to send down an Away Team, they are given a rather cool reception.

Riker, Data, Troi and Yar beam down and ask for information regarding possible survivors. The ruler is evasive and says that she is not yet prepared to answer their questions. When she does answer them, she reveals that there are four survivors who are now radical fugitives from Angel One society.

On the Enterprise, Wesley Crusher and another boy contract a respiratory ailment.

The Enterprise plans to scan the surface of angel one for survivors. The Elected One agrees to this so long as the Enterprise crew promise to take the rebels with them, since they are an unwanted disruptive force.

On the surface, Riker is given a garment to wear for his audience with the Elected One. Yar and Troi are at first annoyed by Riker's submission to the ruler's sartorial demands, but are amused when they see Riker dressed in the skimpy outfit.

Picard contracts the virus which afflicted Wesley, and orders Geordi to take the bridge.

The survivors are located. Data, Yar and Troi are beamed to their position. A man there, Ramsey, greets them as though he'd been expecting them.

On the Enterprise, 82 more cases of the virus are reported.

The survivors of Odin reveal that, while they have families now, they are prepared to leave the planet.

Riker and the Elected One get along very well, as she makes no effort to conceal he feelings of physical attraction for Riker.

Elsewhere, Ramsey explains that he and the other survivors felt alienated in the matriarchical society. They change their minds and decide to stay, and Data points out that they cannot be forced to leave.

On the Enterprise, there are now 300 people ill with the virus.

Data, Yar and Troi return to the palace of the Elected One to report to Riker. The Elected One is angry that the Enterprise isn't going to take the radicals away. She claims to have no choice but to sentence Ramsey and the others to death.

Aboard the Enterprise, Dr. Crusher comes up with a temporary remedy when she discovers how the virus is transmitted. It has a pleasing scent and when people inhale deeply to enjoy it, it goes deep into their lungs. The Enterprise is subjected to further pressure when it receives orders to aid an outpost which is being threatened by the Romulans.

On Angel One, Ramsey and the others are captured, and condemned to death unless they agree to leave the planet.

Riker tries to convince Ramsey to leave on the Enterprise, but he and his people refuse. Riker tries to force them, but Dr. Crusher won't let them be beamed up while the virus is still a threat.

Data is beamed up to pilot the ship since he is not affected by the virus. Data tells Riker that they have 48 minutes before they must leave orbit.

The execution of Ramsey and his people is planned. It is to be carried out by means of disintegration.

Riker points out that the execution could make Ramsey's people martyrs, ans make them symbols of discontent, or even of evolution, instead of revolution. The Elected One rescinds the death order.

Dr. Crusher comes up with a cure for the viral infection.

The rst of the Away Team beams up and they are innoculated as the Enterprise heads for its mission in the Neutral Zone.

EPISODE FIFTEEN: "11001001"

Written by Maurice Hurley and Robert Lewin

Directed by Paul Lynch

Guest Cast: Carolyn McCormack, Iva Lane, Kelli Ann McNally, Jack Sheldon, Abdul Salaam El Razzac, Ron Brown, Gene Dynarski, Katy Boyer, Alexandra Johnson

The Enterprise reports to Starbase 74 to undergo repairs to the holodeck. The repair team includes a team of Binars who work on the computer. The Binars come from a world where a humanoid race has intermixed with computers.

Wesley observes that more Binars arrive to join the original team. When questioned, the Binars explain that since they must complete their repairs more quickly than they originally thought, they need more help. Although Wesley is troubled, Riker finally decides that there's nothing to be worried about.

As more and more people exit the Enterprise, unoccupied areas of the ship are shut down to clear space in the computer banks.

Many crew members go on shore leave at the Starbase. Data tries his hand at painting to see if he's capable of being creative.

With the work on the holodeck completed, Riker uses the holodeck to create a nightclub in New Orleans on Bourbon Street, complete with sultry brunette. When Riker enters the program, he meets the girl, who is named Minuet.

Riker plays a trombone in the bar and Minuet watches admiringly. When Riker starts thinking about leaving to return to work, Minuet dissuades him by wanting to dance. Riker is very interested in her. When he asks how real she is, Minuet replies, "I'm as real as you need me to be."

Captain Picard enters and sits down at the bar with Riker and Minuet. She speaks to him in French and impresses tells her how impressed he is with her adaptability.

Wesley contacts Data about a problem in Engineering with the magnetic containment field. Data detects that it is deteriorating. If this continues, the anti-matter will be released. Data orders that everyone abandon ship. He and Geordi program the Enterprise to leave so that when the anti-matter is released, the ship will be far enough away not to be a hazard to anyone.

The ship is abandoned, but the alarms do not penetrate the holodeck. Riker and Picard remain on board, unaware of the process, and whenever Picard tries to leave he is distracted by Minuet.

The Enterprise leaves Starbase 74 under computer control. Only then is it realized that the two ranking officers are still on board their ship.

Just as the Enterprise exits the starbase, Data detects that the magnetic containment field has stabilized. The ship is out of danger. By this time, the ship has prepared to enter warp speed, and vanishes.

When Picard tries to leave again, Minuet tries too hard to convince him to stay, which tips him off that something isn't right. He calls for the exit and finds his ship empty, undergoing a crisis alert.

Picard contacts the computer and learns what has happened, including that the ship has been evacuated. He is certain that the vessel has been hijacked by the Binars. Picard and Riker decide that it would be better the vessel be destroyed than that it fall into the hands of hostile forces. They activate the auto-destruct sequence and have themselves beamed to the bridge. There they find the Binars unconscious.

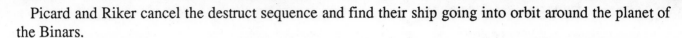

Picard and Riker cancel the destruct sequence and find their ship going into orbit around the planet of the Binars.

The Enterprise computer is filled with information. They return to the holodeck, guessing correctly that Minuet had been created by the Binars to keep tham aboard the Enterprise. She explains that a nova had knocked out the computer on their world and they need another computer to reactivate it. This is why they stole the Enterprise.

Returning to the bridge, Riker and Picard try to access the computer but cannot get in. Picard contacts Data at the starbase. After assuring them that they are well, he asks Data what the access code might be. They finally figure out what it is and access the information which is transferred to the computer on Binars, reactivating that world.

The Binars revive. When Picard questions them as to why they stole the Enterprise rather than asking for help, the Binars explain that there was a chance they might be turned down. They couldn't take that risk. They surrender themselves to be returned to Starbase 74 for a hearing.

Riker returns to the holodeck, but although the New Orleans setting remains, he can no longer summon Minuet. She had been a part of the Binar's programming. He misses her, as she had been a fascinating character to know.

EPISODE SIXTEEN: "TOO SHORT A SEASON"

Teleplay by Michael Michaelian and D.C. Fontana

Story by Michael Michaelian

Directed by Rob Bowman

Guest Cast: Clayton Rohner, Marsha Hunt, Michael Pataki

On a distant planet, a group of terrorists have taken an ambassador and his staff hostage. The planetary ruler, Karnas, contacts the Federation, revealing that the terrorists want Admiral Mark Jameson as negotiator. Jameson had negotiated a previous hostage situation there successfully 45 years before.

Jameson and his wife are beamed aboard the Enterprise and the admiral is designated senior officer.

Karnas contacts Picard while the Enterprise is en route to his world. He says that the terrorists will only negotiate with Jameson in person. Picard believes that Karnas knows more than he is saying.

Dr. Crusher mentions, in passing, that she'll have to schedule Jameson for a routine physical, a prospect which seems to disturb him.

Alone with his wife in their quarters, Jameson steps from his wheelchair, and seems to be a little stronger but then suffers a sudden spasm. He won't let his wife summon the doctor and insists that its just natural body changes.

Dr. Crusher talks with Picard and wonders why Jameson gave her medical records which show his last physical was two months before. When Jameson demonstrates his ability to walk and leave his support chair, she wonders how he could have recovered from Iverson's Disease, which is incurable. When he has another spasm, his wife calls sick bay. Tests reveal an unknown substance in the Admiral's body.

Picard confronts Jameson and learns that the Admiral obtained a black market drug from the people of Cerberus II, whom Jameson had once helped. He had been taking the drug slowly, as intended, until the hostage situation developed— then he took the rest of the drug to accelerate the process. He's never revealed this to his wife, and she becomes furious with him when the truth is revealed.

Later, Jameson contacts Karnas privately. He realizes that Karnas is lying— there are no terrorists. It is Karnas who has taken the hostages in order to realize his revenge against Jameson.

Jameson tells Picard that he wants to get to the planet early and rescue the hostages, whom he believes are in the tunnels under the city.

Dr. Crusher tells Ann Jameson that her husband's condition is not stabilizing and he may very well die.

Picard wants to know what secret Jameson is hiding. The Admiral reveals that 45 years before, when he secured the release of hostages from Karnas, he did so by giving the man the weapons he wanted. Then, to balance this inequity, he gave the same weapons to Karnas' enemies. In this way, Jameson thought he could stay within the boundaries of the Prime

Directive. But the result of his actions was 40 years of warfare on the planet, which ended only five years earlier.

Jameson, who is now some sixty years younger than he was when his voyage on the Enterprise began, leads the Away Team despite Picard's objections. Picard won't stand by idly, so he accompanies the Away Team himself.

They beam down into the tunnels, but Jameson finds them different from what he remembered. They cut through a new wall and are attacked. The battle is fierce. When Jameson has another spasm, Picard has the away team beamed up.

Jameson is gravely ill but offers to trade himself to Karnas for the hostages. When Picard, Jameson and dr. Crusher beam down, Karnas accuses them of trying to perpetrate an absurd trick upon him. Karnas wants revenge on Jameson and insists that they produce the real admiral or he'll start killing the hostages.

Finally Jameson convinces Karnas of the truth. He dies in front of Karnas after Ann beams down to be with her husband. Karnas relents and agrees to release the hostages.

EPISODE SEVENTEEN: "WHEN THE BOUGH BREAKS"

Teleplay by Hannah Louise Shearer

Directed by Kim Manners

Guest Cast: Dierk Torsek, Michele Marsh, Dan Mason, Philip N. Waller, Connie Danese, Jessica and Vanessa Bova, Jerry Hardin, Brenda Strong, Jandi Swanson, Paul Lambert, Ivy Bethune

While Riker is walking down a corridor on his way to the bridge, a young boy named Harry runs right into him. Harry was trying to run away from calculus class.

On the bridge, Riker is told that they are near the legendary location of the planet Aldea, a mystery which Riker has long been interested in.

Amazingly, they do detect a planet which is using a cloaking device, a device which is dropped as the Enterprise nears.

They are contacted by a woman who welcomes them to her world. She says the Aldeans want to discuss something with the Enterprise crew, and two Aldeans beam themselves to the bridge. They invite Picard and his people to a gathering. The Aldeans then beam Riker, Dr. Crusher and Deanna Troi down to the planet.

While they're planetside, powerful beams probe all decks of the Enterprise but seem to contact only the children.

The Aldeans explain to Picard that they have no children and want to trade technological secrets for some of the children on the Enterprise. Riker rejects the suggestion out of hand. The trio are beamed back to the Enterprise, and several children, including Wesley Crusher, disappear from the ship via the Aldean's transport beam.

The Aldeans contact Picard to negotiate a trade but the captain is too furious to even discuss it. He demands the return of the children.

The children are friendly with the Aldeans, but Wesley demands that they be returned to their parents.

The children are dispersed to different people and are well treated, being matched with parents who have similar talents.

On board the Enterprise, Data detects weaknesses and fluctuations in the force shield around Aldea. He works on a way to break through.

Wesley is shown a computer, called a "Custodian." By asking the Aldeans questions, he quickly figures out that they don't understand a great deal about their own technology.

Captain Picard and Dr. Crusher are beamed down for negotiations, but they are not allowed to see the children. Dr. Wesley is allowed to see Wesley, though. She slips him a small medical monitor which he uses to scan one of the Aldeans. He then secretly returns it to her.

When negotiations do not proceed well, Picard and Crusher are beamed back aboard the Enterprise. The vessel is then hurled three days from Aldea in a matter of moments. Picard is told that if he refuses to cooperate, the Enterprise will be hurled decades away.

The Enterprise returns to Aldea. Dr. Crusher has completed her analysis of the scan and determined that the Aldeans are dying, as a race, but can't yet determine why.

Wesley continues to complain and protest. That night he learns where all of the children are from the Custodian. He goes to each of them, gathering them together to organize passive resistance in the form of a hunger strike.

Meanwhile, Dr. Crusher has determined that the Aldeans are dying of a form of radiation poisoning caused by their depletion of their world's ozone layer.

When Crusher and Picard beam down, Data and Riker also beam down at the same moment, and beam through the defensive screen around the planet. The Aldeans want help in dealing with the children's resistance.

Dr. Crusher tells the Aldeans what is afflicting them. The Aldeans refuse to believe it at first and think that its just a trick perpetrated by the Enterprise people as a way of getting their children back.

Riker and Data find a Custodian and get control of the computer so that the Aldeans can't silence Crusher and Picard by beaming them back to the Enterprise.

Finally, the Aldeans accept the truth and they visit the power source of the defense screen, which must be shut down. The children are returned and Picard agrees to have his crew help the Aldeans with their problems.

EPISODE EIGHTEEN: "HOME SOIL"

Teleplay by Robert Sabaroff

Story by Karl Guers, Ralph Sanchez and Robert Sabaroff

Directed by Corey Allen

Guest Cast: Walter Gotell, Elizabeth Lidsey, Mario Roccuzzo, Carolyn Barry, Gerard Pendergast

The Enterprise arrives at a planet where a terraform base is located. The Federation has been asked to check up on the installation by Terraform Command.

When Captain Picard contacts the base leader, Director Mandel, Troi detects fear in the man. He tries to dissuade them from coming down but Picard is insistent and sends down an Away Team.

The Away Team is welcomed by Louisa, who calls herself the "Gardener of Venus." She explains what terraforming is and how the planet chosen to convert must be totally lifeless. This planet had been tested and deemed lifeless by the Federation, maing it perfect for this decades-long project.

Director Mandel greets them and shows them the procedures they are working on. Mandel orders Arthur Malencon to work in a chamber with the laser drill, and Malencon complies, although he shows a strange reluctance and tries to hide. Once inside the sealed chamber, they hear screaming and force the door open. The man had been attacked by the laser drill. Yar immediately beams up to the Enterprise with him. The rest of the Terraforming crew beam up as well. Geordi and Data remain behind to investigate the accident.

Data believes that the drill was controlled. He seals himself in the chamber and has the program reactivated. The laser attacks him, but Data is able to dodge it. When they get the door to unseal, they find that Data is fine, but he's destroyed the expensive laser drill.

Aboard the Enterprise, Director Mandel is angry over the interference that the Enterprise is causing his project. But Picard catches Mandel by surprise by asking him what he's trying to hide. Mandel claims he has nothing to hide, he's just worried about the timetable they must keep in order for the terraforming operation to remain on schedule.

Arthur Malencon, the injured hydraulics expert, dies from his injuries.

Data and Geordi return to the planet to do more investigating of the facility, and encounter strange flashes in a drill tunnel where the laser drill had been aimed. They wonder whether these flashes indicate some sort of life form.

A sample is beamed aboard. They examine it and come to the conclusion that it would have to be inorganic life. It is examined and reacts to the presence of a probe, as well as to a human presence. The computer tests confirm that it is alive.

Mandel is questioned because the presence of the lifeform means that all terraforming must be halted, permanently. Troi reveals that she detects that Mandel knew of the presence of the strange lifeform.

Riker visits Louisa, who has been crying because of the termination of the project. He tries to comfort her.

The lifeform reproduces, thus proving that it is alive. The lifeform links with the computer to attempt a translation of its language into human terms, proving that it is also intelligent. It takes over the Med Lab, which is put under quarantine.

Picard confronts Mandel and they finally learn more about the existence of the lifeform.

The thing continues to reproduce and tries to break the quarantine seal. It again tries to communicate, its words referring to humans as "Ugly bags of mostly water." It wants to kill the terraformers, and has declared war on the Enterprise.

They attempt to beam the lifeform back down to the planet, but it resists the transporter beams and redirects the power. They figure out how it was threatened on the planet, and that it is photoelectric. By reducing the lights in the lab, they force the lifeform to end hostilities. The crystal is beamed back down to the planet. The lifeform tells the humans to return in 300 years.

The terraformers are evacuated and the planet is placed under quarantine.

EPISODE NINETEEN: "COMING OF AGE"

Written by Sandy Fries

Directed by Michael Vejar

Guest stars: , Estee Chandler, Daniel Riordan, Brendan McKane, Wyatt Knight, Ward Costello, Robert Schekkan, Robert Ito, John Putch, Stephan Gregory, Tasia Valenza

On the Enterprise, Wesley tries to console his friend Kurland. Kurland has been defeated by Wesley in a contest to earn the chance to try out for entrance to Starfleet academy. The Enterprise is in orbit over the planet Relba where the group of candidates are to be tested.

After Wesley beams down, Admiral Quinn beams aboard and asks to meet Picard— alone. Commander Remmick of the inspector General's office is with Quinn and will be conducting a full investigation of the Enterprise. They believe something may be wrong on the ship but are not prepared to say what they are looking for.

Down on Relba, Wes meets Oliana Mirren, one of the other candidates.

She's an attractive young woman who is nervous about the upcoming tests.

He also meets the other candidates, Rondon and Mordak. Mordak is already widely known and respected. Wesley is surprised to learn that he isn't already in Starfleet.

On the Enterprise, Remmick is observing as well as annoying everyone. Riker asks Picard what Remmick is doing there, but Picard is not at liberty to say.

Wesley takes a hyperspace physics test. When he realizes that it is really a trick question, he passes it easily, to the mild annoyance of Oliana Mirren. She tells Wesley that if he wasn't so cute, he'd be obnoxious.

Remmick questions Riker about seeming discrepancies in the Captain's log, but Riker doesn't like the tone or direction of the questions. Remmick questions Geordi about the incident in "Where No One Has Gone Before" and asks Troi about Picard's mental state in "The Battle."

Wes is concerned about the upcoming psych test which is based on exploring someone's deepest fear. He discusses this with Worf.

Crewman Kurland steals a shuttle, stating that he's transferring to a freighter. Picard orders the man back just before the shuttle malfunctions. Picard miraculously talks the shuttle in to safety by giving Kurland specific directions on how to save himself.

On Relba, Wesley is bullied and reacts agressively, according to the alien's culture, as the alien's people detest politeness. It turns out to have been a test.

Remmick interviews Data and tries to tell him that Picard is not who he appears to be. Data rejects this premise as being totally without foundation. Remmick interviews other crew members, including Picard.

Captain Picard confronts Admiral Quinn, demanding to know what's going on. Quinn says he'll be able to reveal the answer soon.

Wesley is taking another test when he helps Mordak, who finishes first. Chang announces that the psych tests will be in one hour.

Remmick presents his report to Quinn and Picard and reveals that he could find nothing wrong with the Enterprise. After giving his reports, he turns to leave, but pauses to mention that his tour of duty in the Inspector General's office will end in six months. He says that he would like to serve on board the Enterprise then, if it is possible.

Quinn reveals to Picard that something is wrong in the Federation and that he wants to promote Picard to Commandant of Starfleet Academy because he needs someone there that he can trust.

Wesley is waiting to take his psych test when he hears an explosion in the environmental lab. Two men are trapped. Wes helps the injured man but the other one is too frightened to move. Wesley manages to drag the injured man out just before the lab self-seals, trapping the other man inside. This turns out to have been Wesley's psych test. The Academy knew that Wesley feared that he would be unable to make a decision to leave a man behind in a life-or-death situation, because this is how Wesley's father died.

Mordak wins selection to Starfleet Academy. Wesley tells Picard he feels that he has failed the Enterprise, but Picard assures him that this isn't so. Picard failed the entrance tests the first time around, but not the second time.

Picard decides to turn down Quinn's offer of promotion. Quinn wonders if he's just imagining a conspiracy after all.

EPISODE TWENTY: "HEART OF GLORY"

Teleplay by Maurice Hurley

Story by Maurice Hurley and Herb Wright & D.C. Fontana

Directed by Rob Bowman

Guest Cast: Vaughn Armstrong, Robert Bauer, Brad Zerbst, Dennis Madalone, Charles H. Hyman

The Enterprise receives a report of a battle in the Neutral Zone and proceeds there at Warp 7. Data locates a disabled vessel, which they identify as a Tolarian cargo ship.

Life signs are detected aboard the ship but they are indistinct due to interference from the ship's engineering section. An Away Team is dispatched consisting of Geordi, Riker and Data. Geordi wears a visual acuity transmitter which sends the Enterprise images of what he is seeing, which includes things outside the normal range of human vision.

The vessel is heavily damaged, and the three pick their way carefully through the wreckage. Geordi detects severe metal fatigue developing in the bulkhead, which will allow them only five minutes to find survivors.

Data finds the compartment where the survivors were detected and forces the door open. Inside they find three Klingons, one of whom is badly hurt.

They have to get away from engineering quickly in order for the transporter to pick them up without interference. They barely manage to escape as the ship explodes.

Picard greets the Klingons, who claim they were passengers on the ship when it was attacked by the Ferengi, whom they managed to defeat only at great cost. The three Klingons are surprised to see Whorf aboard the Enterprise.

When the two uninjured Klingons are taken to quarters, Picard tells Riker that he doesn't entirely believe their story.

The two Klingons question why Worf is in the Federation and try to provoke him to learn whether or not he's a tame Klingon. Worf is not, and the Klingons, Koris and Kunivas, are pleased that Worf can display anger.

The wounded Klingon is dying so the other three go to be with him, emitting a chant when he dies. Data later explains to Picard that the death ritual is meant to warn the dead to beware, a Klingon is on the way.

While talking to Worf, they let slip that their companion's death was not in battle at the hands of an enemy.

They question Worf about how he came to be in the Federation. he reveals that he was the sole survivor of a Romulan attack and was rescued by a human to grow up on Galt, a farming colony. The other Klingons reveal that they understand his solitude and confess that they are warriors without a war, fugitives who destroyed a Klingon cruiser sent to bring them back to the Kiingon Empire.

The Enterprise detects a vessel approaching— a Klingon ship. The Klingon Captain inquires what the Enterprise is doing in the Neutral Zone. Picard explains that they have rescued some Klingons from a stricken ship. When he says who they are, the Klingon Captain reveals that Koris and the others are fugitives and requests that they be turned over to him.

Picard dispatches a security team for the Klingons. When the security team, commanded by Tasha Yar, arrives, Koris and Kunivas appeal to Worf for help. Worf seems confused. When a child runs into them and one of Klingons picks her up, Tasha thinks a hostage situation is underway, but Kunivas hands the child to Worf, explaining that Klingons do not stoop to taking hostages. They surrender willingly and are taken to a security cell.

Worf learns that the Klingon ship has come to arrest Koris and Kunivas. Worf asks that he be allowed to speak to the captain of the Klingon ship. He pleads for the hostages, asking that they at least be allowed to die as warriors on a hostile world, rather than be executed while bound and helpless. The Cap tain admits that they are all diminished when a Klingon dies in such a manner, but he is bound to take the prisoners back with him. They pose a threat to the Klingon alliance with the Federation.

In their cell, the two Klingons construct a weapon from parts cleverly secreted in their uniforms. The Klingons kill two guards while escaping but Kunivas is killed as well, leaving Koris alone.

Koris goes to Main Engineering and threatens to use his weapon to blast the dilithium crystal chamber. Worf and Picard go to engineering, and Worf talks to Koris, who pleads with him to join him as a warrior, reject the Federation, take over the battle bridge, steal the saucer section and launch a rampage through space. Worf tells Koris that a man cannot be a warrior without duty and honor, and is finally forced to shoot and mortally wound Koris in order to save the Enterprise. Worf goes to Koris and performs the Klingon death ritual, howling a warning as the Klingon dies. Picard and the others are strangely moved by the sight.

Worf reports to the Klingon Captain that Koris and Kunivas are dead. The Captain invites Worf to join him when his tour of duty with the Enterprise is over. Worf says that he would feel honored to do so. After the Klingon ship leaves, Worf tells Picard that he was just being polite and has no real desire to leave the Enterprise. Picard replies that the bridge wouldn't be the same without him.

EPISODE TWENTY-ONE: "ARSENAL OF FREEDOM"

Teleplay by Richard Manning and Hans Beimler

Story by Maurice Hurley and Robert Lewin

Directed by Les Landau

Guest Cast: Vincent Schiavelli, Marco Rodriguez, Vyto Ruginis, Julia Nickson, George De La Pena

The Enterprise has been sent to investigate the disappearance of the Drake, which had been sent to Minos. Upon entering orbit around Minos, their sensors indicate no life signs on the planet, but then they receive a transmission— an armament commercial.

A small landing team, consisting of Riker, Yar and Data, is beamed down. They find an abandoned high-tech weapon but no signs of life. Data states that he believes they are being watched, but since there is no life on the planet, the question is: what is watching them?

Riker encounters the captain of the Drake, who is an old friend of his, but quickly realizes that this is a fraud. The man tries to get information from Riker on the complement and weaponry of the Enterprise. When Riker states that he knows the man is a phony, it disappears, to be replaced by a small flying robot which encases Riker in an energy field. They destroy the robot but the force field remains.

Picard and Crusher beam down to see what has happened to Riker while Data works at removing the force field, which he thinks he can do, in time.

The Enterprise reports energy readings in the area of the landing party. The Away Team is attacked by another of the small robots, and they split up to find cover. While fleeing, Picard and Crusher fall through a hole in the ground, and the doctor is hurt when they hit the bottom of the cavern. Picard has to tend to her wounds. Dr. Crusher guides Picard and helps him.

Meanwhile, Data removes the force field from Riker and tells him that they must find Picard and Crusher.

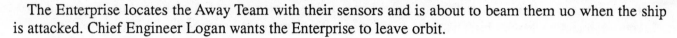

The Enterprise locates the Away Team with their sensors and is about to beam them uo when the ship is attacked. Chief Engineer Logan wants the Enterprise to leave orbit.

They try to compute the pattern of attack of the object, which has a cloaking device, but are unsuccessful.

On Minos, Data and Yar are attacked by small robots again, defeating them with great difficulty. They note that the robots appear every twelve minutes and are more difficult to defeat each time, as though they are upgrading their tactics with data derived from their earlier attacks.

The Enterprise tries to outguess its invisible attacker but fails. Geordi orders the Enterprise out of orbit. They enter warp briefly and then stop.

Geordi puts Logan in charge of the saucer and then does a seperation. Geordi and Whorf go to the battle bridge to control the main section of the ship, and return to Minos.

Picard looks around in the cavern and finds an operational unit with a viewscreen and tracking system, realizing for the first time that the Enterprise itself may be in danger. The projection appears again, programmed to answer questions about the demonstration of weaponry which is presently underway. The weapons being demonstrated work so well that they annihilated the population of the world which created them.

Data and the others find Picard, and the agile android is easily able to leap down 11 meters and save them.

The fourth version of the robot weaponry attacks while Data and Picard try to figure out how the control system works. Finally Picard tells the projection to end the demonstration because he likes what he's seen and wants to buy it. The projection is very pleased. The robot vanishes before it can home in on Riker and Yar.

The Enterprise returns to Minos and encounters the invisible attacker again. Geordi orders the ship to enter the atmosphere. The disturbance created by this action causes the invisible attacker to show up on their detection systems, and they're able to blast it.

Geordi has the Enterprise assume standard orbit and beam up the Away Team. Picard leaves Geordi in charge until the rendezvous with the saucer section as he wants his whole ship back.

EPISODE TWENTY-TWO: "SYMBIOSIS"

Teleplay by Robert Lewin, Richard Manning, and Hans Beimler

Story by Robert Lewin

Directed by Win Phelps

Guest Cast: Merritt Butrick, Kimberly Farr, Richard Lineback

The Enterprise is approaching a star which the crew plans to investigate. The ship's deflectors are hit with X-rays from the erupting sun, but to investigate, they must get closer.

They pick up a distress signal from a freighter in orbit around the fourth planet in the system. The Enterprise moves to assist.

The Enterprise atempts to employ its tractor beam on the ship in distress, but solar flares disrupt it. They contact the small freighter and learn why it is disabled. The computer informs Data how the problem could be repaired, but no one on the freighter seems to know how to replace a control coil. The Enterprise links transporters with the freighter to rescue its six passsengers, but on their first try, they receive its cargo instead. They link transporters again and the freighter disintegrates.

Four people materialize in the transporter— two were lost with the freighter. The first concern of the survivors is not their fellows, but is instead the cargo.

The cargo is Felicium, and the four begin to argue over its ownership since the material traded for it had been aboard the destroyed freighter. Tasha Yar has them removed to an observation lounge, where they continue to quarrel.

Picard requests information about the two planets the people are from, but little is known about them.

Dr. Crusher reveals that two of the people appear to be plague carriers, but that while they show symptoms, there is no apparent cause for them.

Picard talks to the Brekians, the traders, about getting two doses of Felicium for the stricken Onarians. They agree to this.

The plague on Onara, it seems, has afflicted that world's entire population for two centuries. The Brekians manufacture the drug which controls the plague from a plant which cannot thrive on Onara.

When the Onarians get their doses of Felicium, she observes that they respond like drug addicts getting a fix, and perceives from this that everyone on Onara is addicted to Felicium.

Several thousand years before, Onara became technologically advanced. They traded their technology to the Brekians for the drug which controls the plague.

Dr. Crusher opposes allowing this exploitation of the Onarians and wants the truth revealed. Picard is against interfering because it would violate the Prime Directive's non-interference clause by disrupting the cultural symbiosis between the two planets.

Onara contacts the Enterprise, to say that their world is suffering and its people dying.

T'Jon and his people can discharge electricity from their bodies, and he threatens to kill Riker unless the Onarians are given the drug now, with terms to be worked out later. Picard refuses to be blackmailed, and T'Jon relents.

The Brakians agree to provide the Felicium and work out trade terms later. Picard realizes that the Brakians know exactly what they are doing to the Onarians. But the Brakians know that he won't tell the Onarians this since that, too, would be interference.

Reasoning from the Prime Directive, Picard chooses to withhold the control coils from the Onarians. Unable to repair their aging freighters, the Onarians will be forced to find an alternative to the Felicium. The Brakians are upset by this as well.

Picard defends the Prime Directive, insisting that even well-intentioned interference can be disastrous.

EPISODE TWENTY-THREE: "SKIN OF EVIL"

Teleplay by Joseph Stephano and Hannah Louise Shearer

Story by Joseph Stephano

Directed by Joseph L. Scanlan

Guest Cast: Ron Gans as the voice of Armus, Walker Boone, Brad Zerbst, Raymond Forchion, Mart McChesney

The Enterprise is on the way to a rendezvous in the Zed Lapis sector with a shuttle carrying Deanna Troi.

Tasha Yar talks briefly to Worf about her upcoming martial arts competition. He admits that he has bet on her to win.

A distress arrives from the shuttle. It has crashlanded on the planet Vagra II.When the Enterprise reaches the crash site, sensors canbnot penetrate the crashed vessel enough to beam up its occupants. An Away Team, consisting of Riker, Data, Tasha and Dr. Crusher.

They beam down within sight of the shuttle. As they approach it, a strange black slick moves along the ground to block their path. This unknown lifeform generates a tar-like humanoid figure which talks to them. It is named Armus, and it will not let them pass. It doesn't think that their rescue mission is a good enough reason to move out of their way. Tasha Yar tries to pass anyway and it lashes out at her, knocking her to the ground, lifeless. The others attack it with phasers, but to no effect.

The Away Team beams up, but it is too late to save Tasha. There is a black mark on her cheek where the creature touched her.

Armus flows over the shuttle and communicates with Troi. She sensed Yar's death and knows Armus killed her thinking the death would be amusing. Armus is disappointed because Yar did not suffer.

On the Enterprise, Worf becomes acting chief of security. The Away Team returns, with Geordi, but Worf remains at his post on the Enterprise.

Armus covers the shuttle again, and won't let Deanna contact the ship. Deanna realizes that Armus is surprised that the Away Team returned, because it had been abandoned on Vagra II.

On the Enterprise it is noted that the energy field covering the shuttle had momentarily decreased while Armus was covering it. If the energy field were to drop far enough, the occupants of the shuttle could be beamed out safely.

Riker tries to negotiate with Armus. It allows Dr. Crusher to communicate with Troi to learn her condition, and that of the shuttle pilot. While Troi is all right, the pilot is injured.

Then Armus toys with the landing party, demonstrating his power over them.

When Armus covers the shuttle again, Troi communicates with it and learns that is stranded on Vagra II. Argus is the sum total of the evil of an alien race which learned how to bring their negative aspects to the surface and then discard them. Once created in this manner, Armus was abandoned by the purified beings. Troi angers Armus by pitying him. Enraged, Armus kidnaps Riker, enveloping him in his body to torment him. Again, the energy field over the shuttle drops, providing a vital clue for the freeing of Troi.

Troi offers to trade herself to Aramus for Riker, but the offer is refused.

Picard beams down. He wants to see those in the shuttle. Armus demands to be entertained and controls Data's body to point a phaser at the other Away Team members, each in turn, threatening to kill one of them. Finally, Armus relents and regurgitates Riker, but he won't let Picard see Troi.

Riker, Geordi, Data and Crusher are beamed back to the Enterprise.

Armus tells Picard that it wants to leave the planet and lets Picard into the shuttle, hoping he will help the being escape from Vagra II. Picard and Deanna discuss how they might escape— by exploiting the creature's rage.

Outside, Picard talks with Armus about how it was abandoned, and taunts him.

On the Enterprise, they prepare for the parallel transport of Picard, Troi and the shuttle pilot. They succeed when Picard tells Armus that he won't take him anywhere. The creature's rage diverts its energies, and the humans are saved, leaving the evil entity alone, howling at an empty sky.

Picard has the shuttle destroyed so that Armus cannot use it to escape.

On the Enterprise, a funeral is held in the holodeck for Yar. Her image tells of her feelings for her friends as she addresses each individually. Finally she says, "Death is that state in which one exists only in the memory of others, which is why it is not an end. No good-byes, just good memories. Hailing frequencies closed, sir."

EPISODE TWENTY-FOUR: "WE'LL ALWAYS HAVE PARIS"

Teleplay by Deaborah Dean Davis and Hannah Louise Shearer

Directed by Robert Becker

Guest stars:, Isabel Lorca, Rod Loomis, Dan Kern, Jean-Paul Vignon, Kelly Ashmore, Lance Spellerberg, Michelle Phillips

The Enterprise is en route to Sarona 8 for shore leave and Picard is looking forward to it. He is fencing for relaxation when he experiences a momentary time loop in which the events and conversation of seconds before are repeated exactly. He contacts the bridge and learns that it affected the entire ship.

They receive a distress signal from a famous scientist, one Paul Mannheim, who had gone off years before to experiment with non-linear time. They proceed to the coordinates given in the distress call.

Picard knew of Mannhein when he was in Paris. Troi detects intense emotion in Picard when Mannhein was mentioned. She advises the Captain to try to put his feelings in perspective.

Two hours before their schedules arrival, Picard goes to Holodeck 3 and sets it for a bistro in Paris, 22 years earlier. It's set for the time of a rendezvous he didn't keep. The he returns to the bridge and learns that two other locales have reported the same time loop phenomenon.

Arriving at the designated coordinates, they find nothing there, and receive a second message giving them coordinates for a new destination, the planet Vandor. Arriving at Vandor, they receive a message from a woman concerning her sick husband and two people are beamed to sickbay.

Picard arrives, and the woman, Gabrielle Mannheim, recognizes him.

She explains that the rest of their research crew were recently killed in a base on the other side of the planet. She admits that she doesn't know exactly what the goal of her husband's experiments were.

Dr. Crusher reveals that Dr. Mannheim is dying. He seems to be trapped partway into another dimension, and his body can't take the strain.

They experience another time loop.

Two of the crew beam down to the lab but a security device prevents them from materializing.

Paul Mannheim comes through but is very agitated. He says that he's touched another dimension and that part of him is still there. Mannheim knows that the experiment must be stopped.

Dr. Mannheim reveals that they have to go down to his lab and penetrate the elaborate security mechanisms. He reveals as many of the security devices as he can remember, but in his condition his memory is not reliable. He gives them codes which will allow them to beam down safely.

Mrs. Mannheim visits Picard. They recall the time he stood her up in Paris, 22 years earlier. He'd been afraid that if he saw her again, he wouldn't be able to leave.

Troi talks to Dr. Crusher, who is troubled by Gabrielle Mannheim's effect on Picard.

Mannheim asks to see Picard. He's not sure that he remembered all the security codes. He also asks Picard to take care of his wife if he dies.

Picard wants Data to be the only one in the Away Team, because he can handle time distortions better than the others.

Data beams down and is attacked by lasers, but bypasses them. He enters the lab and finds the point of time distortion. Data calculates that the next time loop is in 90 seconds. He must add antimatter at the moment of distortion. The time loop occurs and suddenly there are three Datas, but they combine in time and patch the distortion.

Mannheim recovers and wants to return to his work. His wife agrees to accompany him.

Gabrielle Mannheim enters the Holodeck where Picard has recreated the setting for their unkept appointment. He tells her that he wants to say good-bye properly. She leaves, and Picard returns to the bridge. The Enterprise resumes its original course and heads for shore leave.

EPISODE TWENTY-FIVE: "CONSPIRACY"

Teleplay by Tracy Torme

Story by Robert Sabaroff

Directed by Cliff Bole

Guest cast;, Michael Berryman, Ursaline Bryant, Henry Darrow, Robert Schenkkan, Jonathan Farwell

The Enterprise is en route to Pacfica, a beautiful water planet. They're 22 hours from their destination when the Enterprise receives a Code 47 transmission— a Starfleet Emergency Comminique for the eyes of the Captain only.

Picard is awakened to receive it. He uses the console in his quarters and receives a message from an old friend and fellow officer, Walker Kiel. Kiel warns Picard that Starfleet is in danger, but that he cannot be more specific. Picard is told to meet Walker for a face-to-face entente on a remote planet.

The Captain has the Enterprise alter course and orders that no log be kept. The Enterprise arrives to find three Federation cruisers in orbit around the planet. Three life forms are detected on the surface, and Picard beams down alone to that position.

Picard arrives at the entrance of an abandoned mine and finds Walker Kiel there with two other well-known Starfleet officers, Captain Rixx and Captain Tryla Scott— three of Starfleet's finest. They interrogate Picard to assure themselves that he's not an impostor.

Finally the three reveal their concerns, citing strange orders from Starfleet as well as the mysterious deaths of key personnel. Picard finds the conspiracy theory hard to believe. Walker asks Picard to at least be alert and to stay in touch secretly.

Returning to the Enterprise, Picard confides in Troi the events that have just occurred, and has Data access Starfleet orders for the past six months to search for any unusual entries.

A disturbance is detected nearby in sector 63, and they divert to investigate. They find the debris of a starshio, apparently the Horatio— the ship of Walker Kiel. The sudden and mysterious death of Kiel has a profound effect on Picard. He no longer considers Kiel's theories unbelievable. The timing of the death is too critical— Walker Kiel was killed to silence him.

Data discovers something in his record scan. He tells Picard about odd reassignments which seem to form a pattern to gain control of certain regions— perhaps as a prelude to invasion. Picard reveals what he knows to the bridge crew. He has them alter course and head directly to Starfleet headquarters— on Earth.

Upon arrival, Picard requests a personal meeting with Starfleet Command. They oblige, and invite Picard and Riker to be their dinner guests.

Starfleet Admiral Gregory Quinn beams over to the Enterprise, bringing a small black case with him. In it is a small creature which he keeps hidden. Picard quizzes the Admiral and is disturbed by what he learns. Picard warns Riker to keep his eye on Quinn. Picard then beams down and meets with the head of Starfleet.

On the Enterprise, Quinn attacks Riker and knocks him around as though he were toying with the man. Quinn refers to a recently discovered life form, superior to humanity. Riker summons security, but Quinn knocks out Geordi and atacks Worf.

Dr. Crusher arrives and uses a phaser on Quinn, knocking him out after three blasts. She has Quinn taken to sick bay where a scan reveals something in his body, attached to his neck.

At Starfleet, Picard secretly contacts the Enterprise and learns what has happened. He is summoned to dinner, but when he removes the lid from his dish, he discovers it is filled with wriggling grub worms. The other three men at the table are undeterred by this, and munch away quite happily.

Picard tries to flee but as he reaches the door it opens for Riker, who won't let him leave. All indications are that he has been taken over by the creature that Admiral Quinn had brought on board the Enterprise.

Riker explains that while the creature had been intended for Dr. Crusher, it was necessary to use it on him. He sits down to eat and suddenly pulls out his phaser and attacks the Starfleet Council. Creatures crawl from the mouths of the stricken men and flee. Riker and Picard follow them and see them enter the body of Remmick. Riker and Picard use their phasers on the man and his head explodes. As his body disintegrates, it reveals a large creature within, a queen which had been controlling the others. Picard and Riker make sure that it is completely destroyed.

They discover that Remmick had been sending a homing beacon from Earth to a remote sector of the galacy, obviously the home of the creatures. Is the worst really over?

EPISODE TWENTY-SIX: "THE NEUTRAL ZONE"

Television story and teleplay by Maurice Hurley

From a story by Deborah McIntyre and Mona Clee

Directed by James L. Conway

Guest Cast: Marc Alaimo, Anthony James, Leon Rippy, Gracie Harrison

Captain Picard is temporarily off the Enterprise at Starbase 718 and the Enterprise is awaiting his return. An old Earth satellite crosses their path. Riker wants to ignore it but Data is curious and wants to explore the relic, as it dates from the 20th century. Riker has Worf accompany him but orders Data to be back before Picard returns.

Data finds an old computer which is barely functional and gets a disc from it. He and Worf find the ship filled with chambers containing bodies. Some of the chambers are cracked but they find three that are intact, containing people who seem to be in suspended animation.

As Picard's shuttle nears the Enterprise, Data reports his find. He has the three bodies beamed to sick bay, and Data and Worf return to the ship.

Picard orders a course which takes them through the Neutral Zone separating the Romulan Empire from the Federation. Some outposts in the Neutral Zone have gone silent and the Enterprise has been sent to investigate. Picard wonders why the Romulans would be active now when the Federation has heard nothing from them in 50 years.

Dr. Crusher thaws out the three people and learns that each had been frozen after death through the process known as cryonics, a 20th century fad which was abandoned in the early 21st century. Each body had been frozen soon after death; Dr. Crusher has been able to repair the damage that killed them. She now has them sedated.

Picard reluctantly has them awakened. The woman wakes up, sees Worf and faints. According to the disc Data recovered, she is Clair Raymond. When she died suddenly, her husband had her put in cryonic preservation.

The other two people are Sonny Clemons, a good-ole-boy type, and a formerly-rich industrialist named Ralph. Picard leaves them in the care of Dr. Crusher, and Riker explains to them where and when they are.

Troi talks to Picard about Romulans, and how they are fascinated by humans. She says they should meet. Romulans would wait for humans to make the first move and then respond.

Picard has a meeting with his bridge crew six hours before their arrival at the Neutral Zone. Riker thinks the Romulans want a confrontation to see how much the Federation has advanced technologically in 50 years. Data points out that Romulan intentions might not be hostile.

Ralph demands that they contact Geneva to check on his stock holdings and accumulated wealth. He's annoyed that no one seems interested in helping him make his phone calls from the ship. When Ralph summons Picard as though he were a steward on a cruise ship, Picard tells Ralph that a lot has changed in 370 years, and that he should be prepared for that.

Clair begins to cry, remembering her children, who are now long dead. Picard summons Troi to help her. Troi uses a computer terminal to try to trace the history of Claire's family.

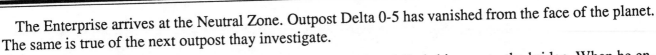

The Enterprise arrives at the Neutral Zone. Outpost Delta 0-5 has vanished from the face of the planet. The same is true of the next outpost thay investigate.

Ralph wanders around the ship until he enters a turbolift and finds his way to the bridge. When he enters the bridge silently, he is at first not noticed.

The Enterprise detects the approach of something but Picard refuses to attack. When the Romulans appear near the Enterprise, Picard won't respond with hostilty. Worf is annoyed because the Romulans killed his parents even though the Klingons and Romulans were allied at the time. He says that Romulans cannot be trusted.

Picard communicates with the Romulans. They explain that they are investigating mysterious attacks on their own outposts. Picard asks for cooperation to learn the truth, but the Romulans find this idea amusing. The Romulans explain that they had been busy with other things but will no longer remain hidden. The impression is given that the Romulans will no longer allow themselves to be confined to the Neutral Zone.

Picard will have the three 20th century people transferred to another ship and taken to Earth. On the way they will have time to adjust to their new lives. Clair has a relative on Earth she plans to look up. Ralph has learned that his fortune has been dispersed.

SEASON TWO

INTRODUCTION

A vast improvement over season one, with some significant changes. Geordi has become Chief Engineer, for one, and Dr. Crusher has gone on to head Starfleet Medical. Her replacement, Dr. Katherine Pulaski, was ably played by Diana Muldaur, but the character's acerbic wit made her seem a low-keyed female version of "Bones" McCoy. The character had her moments, though, such as when she lied about a minor medical matter to preserve Worf's pride, and then took an antidote so she could actually drink the toxic tea in the Klingon tea ceremony that Worf performed to thank her, but in general the character, through no fault of the actress playing her, did not achieve any real chemistry with the other cast members. The one episode featuring her in the spotlight was basically a rehash of "The Deadly Years," in which the good doctor was subjected to rapid aging. Her departure from the show was never to be referred to in the third season.

An addition to the cast that has lasted is that of Whoopi Goldberg, who asked for a role in the series—and got it. She plays Guinan, a mysterious alien of great but indeterminate age who tends bar and dispenses advice in the open ship's lounge known as Ten Forward. Always a supporting character, every revelation about her only seems to raise more questions than it answers. In "Q Who," the episode introducing the Borg, we learn that Guinan and Q had encountered each other two centuries earlier—and that she wore a different form at the time. Q is obviously frightened of her but won't admit it. Although never the focus of any episode, Guinan usually plays a small but pivotal role when she appears, and Goldberg tempers the character's mystery with great warmth and humanity.

Some of the better episodes featured Data, who continues to develop as a character, most notably "The Measure Of A Man" in which his rights as a sentient being are threatened by an ambitious scientist. Brent Spiner's acting skills were given more range in "The Schizoid Man" when a dying scientist places his personality in Data's mind and tries to conceal the truth from the rest of the crew.

One of the best episodes of the entire season was "A Matter of Honor," wherein Riker takes a challenging exchange officer assignment—on board a Klingon ship. The insights into Klingon culture came fast and furious in that story, and popped up again in "The Emissary," which gave Worf a love interest and revealed a few of the aggressive aspects of Klingon sexual behavior.

A sex-crazed alien also figured prominently in "Manhunt" as Deanna Troi's mother Lwaxana tried to snare Picard, then Riker, eventually settling for a holodeck bartender who fascinated her because she couldn't read his mind. The somewhat addled Lwaxana, always an annoying presence, is played by Majel Barrett, known to some as Mrs. Roddenberry. As comic relief, Lwaxana Troi is no Harry Mudd, and this episode doesn't work as an exercise in humor—except for Patrick Stewart's fine comedic turns whenever he cannot avoid Lwaxana, which pretty much parallel the viewer's exasperation with this episode.

A few more weak links include "The Outrageous Okona," which has Data seeking to learn humor from a holodeck Joe Piscopo while the rest of the crew contends with one of the lamest main plots ever to afflict the series, and the season finale "Shades of Gray," a cheater in which a Riker on the verge of death relives scenes from the first two seasons only to be saved at the very last minute by Dr. Pulaski.

Still, all in all, *The Next Generation's* second season flew a great deal higher than the first, and even the weakest episodes are carried with great aplomb by the cast, who have obviously developed a strong working relationship among themselves.

EPISODE TWENTY-SEVEN: "THE CHILD"

Written by Jaron Summer, Jon Povil and Maurice Hurley

Directed by Rob Bowman

Guest Cast: Seymour Cassel,

After Doctor Crusher goes on to head Starfleet Medical, Doctor Pulaski comes aboard as her replacement. At the same time, Geordi (now Chief Engineer) is creating new containment modules that will allow the Enterprise to transport samples of a deadly plasma virus to a science station, where vaccine research will be undertaken. An entity, resembling a point of light, enters the Enterprise and finds Deanna sleeping; she wakes up with a start.

Picard becomes annoyed when he finds that his new ship's doctor seems to be ignoring protocol, having gone to Ten Forward instead of reporting to the bridge. Ten Forward is a rest area, basically a bar, and the hostess is the mysterious, ancient alien Guinan. Picard goes there to find Pulaski, who cuts his protestations short and directs his attention to Deanna. It seems that she has become pregnant. A briefing is held, where it is learned that the fetus is already six weeks old, a mere eleven hours after its unusual conception. At this rate, delivery will occur in another thirty-six hours. The only genetic material involved is Deanna's. A debate ensues: Worf recommends immediate termination, while Data advises letting the unique life form to grow. Deanna settles matters when she states her intention to bear the child.

When the time for delivery arrives, Data stands by Deanna, as there is no father as such. The delivery is completely painless for mother and child. Within 24 hours, the child, named Ian, is already physically four years old. Furthermore, there is no physical sign to indicate that Deanna's body ever carried or delivered a child. When Picard drops in to visit later that day, Ian is eight; he tells Picard not to worry, and that everything is okay.

The plague samples are beamed into the containment units; if even the least dangerous strain gets out, everyone on the Enterprise will be dead within hours.

Picard and Pulaski witness the child allow himself to be burned, as if he wanted to learn about pain and other experiences. Picard asks Ian why he has come, but the child says he is not yet ready to explain. According to Deanna, he has the knowledge within him, but is not developed enough to express it in words.

Something goes wrong with one of the containment units: the strain of plague inside it is growing, and will break through the containment field in two hours. Research reveals that this strain was mutated in a laboratory experiment, by exposure to Eichner radiation. Renewed exposure could provoke growth, and Data in fact detects Eichner radiation on board the ship.

The tricorder leads them to Deanna's quarters, where Ian has already told Deanna that he must leave in order to discontinue the threat to the Enterprise. He dies, or so it seems. Deanna is grief stricken, but the entity emerges and communicates with her. It assumed human form to learn about humans, and thanks Deanna for helping him do so, and then resumes its wanderings through space. With the radiation source gone, the Enterprise is safe once more.

EPISODE TWENTY-EIGHT: "WHERE SILENCE HAS LEASE"

Written by Jack B. Sowards

Directed by Winrich Kolbe

Guest Cast: Earl Boen,

Picard is worried: Riker has joined Worf in a dangerous undertaking. Wandering through a desolate landscape, they are attacked by hideous creature, and must battle for survival. Of course, its a holodeck exercise, the Klingon equivalent of daily calisthenics, although Worf points out that it had been toned down for Riker's benefit.

On the bridge, a black area in space appears on the view screen. A complete absence of matter and energy, it provokes Picard's curiosity, and he moves the ship closer. Probes simply vanish into it, leaving no trace. Worf recommends Yellow Alert status; when asked why, he seems embarrassed, and admits that it reminded him of an ancient Klingon legend of a black space being which ate ships. When the Enterprise moves closer, the void somehow envelops it.

This new "space" seems to lack dimension. When the ship retraces its course, it does not return to its original place, but is still inside the void. When a beacon is dropped, it fades away behind the ship, only to appear before it shortly— even though the Enterprise was on a straight course.

A Romulan ship uncloaks and attacks. A single photon torpedo destroys it utterly. This was too easy, notes Riker, and sensors reveal no debris from the Romulan vessel.

A Federation ship appears next, even though the Yamato should be nowhere near the area. There are no life signs. When Riker and Worf beam aboard, they find themselves lost in a shifting, maze like trap. Tricorder readings show that the ship is not made of the right metals to be a Federation ship. It is some sort of replica. When Riker and Worf beam back, they almost don't make it, and the false Yamato fades out from view just as they are safe.

Openings appear in the void, but constantly disappear as the ship changes course. Eventually, the officers realize that this is some sort of test or experiment, and decide to stop playing along. At this point, a face appears in the viewscreen. It is an entity calling itself Nagilum. It kills a crew member, and decides to learn about all the possible means of death for humans, a process that shouldn't take more than a third of the crew.

Rather than face this, Picard and Riker set the auto-destruct mechanism. As Picard faces the end in his quarters, listening to the piano music of Eric Satie, he is visited by Troi and Data. Data quizzes him about human concepts of death, and Picard discusses various views, including his own. Data and Troi both tell Jean-Luc that he should abort the destruct sequence, and he realizes that they are simulations created by Nagilum.

They vanish, and Picard receives word that his ship is now free of the void. Sensing that this might be another experiment, Picard does not abort the destruct sequence until the last possible second.

Nagilum appears on the screen in Picard's office, telling him that he learned much about humans from this experiment. Picard is not impressed, and the being vanishes, leaving the captain alone.

EPISODE TWENTY-NINE: "ELEMENTARY, DEAR DATA"

Written by Brian Alan Lane

Directed by Rob Bowman

Guest Cast: Daniel Davis, Alan Shearman

Data takes Geordi along to his favorite holodeck program, in which Data is Sherlock Holmes and Geordi is Dr. Watson. While Data gets carried away in the part, Geordi has no fun at all, because Data already knows the solutions in all of Arthur Conan Doyle's stories. Although he understands the process of deductive reasoning, the android does not really know how to savor the mystery itself. Later, Dr. Pulaski contends that Data could not solve a mystery that he doesn't already know the answer to. He accepts the challenge, and programs the computer to create a new Holmesian mystery. Pulaski and Geordi accompany him. As before, he solves it in no time, but only because he recognizes diverse elements from several Holmes stories.

Geordi calls up the computer arch, and programs a mystery that will challenge Data, along with an adversary capable of defeating Data. This is witnessed by the holodeck's Professor Moriarity.

In the altered program, London seems seedier and more dangerous. Moriarity feels "like a new man" and finds that he can summon the arch, himself. Soon, Pulaski is abducted, and Data and Geordi must search for her, only to be distracted by a murder unrelated to their search. Data surmises that the computer is running an independent program. The search continues, but it is too easy, and Data realizes that their adversary— who could only be Moriarity, in this context— wants them to find him. Face to face with the Professor, they find that he has learned a great deal, and wants to know more. When he hands Data a piece of paper with a drawing of the Enterprise on it, the android detective rushes out of the holodeck, only to find that he cannot terminate the program.

He informs Picard of the problem. Moriarity has control of the holodeck. The holographic projections could be wiped out by a particle beam, but this would also kill Pulaski. Suddenly, the ship rocks: Moriarity has gained access to the ship's propulsion and guidance systems.

Picard dons Victorian garb and enters the holodeck, hoping to defeat Moriarity by giving him everything he wants. He concedes defeat to the Professor, hoping that this will bring the program to its end. Unfortunately, Moriarity has developed real consciousness; Geordi goofed by asking for an adversary capable of defeating Data, when he meant to say "Holmes."

Moriarity has transcended his fictional origins. His goals are not evil, he merely wants to live and think. Picard is impressed, but points out that holodeck technology has not progressed sufficiently to allow holodeck creations to exist independently of the deck. Since the technology is related to transporter beams, it may be possible some day, and he promises to store the Moriarity character until the day that it is possible. Moriarity graciously accepts, and the Enterprise is once again under the control of Captain Picard.

EPISODE THIRTY: "THE OUTRAGEOUS OKONA"

Teleplay by Burton Armus

Story by Les Menchen, Lance Dickson and Kieran Mulroney [double-check]

Directed by Robert Becker

Guest Cast: William O. Campbell, Douglas Rowe, Albert Stratton, Joe Piscopo

While passing through the Medina system, where two planets have had tense relations for generations, the Enterprise offers aid to the captain of a damaged freighter. When the humanoid, Thaduin Okona, beams aboard with his damaged guidance system, he turns out to be a charming, brash fellow, and a real ladies man as well. Data is confounded by Okona's jokes, and goes to the holodeck to learn about humor. Skipping a 23rd Century humorist noted for his jokes about quantum mathematics, Data selects instead a 20th Century standup comic, who first shows Data how to do a Jerry Lewis impression. When this doesn't work, he tells Data jokes, which the android proceeds to memorize at high speed. When Data tries to share his jokes, he comes across as a bad impression of a bad comedian; when told that his timing ruined the jokes, he responds, quite innocently, that his timing is digital, which provokes laughter despite its serious intent. He is still baffled by the human concept of humor.

Meanwhile, a small craft, armed with lasers, prepares to attack the Enterprise. Although these weapons are no threat whatsoever, Riker points out bemusedly that protocol requires Yellow Alert status. The ship is captained by Debin of the planet Altec, who claims that Okona is a wanted criminal. When pressed, he admits that he's after Okona for getting his daughter Y'Nar pregnant. Matters are complicated further when a ship from Straleb also arrives, intending to arrest Okona for the theft of the Jewel of Thesia, a national treasure. Straleb is represented by Kushell and his son.

Picard calls Okona to the bridge, but Worf must remove him from a female crewmember's quarters first, for Okona has been making up for lost time.

Face to face with Picard, Okona assures him that he is not guilty of either of the charges against him. Picard does not know what to do until Okona agrees to surrender. He will not say who he's surrendering to until both parties have beamed aboard. He then agrees to marry Y'Nar, only to have Kushnell's son protest. The truth emerges: the two young people had been seeing each other secretly with Okana's help. Kushnell's son had made Y'Nar pregnant, and had taken the Jewel, which was his right as the heir, to give to Y'Nar as a betrothal gift. Okona turns over the Jewel to the young woman, leaving the elder statesmen baffled. He leaves, and Picard gets the two factions off his ship before an argument about the upbringing of the baby can get out of hand.

Having been tutored extensively by the Comic, Data invites Guinan to the holodeck to see him perform. A holodeck audience loves his act, but he realizes that they are programmed to do so, and laugh at everything he does, down to the smallest physical movement. He terminates the program, realizing that he has a long way to go before humor comes naturally to him.

EPISODE THIRTY-ONE: "LOUD AS A WHISPER"

Written by Jacqueline Zambrano

Directed by Larry Shaw

Guest Cast: Howie Seago, Marnie Mosiman, Thomas Oglesby, Leo Damian

The Enterprise is assigned to transport the famous negotiator Riva, an architect of the Klingon peace treaty, to the planet Solais V, where rival factions have warred for fifteen centuries. When Picard beams down to greet Riva, he meets instead the Chorus, three white-clad humanoids who speak for Riva. The ruling line of his world has no gene for hearing, and he uses these companions to express his thoughts for him. Protocol demands that one look at Riva while speaking. Riva is benign but perhaps arrogant, never having failed to settle a conflict, and he is immediately taken with Deanna Troi.

Riva reasons that the warring parties now seek mediation because they are threatened with mutual extinction. With such common ground, a resolution should be simple. But when Riva and the Chorus beam down with an away team, one of the delegates, not wanting peace, tries to kill the mediator. Riker knocks Riva out of the way, but the Chorus is vaporized, leaving Riva without a voice. Back on the ship, Data learns a sign language so he can speak with Riva.

Riva is guilt stricken, and cannot go on. He blames himself for the death of the Chorus. Deanna tries to convince him, but he is too despondent, so she determines to mediate the affair herself. She asks Riva what his secret is. He responds that it is very simple. all he ever did was find some common ground, however small, between the opposing factions, and work from there. Suddenly, he realizes that he can do it after all, and resumes his mission. He will teach the warring parties his sign language. It may take months, but it will create a new common ground for peace.

EPISODE THIRTY-TWO: "UNNATURAL SELECTION"

Written by John Mason and Mike Gray

Directed by Paul Lynch

Guest Cast: Patricia Smith, J. Patrick McNamara, Scott Trost

The Enterprise receives a distress call from the SS Langtry, a Federation supply ship, only to find, by remote viewing, that its crew is dead of old age. The crew of the Langtry was healthy, according to records, except for one officer with an exotic flu which was, however, little more serious than a common nose cold. Apparently, they aged rapidly until they died of natural causes. Picard quarantines the ship and heads for its last known stop, the Darwin Science Station on Gagarin Four.

They discover that the Darwin Station is already experiencing the accelerated aging process, which begins with arthritic inflammation. Were they infected by the Langtry, or was it the other way around? Dr. Kingsley, head of the station, claims that the children there are not affected, having been put in isolation.

Captain Picard and Dr. Pulaski go head-to-head over whether or not it is safe to bring one of the children on board the Enterprise. Eventually, Picard relents, as long as there is a force field containment in place, and the child is sealed in suspended animation. The twelve year old "child" is physically an adult, however, and Deanna senses that he has a telepathic consciousness, despite his being in stasis. All tests indicate that he is not in any way infected, but Pulaski wants to remove the stasis field and awaken him. Again, Picard resists, until she suggests taking the child aboard a shuttlecraft, which will be a close system separate from the Enterprise. With Data as pilot, a shuttle is launched, and the child is beamed aboard and removed from stasis.

Conscious, the child communicates telepathically with the doctor— he can send and receive thoughts. Pulaski is immediately stricken with the aging disease, however, and proceeds to the Darwin Station. The children are in fact the cause, although they are perfectly healthy. Their are genetically engineered; in addition to telepathy and telekinesis, they have active aggressive immune systems, which attack viruses before they even reach their bodies. The relatively harmless flu virus triggered their systems to create an aggressive antibody which is fatal to normal humans, for it alters their DNA, particularly the aging chromosomes.

Although the transporter bio-filter is useless in this situation, Picard, Geordi and O'Brien entertain the possibility that the transporter's trace records could be used to reconstitute Pulaski as she was before the infection.

Unfortunately, Pulaski has an aversion to transporter use, and has never used the Enterprise's system. Her previous ship has not maintained her trace records.

Data returns to the Enterprise and joins the effort to save Pulaski. O'Brien believes that it may be possible to alter the bio-filter to use a DNA sample to reconstitute Pulaski. Data and Riker finally locate some of the doctor's hair in a hairbrush, and use DNA from the intact follicles to program the transporter. The process is risky, and is only one-way; they cannot beam her back if they fail, but will have to scatter her electrons into space. Picard takes the responsibility of operating the transporter, much to O'Brien's relief, and the process works. The staff at Darwin Station will have to leave their "children" behind, but they are saved by the new transporter technique.

The Enterprise returns to the Langtry, and the bridge crew stands at attention while the doomed ship is destroyed with a photon torpedo.

EPISODE THIRTY-THREE: "A MATTER OF HONOR"

Teleplay by Burton Armus

Story by Wanda M. Haight, Gregory Amos and Burton Armus

Directed by Rob Bowman

Guest Cast: John Putch, Christopher Collins, Brian Thompson

A Benzite ensign, Mendoc, joins the Enterprise crew as part of an ongoing officer exchange program. When Picard mentions an opening on the Klingon ship Pagh, Riker volunteers to be the first human to serve with the Klingons. Worf helps him learn about Klingon customs: the First Officer's primary obligation, on a Klingon ship, is to kill his captain if the captain seems weak or indecisive. The Second Officer is likewise obligated to his immediate superior. Riker also prepares by sampling Klingon food in Ten Forward, much to the disgust of Pulaski and other humans.

As Riker is about to beam over to the Pagh, Worf gives him an emergency transponder. While the two ships rendezvous, Mendoc notes a patch of microbiotic organisms on the hull of the Pagh, but says nothing: Benzite procedure requires a complete analysis before making a report.

The Klingons question their new human officer, and Riker swears loyalty to the captain and the ship. When his Second Officer challenges his authority, he beats him soundly, thus winning his respect. Captain K'Argan is greatly amused by this.

The Enterprise discovers the microbe— a subatomic bacteria that eats metal— on its hull, and the Benzite mentions that he'd noticed it on the Klingon ship too. The Enterprise determines that the microbe has eaten a 12 centimeter hole in the Pagh's hull by this point, and follows the Klingon ship to warn it.

Riker impresses the Klingons by eating their food, but stalls when he learns that one dish he'd eaten cooked on the Enterprise is actually eaten alive by Klingons. The two Klingon women aboard express curiosity about Riker, prompting some ribald humor— Riker realizes that they have a sense of humor, even if it isn't very sophisticated, and joins in their laughter. They even discuss Klingon family matters. One Klingon is proud of his father's heroic death, while the other is ashamed that his father was once captured by Romulans, escaped, and now awaits a quiet, natural death on their homeworld.

When Riker returns to the bridge, the Captain has discovered the hole in the hull, and believes that the Enterprise is responsible. The fact that a scan beam (courtesy of Mendoc) was focused on the area for several minutes only fuels his suspicion, which he turns on Riker. Riker stands his ground; having vowed loyalty, he will serve the Pagh even in an attack on the Enterprise. When the Captain demands the Enterprise's security codes and other secrets, however, Riker refuses, since it would violate other oaths he has made. The Captain says that he would have killed Riker on the spot, as a traitor, if he had revealed those secrets; now he may have the honor of dying in battle among Klingons.

Meanwhile, the Enterprise has found a means of removing the microbes, and sends a message out to the Klingons. K'Argan does not believe them, and prepares to attack. The Enterprise, unaware of this, cannot locate the cloaked vessel. K'Argan prepares to fire, and also gives this honor to Riker. Riker says he will obey, but tells the captain that his reasons are wrong, and triggers the transponder. K'Argan demands the device, which Riker yields to him.

The Enterprise locates the transponder beacon, and beams Riker aboard— only to find an angry Klingon captain aboard the bridge instead. Worf subdues K'Argan and puts him under guard. Riker hails the Enterprise, as acting Captain of the Pagh, and demands the surrender of the Federation ship. Picard surrenders, and the Klingons decloak, ready to be rid of the microbe. K'Argan returns to his ship. Riker has cleverly maintained the honor of all involved. His only shortcoming, in Klingon eyes, was that he did not assassinate his superior officer. K'Argan strikes Riker a vicious blow, which Riker does not duck, thus reestablishing K'Argan's authority. Riker returns to the Enterprise, after what may have been the shortest exchange assignment on record.

EPISODE THIRTY-FOUR: "THE MEASURE OF A MAN"

Written by Melinda M. Snodgrass

Directed by Robert Scheerer

Guest Cast: Amanda McBroom, Clyde Kusatsu, Brian Brophy

At Starbase 173, Captain Picard meets Philippa, the woman who prosecuted him in the Stargazer court martial. The local representative of the Federation's judicial arm, she finds that Picard still cannot forget that she acted against him, even though it was simply standard procedure when a ship is lost. Commander Maddox also comes aboard; he is an ambitious cyberneticist who has arranged for Data to be transferred to his command, where he plans to disconstruct the android and download his mind, in order to test the positronic brain he has built. His ultimate goal is to create many more androids for Starfleet use. Data finds the idea interesting, but refuses the procedure on the grounds that Maddox's procedure might risk the loss of Data's personality. To avoid transfer, he resigns from Starfleet at well. Maddox does not regard Data as a sentient being, and seeks to define Data as the property of Starfleet. When Philippa rules in favor of this position, Picard demands a hearing.

As ranking officer, Picard acts as the defense; the prosecution goes to the next highest ranking officer, who in this case is an extremely reluctant Riker. As prosecutor, Riker contends that Data is a machine, made by a man, and thus subject to human ownership. To prove his point, he turns Data off.

Picard tries to determine the nature of sentience. Can Maddox prove that Picard is a sentient being? The issues become cloudy, until Picard draws on an earlier conversation with Guinan, and questions the purpose behind Maddox's desire to create a race of androids like Data. The issue of slavery arises, and Picard declares that a slave race is what Maddox, perhaps unconsciously, has in mind. The final ruling: Data is not property, and has the right to make his own decisions.

EPISODE THIRTY-FIVE: "THE SCHIZOID MAN"

Teleplay by Tracy Torme

Story by Richard Manning and Hans Beimler

Directed by Les Landau

Guest Cast: W. Morgan Sheppard, Suzie Plakson, Barbara Alyn Woods

The Enterprise receives a medical distress call from Graves' World, the immodestly named home of scientist Ira Graves, one of the most brilliant minds in the Federation. An Away Team consisting of Data, Deanna, Worf and a Vulcan medical officer beam down while the Enterprise, with Dr. Pulaski, goes off to the rescue of a damaged colony ship. On Graves' World, they are greeted by the planet's only other inhabitant, Graves' beautiful young assistant, Corinne, who sent the call out of concern for Graves' health. Graves himself is a cantankerous genius who insists that his health his fine, but a medical scan reveals that he is dying. Graves is impressed by Data, the creation of Graves' former student Soong, and the two spend a great deal of time together, as Data sees the scientist as the closest thing to a relative that he has. Graves plans to transfer his knowledge to a computer so that it will not be lost. When talks of his fear of death to Data, the android trustingly reveals his on/off switch.

When the Enterprise returns and prepares to beam everyone up, Data emerges from Graves' office and announces the scientist's death. Later, on the ship, Data seems changed, using phrases that Graves had used while paying a great deal of attention to Corinne. Giving a speech at Graves' funeral, the android heaps lavish praise on the dead man, and is cut off by Picard when he threatens to ramble on and on.

When Picard brings Corinne on the bridge, Data acts jealous, an emotion which Deanna can sense. He even insults Picard. When Geordi examines him, he can find nothing wrong, but a psychological test with Dr. Pulaski reveals that Data's personality has been submerged beneath a second, stronger personality— that of Ira Graves. Later, in Ten Forward, Graves admits this to Corinne, but this frightens her, and he hurts her hand, not realizing the strength of the body he has commandeered.

When Graves/Data goes to a restricted area of engineering, he overpowers Geordi and his crew. Picard confronts him and demand that he give up Data's body. He refuses, and knocks out Picard. He begins to realize the damage that he is doing, damage that he never intended.

Geordi, recovered, finds Data on the floor of his quarters, unable to remember anything since Graves took over his body. They discover that Graves downloaded himself into the ship's computer; although his knowledge will not be lost, his personality did not survive. It seems that Ira Graves' arrogance did not extend to wanton violence, and that he finally accepted that his time to die had come.

EPISODE THIRTY-SIX: "THE DAUPHIN"

Written by Scott Rubinstein and Leonard Mlodinow

Directed by Rob Bowman

Guest Cast: Paddi Edwards , Jamie Hubbard, Madchen Amick, Cindy Sorenson, Jennifer Barlow

Wesley falls head over heals for Salia, a young woman on her way to rule her home planet of Daled IV, where it is hoped that she will unite the factions that have been warring for generations. She is accompanied by her guardian, Anya, who is extremely protective of her charge. Anya refuses to allow Salia to tour the ship; she is highly critical of everything, since she sees everything as a potential threat to Salia. When she encounters a sick patient in sick bay, she insists that Dr. Pulaski kill the crewman to prevent the spread of the disease. When Pulaski refuses, Anya takes matters into her own hands, transforming into a monstrous creature. Worf struggles with her until Picard arrives; Anya resumes her unassuming human form, and Picard confines her to her quarters for the duration of the trip.

Meanwhile, Wesley has taken Salia to the holodeck, where he shows her scenes from many worlds. In Ten Forward, they talk about her future. Wesley insists it will be wonderful, but she's afraid that her responsibilities will be oppressive. Picard asks Wesley to stay away from Salia, to avoid problems, and he reluctantly agrees.

Salia, however, is under no such restriction, and visits Wesley in his quarters. Anya barges in, again in her monstrous for, but Salia faces her down by shifting her own shape. Anya backs down, and she and Salia leave the surprised ensign alone.

When the Enterprise reaches Daled IV, Wesley avoids saying good-bye to Salia, but changes her mind and sees her off after all. She reveals her true form to him. Anya returns to her home on a moon of Daled IV; she and Worf part respectfully, since they recognize each others' warrior natures.

EPISODE THIRTY-SEVEN: "CONTAGION"

Written by Steve Gerber and Beth Woods

Directed by Joseph L. Scanlan

Guest Cast: Thalmus Rasulala, Carolyn Seymour, Dana Sparks

The USS Yamato, another galaxy-class starship commanded by Captain Varley, has ventured into the Neutral Zone, where it experiences serious problems. The Enterprise arrives just in time to see it explode, killing the thousand persons on board. The Yamato barely had time to download its logs into the Enterprise's computer; Picard studies these and learns that Varley believed himself to have discovered the legendary planet of Iconia, peopled by a race that could supposedly travel through space without use of vessels.

Picard, an amateur archaeologist, decides to investigate further, although Iconia is located close to the Romulan side of the Neutral Zone. The Enterprise experiences strange malfunctions along the way, similar to those that plagued the Yamato.

The planet Iconia bears the signs of a civilization bombed out 200 thousand years earlier. A probe is launched from the planet, identical to one that scanned the Yamato. Geordi warns Picard to destroy it before it can scan the Enterprise: the Yamato's destruction was caused by an alien computer program from the earlier probe. The Enterprise's problems are less drastic because they downloaded the program along with the Yamato's logs, and it needs to work its way through the system.

Picard leads an away team to the ancient command center below, where Data manages to decipher the computer by extrapolating the a root language from the tongues of several worlds believed to have been colonized, or conquered by, the Iconians. He triggers a gateway which opens onto a variety of locations, including strange worlds and the bridge of the Enterprise. Picard wonders: were the Iconians really conquerors, or were they bombed out by enemies who feared their advanced technology, and maligned as evil in those enemies' history? And did the Iconians really die— or did they escape to other worlds by means of the gateway?

More important problems arise. The Enterprise is confronted by a Romulan ship, which is also malfunctioning, because it scanned the Yamato's records as well. Data tries to access the Iconian computer, but it is incompatible with his systems, and he malfunctions. Picard realizes that the Iconian technology must not fall into Romulan hands, and sends Worf and Data back to the Enterprise through the gateway, while he arranges to destroy the ancient gateway. Back on the Enterprise, Data "dies," only to revive again, with no memory of his experience. This provides a solution to the problem: download and wipe all affected systems. Geordi does the same to the computer, and regains control of the ship.

Picard jumps through the gateway, only to wind up on the bridge of the Romulan ship, which is about to self-destruct like the Yamato. The Romulan captain is pleased that Picard will die with her ship, but he is located and beamed away; he has Geordi transmit the necessary procedure to the Romulans, and the Enterprise heads out of the Neutral Zone.

EPISODE THIRTY-EIGHT: "THE ROYALE"

Written by Keith Mills

Directed by Cliff Bole

Guest Cast: Sam Anderson, Jill Jacobson, Leo Garcia, Noble Willingham

NASA debris, dating from the 21st century, is found orbiting a planet

much too far from Earth to have been reached by that era's technology. The mystery deepens when the Enterprise's sensors locate a small area of Earth-like atmosphere on the planet's surface, which is otherwise covered with violent ammonia-methane storms. Riker leads an away team down to the anomalous area, where they discover an ancient revolving door. Inside, they find a 20th century casino, complete with sarcastic hotel clerk, who welcomes them to the Hotel Royale. In fact, a "trio of foreign gents" were expected. Riker witnesses a bit of drama: a young bellhop, involved with gangster Mickey D's girlfriend, seems headed for serious trouble. Tricorder readings reveal that all the people in the Royale are not alive; although real, they are neither men nor machines, with no trace of life signs.

Although there seems to be no danger, the away team can't communicate with the ship, and the revolving doors will not let them out. A tricorder scan reveals DNA on the second floor. Riker and his team discover a room with a 283-year-old corpse, which turns out to be a NASA astronaut from the period between 20333 and 2079. (This is determined by the presence of 52 stars on the US flag on his uniform) Colonel S. Richey's effects are few: a second rate novel entitled *Hotel Royale,* and a diary with one entry. It seems that Richey's craft was damaged by an alien life form, killing all the crew but Richey.

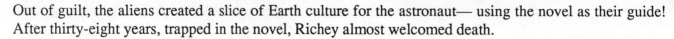

Out of guilt, the aliens created a slice of Earth culture for the astronaut— using the novel as their guide! After thirty-eight years, trapped in the novel, Richey almost welcomed death.

The Enterprises manages to contact the away team, and Riker explains their situation. Picard accesses the novel on the computer, and endures its tortuous prose to the end; the final scenes include Mickey D's murder of the bell boy, after which a trio of foreign gentlemen buy the hotel and leave it in the care of the assistant manager. When Riker witnesses the murder, he realizes a means of escape. Data embarks on a winning streak at the craps table, and parlays a handful of chips into millions of dollars. This breaks the bank, but Riker takes the deed to the hotel as payment, and the away team assumes the characters of the "trio of foreign gents" and saunters out the revolving doors, to be beamed back to the Enterprise.

EPISODE THIRTY-NINE: "TIME SQUARED"

Teleplay by Maurice Hurley

Story by Kurt Michael Bensmiller

Directed by Joseph L. Scanlan

A shuttlecraft, adrift where it couldn't possibly be, is picked up by the Enterprise's sensors, and pulled aboard by tractor beam. Its markings indicate that it is a shuttlecraft from the Enterprise— even though that shuttle is still in its docking bay. Things grow even more confusing when the craft's sole occupant turns out to be Captain Picard, who is also at his place on the bridge. The unconscious Picard2 is taken to sick bay, where his brainwaves are discovered to be out of synch. The shuttlecraft (apparently damaged in an anti-matter explosion) resists attempts to download its logs; its circuits seems to be reversed. Data uses a phase inverter to align it with the Enterprise's power, but finds that it works only when adjusted in the opposite direction than expected. Attempts to revive Picard2 with stimulants have the opposite effect as well.

The shuttle logs reveal that the craft came from six hours in the future. Visual logs reveal that the Enterprise was utterly destroyed, with Picard as the sole survivor, in a strange vortex in space. Picard is assailed with self doubt, for he cannot understand why he would abandon his ship, and wonders if he can avoid making a possibly predetermined mistake.

As the time of the event nears, Picard2 becomes more coherent, but communication is still impossible. When the vortex appears, it draws the ship in with inexorable force, and attacks both Picards with bolts of energy. Deanna senses that it has some sort of awareness, and that it has identified Picard as the "brain" of the ship. The captain realizes that his other self tried to save the ship by drawing the vortex's attention. Picard2 revives and heads for the shuttlebay: Picard tries to get Picard2 to tell him what his other choice was, but Picard2 is barely aware of anything but the crisis at hand. At last Picard2 reveals that he had discarded going through the vortex as too dangerous. Picard shoots Picard2 with a phaser and orders the crew to take the ship through the vortex. The duplicate captain and shuttle vanish as they pass through, to emerge unscathed on the other side.

EPISODE FORTY: "THE ICARUS FACTOR"

Teleplay by David Assael and Robert L. McCullough

Story by David Assael

Directed by Robert Iscove

Guest Cast: Mitchell Ryan

Riker is given the opportunity to command the Ares, a ship about to embark on a long exploratory mission. He has only twelve hours to decide. When his estranged father Kyle comes aboard to brief him on the mission, his uncertainty grows, for he and his father have always had a highly competitive relationship. Their reunion, after fifteen years, is a cold one.

Wesley notices that Worf is acting disturbed, and enlists the aid of Data and Geordi in helping the Klingon. Worf, hoping to immerse himself in danger, asks Riker to take him along when he takes charge of the Ares.

Tension escalates between the two Rikers, the younger one refusing to talk.

Wesley learns that it is the tenth anniversary of Worf's Age of Ascension, an important Klingon ritual. Using the holodeck, they provide Worf with an appropriate anniversary celebration, which involves running a gauntlet of Klingon "pain-sticks." Worf endures the ordeal and thanks his friends for helping him "celebrate,' as it were, this important occasion.

The Rikers finally work out their aggressions in the gym; Kyle gets the better of son Will, but only by cheating, and Will realizes that his father had always cheated in their competitions. Kyle admits that he did, but only as a means of keeping his son motivated. An uneasy rapport is achieved, and Riker decides to stay on the Enterprise rather than assume a captaincy merely because it is expected of him.

EPISODE FORTY-ONE: "PEN PALS"

Teleplay by Melinda M. Snodgrass

Story by Hannah Louise Shearer

Directed by Winrich Kolbe

Guest Cast: Nicholas Cascone, Nikki Cox, Ann H. Gillespie, Whitney Rydbeck

The Enterprise investigates some planetary systems marked by extreme seismic activity. As Riker puts it, planets in this area "live fast and die hard." The planets are all in danger of being destroyed by drastic tectonic shifting. Wesley is placed in charge of the mineral survey team, and is uncertain if he's up to commanding such a vital mission. Meanwhile, Data picks up a message from a child, somewhere in space, and responds, although this may violate the Prime Directive.

As the ship proceeds to the system in question, it becomes apparent that Data's friend is a resident of one of the threatened planets. Since this world has had no contact with spacefaring peoples, Picard is concerned about the Prime Directive, which would seem to dictate that this race be left to its own devices, even though this will mean its certain doom. His officers voice a variety of opinions. For once, Pulaski sides with Data, although she expresses her argument with more emotion than the android. A plea from the child weakens Picard's resolve, however, and he gives Data permission to contact her. When transmission proves impossible, Data is allowed to beam down to the planet.

As this is going on, Wesley has problems with his team, who are all older than he is. He wants a certain test done, but the expert on that subject thinks it will be a waste of time. Wesley consults with Riker, and finally simply tells the other officer that he wants the test done. Much to Wesley's surprise, the officer takes this order cheerfully and without question. The test, in fact, reveals that subterranean layers of dilithium crystals are forming lattice-like structures which transform the planet's heat into tectonic movement. The Engineering staff believes that the process can be halted by converting probes into resonators which, burrowed into the planet's surface, could break up the dilithium crystal lattices.

Data discovers the child alone, for she hid when her family fled, in order to stay with her transmitter. He beams her up with him, much to Picard's chagrin. The plan to stop the tectonic activity works, however, and Pulaski wipes the child's memory of Data and the Enterprise so she can resume her life on her world. Data returns her to her hideaway, but leaves a gift in the sleeping child's hand. Although she will not remember him, he will always remember her.

EPISODE FORTY-TWO: "Q WHO"

Written by Maurice Hurley

Directed by Rob Bowman

Guest Cast: John DeLancie, Lycia Naff

Q gets around his promise to stay off the Enterprise by whisking Picard away in Shuttlecraft 6. Guinan sense the entity's presence, but by then he and the Captain are far beyond the Enterprise's sensor range. Riker begins seeking Picard, but has no success. After some time adrift, Picard agrees to listen to Q, who immediately returns Picard and the shuttle to the ship. In Ten Forward, Guinan recognizes Q, and he seems to feel threatened by her; they met 200 years earlier, and Guinan, according to Q, wore a different form at the time. Q's desires are simple, however; he wants to join the crew of the Enterprise. He contends that the Federation cannot proceed much further in its exploration of the cosmos without encountering things beyond their comprehension; in all modesty, Q offers himself as their guide. Besides, he's been kicked out of the Continuum and has nowhere else to go. Picard does not trust him, and turns down this request.

To prove his point, Q sends the Enterprise seven thousand light years off course. It would take them two years and seven months at Warp 9 to return to Federation Space. Guinan suggests that they head back immediately, for there is great danger, but Picard decides to explore.

Sensors locate a Class M planet with signs of civilization: ancient roads remain all over its surface. Where cities once were, however, there are only vast pits, as if all technology had been ripped off the planet. This is identical to the destruction of outposts along the Neutral Zone. A huge, cubical ship appears, and Guinan tells Picard that it is the Borg, who destroyed Guinan's homeworld and dispersed her people. A Borg, a humanoid extensively implanted with machinery, appears on the bridge and begins draining power. Worf kills it with a phaser blast, and a second Borg appears, and raises a shield when it is fired upon. They seem to adapt almost immediately to anything thrown against them. It takes some components from the dead Borg and returns to its ship. A sort of tractor beam locks on to the Enterprise. It takes heavy photon torpedo action to damage the Borg ship and free the Enterprise.

An Away Team beams over to the Borg ship and discovers that the Borg act as components in a hive mind, plugging into outlets and becoming physically dormant. A nursery is found; the Borg are born biologically but begin implantation almost at birth. They are the perfect fusion of artificial intelligence and biological brains. In their regenerative mode, they don't perceive the Away Team as a threat.

The team beams back and the Enterprise heads out, only to be pursued by the Borg ship, which is almost completely repaired. Photon torpedos now have no effect, and the Borg are able to match any warp speed.

The Borg fire weapons designed to drain shield power, and soon the Enterprise is defenseless.

Q reappears, and Picard admits that Q was right: they do need his help. Q returns the Enterprise to its original location and goes along his merry way, leaving Picard uneasy. The Borg, a threat greater than any previously encountered, are out there, and they are coming toward the Federation.

EPISODE FORTY-THREE: "SAMARITAN SNARE"

Written by Robert L. McCullough

Directed by Les Landau

Guest Cast: Christopher Collins, Leslie Morris, Daniel Bemzau, Lycia Naff, Tzi Ma

Wesley Crusher is about to shuttle to Starbase 515, where he will take his exams. Picard, meanwhile, decides to go along for a medical procedure; Pulaski says that she can do it, but Picard does not want the crew to know about it. Wesley is somewhat intimidated at the prospect of a six hour ride with the Captain.

The Enterprise, under Riker's command, proceeds with a scientific mission, only to receive a distress call from a small vessel, which only has sublight capacity.

The Paklids seem fairly simple people, with no knack for technology, and Geordi beams over to fix their simple guidance system, an easy task for him. Although Deanna believes that Geordi is in danger, it doesn't really seem to be true, but as soon as Geordi fixes one thing, another system goes down. The Paklids, impressed by Geordi's know-how, decide to keep him, grab his phaser, and stun him. They raise Romulan-type shields and ignore all hails from the Enterprise.

On the shuttlecraft, Picard reveals to Wesley that he needs his cardiac implant replaced. Loosening up somewhat, he tells the story of how his original heart was damaged. Wesley is astounded to learn of the young, undisciplined Picard, and the fight which ended with a spear through his torso. This is a side of the Captain few people have ever seen.

While Data tries to get through the Paklid's shields, Deanna sense that they are very tricky, and that they actually programmed their computer to fake the various problems for Geordi's benefit. Furthermore, they want Geordi to make them more phasers. When communication is reestablished, the Paklids stun Geordi repeatedly, and demand all computer information from the Enterprise. The Paklids have no technology of their own, but have borrowed and stolen from just about everybody in their impatience to get ahead. Riker plans to play along with this, and he and the crew stage an elaborate "farewell" to Geordi, who they will miss as their resident "weapons expert." His death will be remembered, says Worf, but he will never achieve the 24th Level, whatever that is:; "24," says Worf, "is the gateway to heroic salvation." The Paklids become convinced that Geordi is a weapons expert, but Geordi is a bit baffled by the Enterprise crew's behavior.

At Starbase 515, Picard's operation takes a turn for the worse, and even the best expert on the base cannot save him, and they put out a call for one who can.

Geordi rigs the Plaklid ship with photon torpedo capacity. When Enterprise sensors pick this up, Riker orders Gomez to fire on the Plaklids after a 24-second countdown. At this, Geordi delays the Plaklids from responding by "adjusting" the torpedo array for maximum efficiency, while actually dismantling the system. When the countdown ends, the Enterprise emits a red cloud of gas. Geordi feigns dismay, and tells the Plaklids that the "crimson force field" has disarmed the torpedos. Overwhelmed by the Enterprise's show of strength, the Plaklids return Geordi to his ship. The "force field' was merely hydrogen discharged through the Broussard collectors.

The Enterprise then speeds to Starbase 515 at maximum warp. Picard awakens from his operation to discover Pulaski at his bedside. She was the expert who saved him, and now everyone knows about his heart. Fortunately, this is not the disaster he had feared.

Finally, Wesley passes his exams, and will be allowed to continue his studies on board the Enterprise.

EPISODE FORTY-FOUR: "UP THE LONG LADDER"

Written by Melinda M. Snodgrass

Directed by Winrich Kolbe

Guest Cast: Barrie Ingham, Jon de Vries, Rosalyn Landor

Starfleet picks up a repeating signal, which Data recognizes as a distress call. It is of Terran origin, utilizing a 22nd Century code dating from the time of the European Hegemony. It originates from the Ficus system.

As this is being considered, Worf, who has been acting strangely, collapses on the bridge.

Records do not reveal any trace of a ship headed toward the Ficus system, but the records of that period are jumbled. Someone had to load the ship, however, and Picard finds the loading manifest for the ship Mariposa, launched in 2123. Its cargo was a strange mix of state-of-the-art technology and primitive, low-tech items such as spinning wheels. A 22nd agrarian movement might account for the low-tech end, but what of the computers?

In sick bay, Pulaski reveals that Worf has a Klingon disease roughly equivalent to measles. Worf is dismayed to learn that he's been laid low by a childhood disease, so Pulaski spares his honor by telling Picard that Worf collapsed because of a Klingon fast he was observing. Worf thanks the doctor by sharing the Klingon Tea Ceremony with her— although she cannot drink the tea, which is fatal to humans, she can take part in the ritual. Impressed, Pulaski gives herself the antidote to the tea so she can share the experience fully.

The Enterprise reaches the source of the signal, a class-M planet threatened by solar flares, and evacuates the entire population of several hundred. They beam up with their livestock, which creates some confusion in the transporter room, and are given a cargo bay as temporary quarters. Their leader is O'Dell, a crazy, hard-drinking Irishman, but the real power is is headstrong, beautiful daughter. Riker is taken with her immediately, and sparks fly. The colonists have some difficulty coping with advanced technology; when Picard asks O'Dell about the computers and such, he is asked if he'd heard anything from "the other colony."

Locating a class-M planet half a light year away, the Enterprise proceeds on the assumption that this is the home of the second colony.

They find a planet of scientists, headed by Wilson Granger, who is "not exactly" a descendant of the Mariposa's Captain Walter Granger. When an away team, with Pulaski and Riker among its number, beams down, they discover several men identical to Granger, and a number of identical women as well. In Granger's office, Pulaski scans him, and realizes that the planet is populated by clones. It seems that only five of the Mariposa's passengers reached the planet. Cloning was their only option. Sexual reproduction has faded out and become a repugnant concept. The Mariposans are faced with the problem of replicative fading: their gene pool is weakening. When they cannot get tissue samples freely, they abduct Riker and Pulaski, and steal cells from their stomach linings. Back on the Enterprise, they realize what has happened, and a furious Riker beams down and destroys his clones.

It becomes apparent that what the Mariposans really need is breeding stock. Further cloning, even with new cells, will only prolong their problems another generation or two. After some maneuvering, Picard manages to unite the two colonies: the Mariposans will have to learn to reproduce the old-fashioned way, and polyandry will have to be the norm for a century or so.

No one can tell how this will work out, but at least it's out of Picard's hands at last!

EPISODE FORTY-FIVE: "MANHUNT"

Written by Terry Devereaux

Directed by Rob Bowman

Guest Cast: Majel Barrett, Robert Costanzo, Rod Arrants, Carel Struycken, Robert O'Reilly, Rhonda Aldrich, Mick Fleetwood

A pair of Antedian delegates on their way to the Pacifica conference beam aboard. Tall, fish-headed beings in long silver robes, they are in a self-induced catatonic state until sick bay can provide them with the necessary life support. The Enterprise is hailed by a small transport vessel, and Deanna is dismayed even before the rest of the crew discover that it carries her mother, Lwaxana Troi. She has been appointed Ambasadress to the Pacifica conference, and must be accorded full diplomatic treatment. She immediately invites Picard to a diplomatic dinner, but neglects to invite anyone else: she's out to snare the good captain with her romantic wiles.

Picard catches on quickly enough, and invites Data to join them for some after-dinner conversation. The android is all too willing to entertain them with anecdotes of various scientific matters, which Picard willingly endures rather than be alone with Lwaxana.

Deanna tells Dr. Pulaski that her mother is going through "The Phase," during which Betazoid women quadruple their sex drive, which also impairs their telepathic powers, at least with men. All her energies are directed to winning a husband by any means.

Faced with this, Picard flees to a Dixon Hill holodeck program for the duration of the trip to Pacifica. This is not as peaceful as he'd hoped, since various characters keep trying to kill "Hill." Unfortunately, the program must conform to the parameters of the published Dixon Hill novels. Finally, he asks holographic secretary Madeline to join him for drinks at Rex's Bar, where he has a meeting with Rex. Madeline hands him a gun, which she says he'll need.

Lwaxana, unable to locate Picard, chooses another mate, and astounds the bridge crew by announcing her impending marriage to Will Riker. Riker joins Picard on the holodeck, accompanied by Data. Lwaxana eventually tracks them down, only to be hit on by Rex the bartender, who is after her wealth. She is immediately taken by Rex, and is intrigued because she cannot read his thoughts. The officers withdraw, leaving Lwaxana with her holographic beau.

Upon arrival at Pacifica, the delegates prepare to beam down. Lwaxana, who took the truth about Rex remarkably well, reveals that the Antedians are actually assassins, who plan to blow up the entire conference with undetectable explosives hidden in their robes. They are disarmed, and she beams down, but not after taking one more shot at Jean-Luc Picard.

EPISODE FORTY-SIX: "THE EMISSARY"

Television story and teleplay by Richard Manning and Hans Beimler

Based on an unpublished story by Thomas H. Calder

Directed by Cliff Bole

Guest Cast: Suzie Plakson, Lance LeGault, Georgann Johnson

Worf wins another poker game and dispenses the following bit of cultural information: Klingons never bluff.

The Enterprise is assigned to rendezvous with an important emissary, who is travelling at high warp speed in a stripped-down probe. When the probe is beamed aboard, the emissary proves to be a half Klingon, half human woman, K'Ehleyr, whose mission involves a Klingon ship with a crew that has been in cryonic suspension for seventy-five years. The Enterprise must try to reach them in time to delay their awakening, for they will believe that the Federation/Klingon war is still going on.

K'Ehleyr is a familiar face to Worf; she feels they have an unresolved relationship. Worf disagrees, and they argue constantly. When they meet in a holodeck battle simulation, Klingon passions are aroused (not a pretty sight), and old business soon becomes new business. Worf feels obligated to take the vow of mating, but K'Ehleyr, who is scornful of Klingon traditions, declines.

The Enterprise reaches the Klingon ship too late, and is attacked. A vicious battle seems imminent, until Worf has a brainstorm. He poses as the captain of the Enterprise, with K'Ehleyr his second in command, and convinces the Klingon captain that the war is over— with the Klingons as the victors. His poker playing skills save the day.

EPISODE FORTY-SEVEN: "PEAK PERFORMANCE"

Written by David Kemper

Directed by Robert Scheerer

Guest Cast: Roy Brocksmith, Armin Shimerman, David L. Lander

In the light of the potential Borg threat, the Enterprise takes part in a war game. Riker is given command of the starcruiser Hathaway, an eighty-year-old relic which he has 48 hours to get into shape. Both ships, of course, will convert their weapons to harmless laser pulses, which their computers will interpret in terms of "real" damage. En route to the Hathaway, they pick up master strategist Kohlrami, who is to act as observer. His race has had such a reputation as brilliant stategists that no one has attacked their planet for over nine thousand years. Kohlrami is also a master of the game Strategema, and easily defeats both Riker and Data.

Riker takes command of the Hathaway, with Geordi, Wesley and Worf among his crew. The Hathaway has no warp drive, until Wesley returns to the Enterprise briefly to check up on a science experiment, which he beams over to the Hathaway. This device will give them two seconds at warp two. When the games begin, Worf tricks the Enterprise sensors into seeing a Klingon warbird, which distracts Picard long enough for Riker to score a significant "hit." When a Ferengi warship appears, Picard assumes it is another illusion, until it attacks with real weapons. The Ferengi are curious: why would one Federation ship fire on another? Nothing makes sense to them but acquisition, so they assume that the Hathaway hides something of great value, and demand that it be turned over. Data proposes a daring plan: if the Enterprise fires photon torpedos at the Hathaway, and the Hathaway uses its limited warp ability to outrun the explosion, then the Ferengi will have nothing to motivate them to attack the Enterprise. The plan works, and the Ferengi flee when Worf tricks their sensors into seeing another ship.

Data plays Strategema with Kohlrami, who gives up when Data breaks all records. Data's strategy was not to seek victory but to maintain a balance, thus frustrating an opponent whose only goal was to win.

EPISODE FORTY-EIGHT: "SHADES OF GREY"

Teleplay by Maurice Hurley, Richard Manning and Hans Beimler

Story by Maurice Hurley

Directed by Rob Bowman

While surveying an uncharted planet, Riker is stung by an indigenous life form. When he tries to beam up, the transporter registers a micro- organism in his system that cannot be filtered out. Pulaski (in her last episode) authorizes a medical override. In sick bay, it is determined that the microbe has bonded with his nervous system on the molecular level, and is taking over his spinal cord. The unconscious Riker is placed on direct brain stimulation, which retards the microbes fatal progress to his brain. The brain stimulation causes Riker to relive past events. The endorphins released by the emotions of these memories have an effect on the microbe, and Pulaski, with Deanna's help, tries to find the right emotional "frequency" to save him.

He goes from pleasant memories to passionate ones, and at last to violent scenes from his past (all scenes from previous episodes); a cascade of crises recalled becomes so intense that it risks his life, only to drive the infection out and save him.

SEASON THREE

INTRODUCTION

An even more varied and interesting season, it might even have been perfect if it hadn't had yet another Lwaxana Troi episode. Despite this, it had some of the strongest scripts to date, and the season actually ended on a strong note rather than lying down and dying. Dr. Beverly Crusher returned to her post, with no explanation, and her temporary replacement's departure was never mentioned at all.

Two episodes, "The Survivors" and "The Bonding," were both very good, but were aired too close together in that they shared the basic idea of benevolent aliens complicating matters for the Enterprise crew in a well meaning attempt to right a wrong. "Who Watches The Watchers" examines the problems posed by the Federation's covert studies of other worlds, and "The Enemy" is a gripping survival tale in which a blinded Geordi must win the cooperation of a Romulan so that they may both survive. The Romulan menace is dealt with in a highly intriguing script, "The Defector."

Data's experiences grow in "The Offspring," in which he creates another android as his daughter and develops a relationship with her, only to lose her tragically. Data also figures prominently in one of the season's best, "Tin Man," in which he is the only one who can relate to Betazoid emissary Tam Elbrun, who is afflicted with telepathic abilities too all-encompassing for him to control. In "The Most Toys," Data is abducted by a single-minded collector, and must decide if it is right to use violence to prevent violence. His final decision is quite surprising.

A new character, Reginald Barclay, appears for the first time in "Hollow Pursuits," which reveals that not everyone in the 24th Century Federation is as perfectly well-adjusted as it would sometimes seem.

Even the obligatory Q episode, "Q Who," is a good one, as Q is stripped of his powers and goes to the Enterprise for safety when old enemies track him down.

In "Yesterday's Enterprise," a shift in the time lines brings back Tasha Yar, who must sacrifice herself to insure that the alternative history that preserved her life will never come to pass. Worf's past catches up with him in "Sins of the Father," setting in motion chains of events which may have far reaching consequences; these are two of the best of the season.

Needless to say, "Sarek" is a real treat for old-line fans of the Enterprise, as Mark Lenard beams aboard as Spock's father—and we learn that a very young Lieutenant Picard attended Spock's wedding! Of all the episodes referring to the old show, this is the most original, dealing with a disease that sometimes affects Vulcans after they enter their two hundreds.

The season ends with a real cliffhanger: the Borg invade Federation space, kidnap Picard, and turn him into one of their own, putting Riker in the Captain's seat. As the Borg ship comes racing after the Enterprise, Riker must weigh the life of his crew against that of Picard, and the season concludes with Riker ordering Worf to fire against the ship bearing Picard—and the words "To Be Continued!" Reportedly this cliffhanger existed in life as well, as Patrick Stewart was strongly considering not returning for a fourth season and his transformation into a Borg could easily have marked his permanent exit had negotiations gone other than they did.

EPISODE FORTY-NINE: "EVOLUTION"

Teleplay by Michael Piller

Story by Michael Piller and Michael Wagner

Directed by Winrich Kolbe

Guest Cast: Ken Jenkins

Wesley is called to the bridge. He's overslept, and rushes to his post. The Enterprise is approaching a binary star system, where material from a red giant is drawn toward a neutron star. Every192 years, a buildup of stellar matter produces a spectacular explosion, and Dr. Paul Stubbs is on board to launch a special probe, "The Egg," which will gather data from the event. This represents Stubbs' life's work.

Suddenly, the ship goes briefly out of control, almost veering into the stream of stellar matter. No malfunction can be detected.

Dr. Crusher returns to her post, and is concerned about Wesley. She doesn't sense his dependence any more, which will require some adaptation.

In sickbay, a food slot malfunctions, even though the computer insists that it is working perfectly.

The Enterprise goes to Red Alert when it senses a Borg vessel. The shields go down, and the Borg prepare to fire— only to disappear without a trace. The computer seems to be going haywire; there was no Borg ship. The ship is rocked, and all the computer will produce are chess moves. Stubbs is angry— if he misses this chance, his work is all in vain. Picard is more concerned that his ship is stranded right where the explosion will take place, but Stubbs values his experiment more than the lives of the crew.

It seems that the ship's computer core has been tampered with. Wesley realizes that it's his fault. He removed two nanites— microscopic robots desogned for cellular repairs— from sickbay for an experiment to see if they could work together. The nanites escaped, reproduced, and infiltrated the computer. They seem to be evolving, too, and eat computer memory core. They might even have some sort of collective intelligence.

Stubbs enters the computer core area and tells Geordi that gamma radiation might clear the cores. When Geordi responds that that would kill the Nanites, Stubbs agrees, and fires a blast of gamma radiation at the core, killing the Nanites in it.

The Nanites retaliate by altering the atmosphere of the ship. Manual control restores normal air, but Stubbs has inadvertantly proven that the Nanites have intelligence. That night, they locate him and hit him with a bolt of energy. Picard plans to use gamma radiation after all, but Data manages to communicate with the Nanites, and allows them to use him as a host.

Picard explains what has happened to them, and gives them the standard Starfleet "peace between entities" speech. The Nanites explain that they needed raw materials for replication, but meant no harm. Stubbs apologizes for his thoughtless action.

The Nanites have evolved beyond the need to use the Enterprise, and help repair the computer cores in time for Stubbs and the Enterprise crew to witness the stellar blast from a safe distance. Picard arranges for a planet for the Nanites, and the Crusher family resolves its disagreements.

EPISODE FIFTY: "THE ENSIGNS OF COMMAND"

Written by Melinda M. Snodgrass

Directed by Cliff Bole

Guest Cast: Eileen Seeley, Mark L. Taylor, Richard Allen

After 111 years, the Federation receives a communication from the mysterious Sheliak. They have discovered humans on Tau Cygna V, a planet ceded to them by a treaty, and demand their removal so they can colonize. The Federation has no knowledge of humans on that world. It is blanketed by heavy hyperonic radiation, which is fatal to humans. It is possible that humans could adapt, however, and the Enterprise is sent to investigate. The Sheliak regard humans as inferior beings, and will exterminate them if their deadline is not met.

Sensors, affected by the radiation, do sense life forms, but transporters and phasers are completely useless. Data, who is unaffected, shuttles down, where he finds a thriving community of 15 thousand settlers.

It would take over four weeks to shuttle them all up to the Enterprise, and there are only three days until the deadline. Even worse, Data cannot convince Gosheven, the colony leader, that there is a threat. Gosheven is proud of colony and its accomplishments, especially its water system, and will not consider leaving these monuments.

Ardrian McKenzie, a young woman interested in cybernetics, offers to help Data. They discover that not everyone agrees with Gosheven, but still, few are interested in leaving.

Picard hopes to find a loophole in the treaty, which required 372 Federation legal experts to negotiate, but the Sheliak refuse to talk. With a Federation colony ship three weeks away, Picard decides to intercept the Sheliak colony ship and delay it.

Gosheven calls a meeting, which Data attends. The android uses various arguments, which provoke much thought, but Gosheven rallies his people again. Still, there are dissenters, and they meet at McKenzie's house. Gosheven intrudes, and shoots Data with an energy weapon. The meeting breaks up.

With McKenzie's help, and his diagnostic circuits, Data revives, and decides that words are not enough. He rigs his phaser, using parts of his neural processor, to work despite the radiation, and sends a message to Gosheven telling him that he plans to destroy the acqueduct. Data finds the area protected, but stuns the armed guards, and sends a maximum-power phaser burst up the waterway, demonstrating his power. If one android can do this, he tells them, think what the Sheliak can do. This finally convinces the colonists that evacuation is a good idea, and preparations begin.

Picard manages to stall the Sheliak when he finds a clause in the treaty which enables either side to call in a third-party arbitrator in any dispute. As arbitrators, he chooses a race that won't emerge from hibernation for nearly six months. Faced with this, the Sheliak cede Picard his requested three weeks. Data returns to the Enterprise, as the evacuation begins.

EPISODE FIFTY-ONE: "THE SURVIVORS"

Written by Michael Wagner

Directed by Les Landau

Guest Cast: John Anderson, Anne Haney

The Enterprise races to a Federation colony under attack, only to find all life obliterated from Delta Rana IV— except for a few acres of lush land occupied by two survivors, a pair of Earth botanists in their eighties. There seems to be no clue as to why Kevin and Rishanna Oxbridge were spared from the global destruction by their attackers. Enterprise sensors cannot detect any sign of the massive space ship responsible. The Oxbridges are perplexed by their survival, but seem perfectly content to remain where they are. Data is intrigued by one of their artifacts, an ancient music box topped by a pair of mechanical dancers. On board the Enterprise, Deanna Troi finds her mind assailed by an endlessly repeating piece of music, the same one played by the Oxbridge's music box. The Away Team leaves, but not before Riker gives them a communicator and tells them that the Enterprise will remain in orbit for a few days.

While Deanna begins to unravel under the pressure of the inescapable tune, the Enterprise is suddenly attacked by the alien ship, which appears almost out of nowhere. It fires on the Enterprise but does no damage, then flees, with the Enterprise in pursuit, until Picard realizes he's being toyed with and returns to Delta Rana IV. The Oxbridges cannot last long, even with their generator, because the water table is tainted, so the Captain beams down with a matter replicator for them. He questions them, but all he can learn is the Oxbridge holds a strong moral position against killing, and refused to join in the defense of the colony. Perhaps this was why he and his wife were spared. Picard is still suspicious; as soon as he beams up, the Enterprise is attacked again by the same ship, only to have its shields destroyed and its weapons systems rendered inoperable. The aliens do not pursue when the Enterprise flees, but orbit the planet.

Picard waits for an hour and returns again. The ship is gone again, much as he anticipated. He beams down again, and tells the Oxbridges that he will never enter their house again, but that the Enterprise will stay in orbit around Delta Rana IV as long as they are alive. As soon as he beams up, the aliens reappear. When Picard refuses to respond to its imminent attack, it veers off and destroys the Oxbridges instead. Picard then orders Worf to fire upon the ship, which disintegrates completely when hit by a single photon torpedo.

Sensors indicate no life on the planet, but Picard waits. After a few hours, the Oxbridge home reappears. Picard claims that he is acting on the assumption that there is only one survivor of the alien attack, which baffles Riker. The Oxbridges are beamed onto the bridge, where Picard confronts them with his deductions.

He believes that the entire colony was destroyed, including Oxbridge's wife. At this, she vanishes. He continues: the house, the trees, and the wife were all re-creations. The alien ship that fought the Enterprise was one, too, and when Picard set the conditions for his departure they were all too quickly fulfilled. "Kevin Oxbridge'" vanishes, and reappears in sick bay, where he removes the music from Deanna's mind. He had used it to block her from learning his true nature. He reveals that he is a being thousands of years old which fell in love while in human form and married Rishanna. She never knew his true nature. When the colony was attacked by a warlike alien race, she joined the resistance and died. His grief and rage was so great that, in a moment, he destroyed the attackers— not just those in the ship, but all fifty billion of them, everywhere in the universe. The guilt of that genocide overwhelms him.

The being returns to the planet, to recreate his former life and deal with his guilt alone, for, as Picard notes, there is no law to deal with such a crime.

EPISODE FIFTY-TWO: "WHO WATCHES THE WATCHERS"

Written by Richard Manning and Hans Beimler

Directed by Robert Weimer

Guest Cast: Kathryn Leigh Scott, Ray Wise, James Greene, Pamela Segaul, John McLiam

An anthropological team observing the proto-Vulcan inhabitants of Mentaka-III experiences a power failure in its holographically concealed station, and one of its members is thrown clear of the area by a blast. The Mentakans are a Bronze-age level culture technologically, but they are very sensible people who have long lived without superstitions. The arrival of an Enterprise Away Team coincides with the post's discovery by two Mentakans. Liko, a man who is still grieving his wife's death a year earlier, peers into the outpost, only to be shocked by some stray energy which causes him to fall from a great height. Doctor Crusher descends to help him, and beams him up to the Enterprise. This is witnessed by his daughter Oji, who is hiding nearby. Liko awakens briefly on the Enterprise, and, through a haze, sees Picard, who is obviously in charge. Crusher tries Pulaski's memory wiping technique, but it doesn't work, and when he awakens on Mentaka-III he believes that he has seen a god out of his people's ancient legends.

Troi and Riker are altered to resemble Mentakans, and, outfitted with implanted transmitters, beam down to locate the missing scientist Palmer. They are welcomed to the village, where Liko is telling his people of the miracle that brought him back to life, and of the god he calls "The Picard."

The other Mentakans are sceptical, especially the village leader, a woman named Nouria. Other villagers soon arrive with the injured Palmer in tow. Liko surmises that Palmer is a servant who has failed The Picard— perhaps they can win The Picard's good will by punishing him. While the villagers debate this, Troi slips out, and returns claiming to have seen another stranger. When they go to investigate, Riker makes off with Palmer, only to be pursued by a bow-wielding Mentakan. He manages to beam up unobserved, but Troi is held by the Mentakans now.

There seems to be no way to rescue Troi without compromising the Prime Directive, so Picard beams Nouria to the Enterprise to convince her that he is not a god. She grasps the concept of that there are different levels of social and technological development, and that Picard is not supernatural, but still thinks that he has the power to bring back the dead until he takes her to sick bay and allows her to witness the death of one of the injured anthropologists. He returns to the planet with her, only to face the unstable Liko, who begs for the return of his dead wife. Liko tries to prove Picard's powers by shooting him with an arrow; his daughter pushes him, and Picard is only wounded in the shoulder. He bleeds, which convinces Liko that he is mortal after all.

The Mentakans understand Picard's explanation of the Prime Directive, and bid him farewell after he dismantles the observation post.

Picard is impressed by their intelligence and determination, and is certain that they will some day take their place in the stars.

EPISODE FIFTY-THREE: "THE BONDING"

Written by Ronald D. Moore

Directed by Winrich Kolbe

Guest Cast: Susan Powell, Gabriel Damon

Worf leads an Away Team to ancient ruins on a planet depopulated by war millennia earlier, but an explosive device left over from that conflict explodes, killing the ship's archaeologist, Lt. Marla Astor. Her 12 year old son Jeremy, who lost his father a few years earlier, is on board the Enterprise, and Picard once again faces the unhappy task of breaking the news, as he once did to Wesley Crusher.

Geordi beams down to the lifeless planet and discovers more of the bombs— which have been dug up and disarmed. Worf feels responsible for Astor's death, which was senseless, and at the hands of a long-dead enemy which Worf cannot take vengeance against. He considers performing the Klingon bonding ceremony with Jeremy, but Deanna advises him to wait, as the boy has not yet started to deal with his emotions.

An energy field is detected on the planet, near the explosion site, and Deanna detects a presence. Geordi detects fluctuations in the anti-matter containment pods. While Jeremy is watching video records of his family, his mother reappears in their quarters and tries to take him to the planet below.

Worf discovers this but is told not to interfere. When Picard confronts Astor, she vanishes. When Deanna takes Jeremy back to his quarters, Astor is there again, and the rooms have been transformed into Jeremy's home on Earth, right down to his favorite cat. Jeremy is convinced that it is all real.

The being posing as his mother does not understand the other humans' interference, since all she wants to do is make him happy.

Geordi discovers that he can cut off the energy's access to the Enterprise by adjusting the shield harmonics. It works, and the illusion vanishes, but the energy field leaves the planet and enters the vessel. The illusion is restored, while the energy goes through the ship's systems, learning all about them.

Picard tries to reason with "Astor" and learns that she was created by a race of energy beings who vowed to stop all wars after another race, made of matter, destroyed itself. He must convince the beings that it is not in the boy's best interest to be given a comforting illusion. He must be allowed to mature, despite the pain that often accompanies that process.

Wesley joins the conversation and talks about his own father's death. Jeremy finally expresses his anger at Worf, who reveals his own parents' deaths, and offers to help the boy.

The aliens realize that the real Marla Astor will live in her son's memory, and withdraw to the planet. Worf and Jeremy perform the Bonding ceremony, which honors their dead mothers and makes them brothers.

EPISODE FIFTY-FOUR: "BOOBY TRAP"

Written by Ron Roman, Michael Pilar, Richard Danus and Michael Wagner

Diredted by Gabrielle Beaumont

Guest Cast: Susan Gibney

The Enterprise, on its way through an asteroid field that was the site of an ancient space battle, discovers the perfectly preserved remains of a thousand-year-old Promelian battle cruiser. Picard, Data and Worf beam down and discover the bodies of the crew still at their stations; a memory coil provides them with the Promelian captain's last message, in which he praises his crew and takes all responsibility for his ship's fate.

When the Enterprise tries to leave the area, it cannot, for something is draining its power. At the same time, it is being bombarded by lethal radiation, which will destroy the shileds in several hours. The Enterprise has fallen into the same booby trap that destroyed the Promelian vessel.

Geordi usues holodeck simulations to study the problem, and finds himself working with a simulation of Dr. Leah Brahms, the designer of the Enterprise's propulsion systems. Data recovers more memory coils from the dead ship and eventually repairs them. They reveal that the trap involves energy assimilators hidden in the asteroids: these devices draw off power and transform it into radiation. Any power use fuels it, even that of the shields. Geordi and "Leah Brahms" try to work up computer simulations that will enable the Enterprise computer to run the ship, making split-second alterations that might save them, but none of the simulations are successful. Finally, in a moment of inspiration, Geordi turns the whole idea around: why not cut the power completely? Picard accepts the idea as their best chance, and takes the con himself. After a single impulse burst sets the ship in motion, everything but basic life support is shut off, and the Captain uses simple thrusters to direct his drifting vessel through the asteroid field. When their momentum seems about to give out, he uses the gravity of a large asteroid to swing the Enterprise around and out of harm's way.

The assimilators are destroyed with photon torpedos. Geordi shuts down the holodeck, and finds that he has become attracted to the "Leah" simulation.

EPISODE FIFTY-FIVE: "THE ENEMY"

Written by David Kemper and Michael Piller

Directed by David Carson

Guest Cast: John Snyder, Andreas Katsulas, Steve Rankin

Riker, Worf and Geordi investigate a distress call on a world ravaged by electromagnetic storms which interfere with all technology. They find a Romulan scout craft, destroyed after it crashed, and a wounded Romulan nearby. Geordi is separated from his companions and falls into a deep cavern. They beam up without him, but cannot locate him with their sensors.

Geordie locates metallic ore with his visor and uses his phaser to fashion pitons, with which he escapes from the cavern. The Enterprise drops a neutrino beam probe, which emits a beam visible to Geordi's visor. All he needs to do is locate it and alter its frequency. He sees it, but is taken captive by another Romulan. When they are threatened by a rock slide, he helps the Romulan to a sheltering cave, but the Centurion still regards the human as his prisoner.

The Romulan on the Enterprise will die unless he receives a compatible blood transfusion. The only crew member whose blood will serve is also the one who hates the Romulans most: Worf. Data intercepts a Romulan response to the distress call, which reveals that a Romulan ship is six hours away from the Neutral Zone border. Picard warns them not to enter Federation space. They insist that the Enterprise meet them at the border in five hours and turn over the injured Romulan, but Picard will not abandon Geordi.

On the planet, Geordi realizes that the electrical storms are affecting their nervous systems. He finally succeeds in convincing his captor that they must depend on each other for survival, only to have his neural interface with his visor fail. Now he can't see the beacon.

Worf refuses to give blood for the Romulan. The Romulan, in turn, says he would rather die than accept Klingon blood. The Romulan ship passes the border and heads toward a confrontation with the Enterprise.

Since Geordi's visor is still functional, his new-found ally suggests rigging it to his tricorder. Acting as Geordi's eyes and hands, the Centurion completes the connection, creating a crude neutrino detector. With this, they manage to reach the beacon.

The Romulan aboard the Enterprise dies. The Romulan ship arrives, ready for battle. The beacon changes, but Geordi can't be beamed up with the shields raised, so Picard makes a gesture of peace and lowers them. Conflict is averted, and the Centurion is returned to the Romulans, who return to the Neutral Zone.

EPISODE FIFTY-SIX: "THE PRICE"

Written by Hannah Louise Shearer

Directed Robert Scheerer

Guest Cast: Matt McCoy, Elizabeth Hoffman, Castulo Guerra, Scott Thomson, Dan Shor, Kevin Peter Hall

When an apparently stable wormhole appears in the Barzan system, the premiere of that world opens negotiations for exploitation rights, since the inhabitants of Barzan lack the resources to utilize it themselves. Apparently, the wormhole opens on a sector which can only be reached in a hundred years at Warp 9; through the wormhole, the trip will only take a few seconds. The Federation is represented by its top negotiator, Mendoza. The Caldonians are also present for the talks, hosted by Picard on board the Enterprise. A Ferengi delegation appears, demanding to be let in on the proceedings. The Premiere invites them to participate; as usual, they are greedy and vulgar.

Ral, a human negotiator employed by the alien Chrysalians, comes aboard, and is immediately attracted to Deanna Troi. She is also attracted to him, and their romance develops quickly. Meanwhile, the Ferengi delegate administers a chemical to Mendoza by shaking hands, incapacitating him with an extreme allergic reaction. Riker takes Mendoza's place at Picard's insistence, for the captain is certain that his First Oficer's poker skills will serve him well at the bargaining table.

Since the information about the wormhole is based on a single probe, Geordi and Data prepare to travel through it in a shuttle at its next appearance. The Ferengi sense treachery and send their negotiator's two assistants into it in a Ferengi pod.

Ral reveals to Deanna that he is one quarter Betazoid, a fact he generally keeps secret. Caught up in romance, she does not give this much thought at first.

Geordi and Data pass through the wormhole with the Ferengi close behind. They discover that their location is 200 light years off from the expected sector. The far end of the wormhole is unstable, and shifts position. Eventually both ends will be completely unstable. They try to convince the Ferengi of this, but the suspicious big-eared creeps won't listen.

Ral uses his wiles to talk the Caldonians from withdrawing their bid on the wormhole, reducing the competition.

Geordi can see the wormhole a few moments before it becomes visible, through his visors ability to see subatomic energy patterns. He and Data enter it early, but the stubborn Ferengi crew will not follow. When the wormhole becomes visible to them, it only holds its position for a second before disappearing completely, leaving them stranded.

Deanna begins to suspect that Ral is using his secret powers to gain an unethical edge in the negotiations, and their romance begins to fracture.

Ral talks to Riker in Ten Forward, but the First Officer is in his best poker playing mode and can't be bluffed. Ral makes a mistake when he tries to disrupt Riker's cool façade by mentioning that he plans to take Deanna away with him. Riker tells the smug empath that he is entirely in favor of anything that will make Deanna happy. Still, Ral claims that he is willing to make his final bid before the shuttle brings back its conclusions. Even Riker will not commit to such a move.

The negotiations resume, only to be interrupted when the Ferengi ship fires on the Enterprise. Riker must go to the bridge. The Ferengi claim the Federation has rigged the negotiations, cutting the Ferengi out of the action. They fire on the wormhole, a pointless maneuver, and the Enterprise easily destroys their missile. Ral and the Premiere come on the bridge and Ral announces that he has closed the deal.

Deanna senses that the Ferengi are not really angry, and that they are lying. Ral takes charge of the "crisis" and gets the Ferengi to back down by cutting them in on the wormhole deal. Deanna figures out what's going on and reveals Ral's secret: he and the Ferengi staged the entire conflict to get Riker out of the way. Before the deal can be undone, Data and Geordi return and reveal that the wormhole has no practical value. Ral's employers are still stuck with holding up their end of the bargain, and Riker has called another bluff without losing a thing. Riker offers his congratulations to Ral for his hollow victory.

Undaunted, Ral tries to get Deanna to come with him, but she turns him away, since he seems to have no scruples about using his Betazoid abilities to take advantage of others.

EPISODE FIFTY-SEVEN: "THE VENGEANCE FACTOR"

Written by Sam Rolfe

Directed by Timothy Bond

Guest Cast: Lisa Wilcox, Joey Aresco, Nancy Parsons, Stephen Lee, Mark Lawrence

Akhama Three, a world once torn by clan warfare, has achieved unity after many generations. One faction, which split off years earlier, is a group of thieves and scavengers known as the Gatherers. When traces of Akhama blood is found at a raided science station, Picard goes to the Sovereign of that world and convinces her to talk to the Gatherers in an effort to reintegrate them into the society of their homeworld. The Sovereign, Marouk, is accompanied by her cook and food taster, the beautiful Yuta, who catches Riker's eye.

A Gatherer outpost is located, and Riker leads an away team. After ending a brief battle by means of a ruse, they convince the ranking Gatherer, B'rull, to talk to the Sovereign. Marouk and Yuta beam down. While Marouk and B'Rull talk, Yuta confronts an old Gatherer of the Lornak clan, who is astounded to recognize her. When she touches him lightly, he dies. She is the last of her clan, she says, but she will outlive his clan nevertheless.

When the body is discovered, it is believed that he died of natural causes, but Crusher beams the body up for examination. B'Rull, meanwhile, has agreed to lead the Sovereign to the Gatherer leader Chorgon.

Crusher discovers that the Lornak man had a perfectly healthy heart despite his age. His cardiac arrest was caused by a micro-virus, apparently tailored to his genetic pattern, which blocked the impulses of his autonomic nervous system. In a word, he was murdered. The virus could be carried without harm to the carrier, only to be deadly for anyone with the right DNA.

Uta, attracted to Riker, visits him in his quarters, but she cannot deal with him as an equal, having been sworn to servitude for so long. She is free to leave the Sovereign by choice at any time, but she has some secret which limits her choices. Riker tries to comfort her, but must go to the bridge when a Red Alert is announced.

The Gatherers have fired on the Enterprise, but Picard knocks out their shields and beams over for talks with Marouk, who, as always, takes Uta along. As the rocky negotiations get underway, Crusher studies the Akhamanian medical records and discovers a similar murder. Fifty three years earlier, the Lornaks eradicated another clan, and their leader died while awaiting trial— of cardiac arrest. Visual records show a surprising link between the two cases: Uta. Apparently, she hadn't aged a day in over fifty years. Another link is also discovered: Chorgon is also a member of the Lornak clan.

Riker beams over to the Gatherer ship just as Uta is about to give Chorgon a fatal glass of brandy. He confronts her, but she tries to complete her task, for Chorgon is the last Lornak, and she was the one chosen from the five survivors of her clan to undergo genetic life extension and carry out their final revenge. Riker fires a phaser at her twice, but she can resist maximum stun settings. He gives her a final warning, and raises the setting. When she makes a final attempt to kill Chorgon, he vaporizes her.

Although Marouk arranges a truce with the Gatherers, this is little consolation for Riker, who is haunted by the painful duty he has performed.

EPISODE FIFTY-EIGHT: "THE DEFECTOR"

Written by Ronald D. Moore

Directed by Robert Scheerer

Guest Cast: James Sloyan, Andreas Katsulas, John Hancock

Near the Neutral Zone border, the Enterprise detects a Romulan scout ship being pursued by a larger Romulan vessel. The pilot of the scout asks the Enterprise for asylum, and is rescued after passing over into Federation space. He claims to be a minor logistics officer with important information: the Romulans are preparing for war, and have built a hidden base in the Neutral Zone, within easy striking distance of Federation outposts. Picard does not trust him, even though he claims he wishes to avert war; the possibility that he is a spy is great, since analysis of the fight indicates that the Romulan warship slowed down to let him escape. In the past, the Romulans have often tricked opponents into appearing to be the aggressor, thus establishing their "right" to war. Still, a probe picks up traces of low level subspace transmissions in the area of the alleged outpost.

When Data takes the Romulan to a holodeck simulation of a valley on Romulus, the defector admits that he is actually an Admiral who had been censured for counselling against war. He has defected to prevent his Empire from destroying itself, and gives up a wealth of information. Picard risks entering the Neutral Zone to investigate the base, only to find nothing there except two Romulan ships ready to do battle. The Admiral had been fed misinformation to test his loyalty.

Picard faces off the threats of the Romulans with a cool front. Outgunned, he seems to be bluffing, until he reveals an a ace up his sleeve: the Enterprise has been accompanied by cloaked Klingon warships all along. The Romulans clear out once the tables are turned, and Picard heads the Enterprise back to Federation space, only to find that the Admiral has poisoned himself. He leaves behind letters for his wife and daughter, which can never be delivered as long as the Romulans maintain their hunger for war: the defector was brave enough to stand up for peace in a violent society.

EPISODE FIFTY-NINE: "THE HUNTED"

Written by Robin Bernheim

Directed by Cliff Bole

Guest Cast: Jeff McCarthy, James Cromwell

The planet of Angosia, which has achieved peace, applies for Federation membership. The Enterprise, in orbit, helps the Angosians catch an escaped prisoner, Roga Danar, who continually evades them until Data second-guesses his next move. He is held on the Enterprise until the Angosions can pick him up. Deanna Troi senses the prisoner's pain, and goes to him, to discover the truth of his violent nature. In fact, his basic nature appears to be peaceful, only to have been altered to make him a perfect soldier. Investigation of his records is baffling: he has no criminal record, and his military record is exemplary. The Angosians, it seems, turned their volunteers into soldiers through biological and mental tampering. Once their war was won, they shunted their soldiers off to a lunar colony, where they were provided with a comfortable existence. This was not enough for Roga Danar.

Despite security precautions, Danar escapes during the transfer. Certain modifications made to his body enable him to fight the transporter beam, as well as making him invisible to the ship's sensors. He leaves traces intentionally, however, leading Data to conclude that he is misdirecting them.

Worf finds traces of him in Cargo Bay Two; a pressure suit is missing. Attention shifts to the airlocks, but Dana is actually still hiding in the cargo bay. Worf discovers him, and they fight, until the power goes out when an overloaded phaser, left by Danar, explodes in a Jeffrey's Tube. Danar knocks out Worf, powers the cargo bay transporter with a phaser, and beams onto the Angosian police shuttle, getting the drop on his would-be captors. He then leads a revolt, and faces off the government at gunpoint. The soldiers are not programmed to fight unarmed opponents, but can defend themselves if attacked: will the government try to coerce them, or listen to their position? The Prime Minister asks Picard for help, but Picard invokes the Prime Directive, leaving the Angosians to work out their own problems.

EPISODE SIXTY: "THE HIGH GROUND"

Written by Melinda M. Snodgrass

Directed by Gabrielle Beaumont

Guest Cast: Kerrie Keene, Richard Cox

On Rutia IV, while helping victims of a terrorist bombing, Dr. Crusher is kidnapped. The Ansata terrorists have been fighting the Rutian government for years, and have an undetectable mode of transport. They need a doctor because their DNA itself has been warped by constant use of the Inverter, which transports by means of a dimensional shift. Their leader, Finn, hopes to draw the Federation into the conflict. Already concerned that the Federation is providing medical supplies to his enemies, he becomes convinced, despite Crusher's protestations, that the Federation has chosen sides.

Examining a coil taken from a captured terrorist, Data and Wesley are baffled until Wesley remembers early experiments in dimensional shifting. Picard realizes how the Ansata are transporting, and why they need a doctor; Wesley develops a program that will trace the power source, although the device must be used a sufficient number of times to get a fix on it.

Riker's presence as an observer at interrogations convinces Finn that the Federation is his enemy. An attempt to destroy the Enterprise fails, but a second foray results in the capture of Picard. The Ansata demand that the Federation impose an embargo on Rutia within twelve hours. By now, Wesley has located the pwer source, and an away team beams down to rescue the Captain and Dr. Crusher. In the melee, Rutian police kill Finn, but the struggle seems destined to go on for a long time.

EPISODE SIXTY-ONE: "DEJA Q"

Written by Richard Danus

Directed by Les Landau

Guest Cast: John deLancie, Corbin Berenson

The Enterprise attempts to keep a planet's moon from dropping out of orbit, but their efforts seem futile. When Q appears on the bridge, naked and claiming to have been stripped of his powers, Picard immediately suspects that he has a hand in the imminent disaster. Q is actually telling the truth, however, and cannot remedy the situation. Placed in the brig, Q tries to adapt to mortality, but is frightened by such unfamiliar sensations as sleep and hunger. When the Enterprise is probed by a mysterious force, it becomes obvious that Q's enemies are out to get him in his vulnerable state, and the ship is attacked by a diffuse energy being. The being can be repulsed by adjusting the shield's harmonic structure. Meanwhile, Q tries to help Geordi with the moon, but his best suggestion is to change the gravitational constant of the universe, something the humans cannot do. This does inspire Geordi to try to reduce the moon's gravity by enclosing it in a warp field. The attempt to do this works, but is cut short when the alien uses the drop in shield power to attack Q again. Data is damaged trying to help Q. The Enterprise nearly enters the planet's atmosphere, but gets back on course and raises the shields. The moon's descent has been delayed but not stopped.

Although being human is unbearable to him, Q admits that Data is a better human than he is, and, bored with mortality, takes a shuttle to face the energy being and spare the Enterprise further attacks. When Picard tries to get the shuttle back, nothing works on it; unknown to the Enterprise crew, another Q (Corbin Berenson) has stepped in. Since Q has shown a modicum of selflessness, his powers are restored, enabling him to get rid of the energy being. Returning to the bridge with a mariachi band, he serenades his Federation friends. Picard is not amused, and asks Q to leave. He gives Data a parting gift, allowing him to experience laughter for a few moments, and also sets the moon back in a perfect orbit, sparing the planet below.

EPISODE SIXTY-TWO: "A MATTER OF PERSPECTIVE"

Written by Ed Zuckerman

Directed by Cliff Boles

Guest Cast: Craig Richard Nelson, Gina Hecht, Mark Margolis

Riker is accused of the murder of Dr. Nel Apgar when the Taneka IV orbiting research station explodes just as he beams back to the Enterprise. A power drain would seem to indicate that he fired a phaser at the reactor core just as he beamed away. On Taneka IV, a variation of the Napoleonic Code holds sway: the accused is guilty until his innocence is proven. Picard resists extradition, and talks Taneka's Investigator Crag into reviewing the case on the Enterprise holodeck.

Dr. Apgar had been working on producing Krieger waves. The Krieger converter on the station was the focus for an energy generator on the planet's surface, but apparently was not ready. In Riker's version of events, Apgar resented the intrusion; he seemed concerned that Riker would block his access to a certain element needed in his research. To further complicate matters, Mrs. Apgar tries to seduce Riker. When Apgar intrudes on this, he hits his wife, and falls to the floor when Riker sidesteps a blow meant for him. The next day, after Mrs. Apgar and an assistant have beamed down to the planet, Riker returns to the Enterprise.

In Mrs. Apgar's version, Riker tried to seduce her, then tried to force her to do his will. When Apgar intervenes, Riker hits him, and warns that charges filed would result in a negative report to the Federation.

As the hearing goes on, the Enterprise is subjected to periodic bursts of an unknown radiation.

Apgar's assistant relates Apgar's version of events as he told it to her; on Taneka, hearsay is admissible evidence. According to Apgar, Riker and his wife seemed equally culpable in their infidelity, and the doctor beat up Riker in his righteous anger. Since the Enterprise is in Tanekan space, extradition must take place, and evidence to prove Riker's innocence seems nonexistent.

Geordi, Data and Wesley solve the case in time. The radiation bursts occur at regular intervals; except for a slight time variation, the explosion also occurred at a multiple of this interval. Apgar had actually succeeded in creating Krieger waves, but was stalling the Federation in the hopes of developing them into an offensive weapon he could sell to the highest bidder. Riker was a potential threat because he could cut off the supplies Apgar needed. Apgar tried to stage a transporter accident by striking the transport beam with Krieger waves, but the wave was deflected from Riker's position— which accounted for the time lag— and blew up the reactor core instead. The radiation plaguing the Enterprise was, in fact, Krieger waves, converted from the planetary generator by the holodeck's recreation of Apgar's fully functional converter. Crag is not convinced until Geordi stages one last holodeck program, timed to coincide with the energy transmission; the destruction of the station is recreated, proving Riker's innocence.

EPISODE SIXTY-THREE: "YESTERDAY'S ENTERPRISE"

Teleplay by Ira Steven Behr, Richard Manning, Hans Beimler and Ronald D. Moore; from a story by Trent Christopher Ganing and Eric A. Stillwell

Directed by David Carson

Guest Cast: Denise Crosby as Tasha Yar, Christopher McDonald, Tricia O'Neil

Guinan introduces Worf to the pleasures of prune juice, which the Klingon pronounces "a warrior's drink." He is called to the bridge when a strange phenomenon—a temporal rift—appears in the path of the Enterprise. A Federation ship emerges from the void; as it does so, the timelines shift, and the Enterprise becomes a war vessel, for the Federation has now been fighting the Klingon Empire for the past twenty-two years.

Worf is no longer on the ship—but Tasha Yar is, never having encountered the creature Armus in "Skin of Evil." The other ship is the Enterprise-C, which vanished around the time of the failed peace talks with the Klingons.

Guinan senses that something is amiss, and tries to convince Captain Picard that the earlier Enterprise, damaged in a battle with Romulans, must go back to its own time despite its almost certain destruction. Reluctantly, Picard comes around to this view; the Enterprise-C seems to be a key factor in history, for it was actually defending a Klingon outpost from a Romulan sneak attack before its trip through time. Had it succeeded, the Klingons may have been impressed by the sacrifice. Picard confides to the other Enterprise's captain, Rachel Garrett, that the war is going badly for the Federation— a war which has already cost four billion lives.

Tasha Yar becomes involved in her work with Lieutenant Castillo of the ship from the past, and becomes increasingly aware that something is wrong with her presence on the ship. Guinan tells her that her death in the other timeline was senseless. The two Enterprises are soon under attack from a greater Klingon force, as the Enterprise-C prepares to return through the destabilizing rift. When Captain Garrett is killed, Tasha Yar volunteers to join Castillo on his doomed ship, in order to gain a meaningful departure from the world. The Enterprise-D is outgunned and seemingly doomed when the timelines are restored; things return to normal, and Lieutenant Worf reports only a brief fluctuation in the sensor readings. No one has any knowledge of the alternative reality just avoided except Guinan, who joins Geordi in Ten Forward and asks him to tell her about Tasha Yar.

EPISODE SIXTY-FOUR: "THE OFFSPRING"

Written by Rene Echeverria

Directed by Jonathan Frakes

Guest Cast: Hallie Todd, Nicolas Coster

Data has been working on something in private ever since he attended a cybernetics conference. He unveils it to Troi, Wesley and Geordi: he has build an android like himself, which he has named "Lal." Lal, a humanoid without distinct features, calls Data 'father' and chooses the form of a young human woman for her permanent appearance.

Picard is a bit perturbed not to have been informed, and finds the father/daughter aspect of the androids' relationship a bit disturbing at first.

Despite this, he takes Data's side when a Starfleet Admiral expresses his intent to remove Lal from Data's care and take her away for study, going so far as to contradict a direct order from the Admiral. He feels that the Admiral is not recognizing or respecting the rights and liberties that the androids posess as sentient beings in the Federation. Ironies build up: Picard himself has never had children, but the Admiral, who is a father several times, seems, at least outwardly, to be quite heartless in this matter, and promises Picard that his stand may cost him dearly.

Lal is learning more daily, both from experience and from a series of neural transfers from Data's brain, and she is becoming more and more aware of her difference from other beings. There are signs that she has, in some ways, surpassed her father. One is her self-developed ability to use contractions in her speech, something Data cannot do. The other change becomes evident when she realizes that the Admiral intends to separate her from her father and the Enterprise. She runs to Deanna's quarters— not to Data's, as her programming would have her do in times of malfunction— and reveals that she is actually feeling fear. She has achieved real emotion, but only as her systems begin to fail. Data and the Admiral strive to repair her, but her neural pathways shut down faster than Data can restore them. The Admiral is shaken by the experience, realizing much too late that there was more involved here than mere cybernetic devices. Data informs Lal that he must shut her down permanently; she thanks him for her life, and tells him that she loves her. Data cannot truly tell her the same, for he cannot feel love, but love is evident in his actions even though he does not realize it.

In the end, Data transfers all her memories to his brain; Lal, whose name means "beloved" in Hindi, will remain with him forever.

EPISODE SIXTY-FIVE: "SINS OF THE FATHER"

Teleplay by Ronald D. Moore and W. Reed Moran

Based on a teleplay by Drew Deighan

Directed by Les Landau

Guest Cast: Charles Cooper, Tony Todd, Patrick Massett, Thelma Lee

The Enterprise crew is in for a rough ride when a Klingon exchange officer temporarily assumes Riker's duties. The over-worked crew can't help but notice that Worf is the only one escaping the Klingon's discipline; what they fail to realize is that being polite and condescending to a fellow Klingon is a very pointed way of insulting him. Worf at last cannot stand it any longer, and is ready to fight the visitor, only to learn that the Klingon is actually his younger brother, and that his insults were a test. Now that Worf has shown his worthiness, his brother reveals his secret: when Worf and his parents went to the outpost later destroyed by the Romulans, the younger brother was left behind, presumed dead by the Empire but actually raised by another family. He has sought out Worf after all these years because their father has now been accused of helping the Romulan's notorious attack, and only the eldest son can challenge charges of treachery in the High Council. Otherwise, the stigma of a traitor will be borne by their family for seven generations. One further catch: if Worf's challenge fails he will be executed.

Picard has Data access all the records of the massacre. The charges against Worf's father were based on the records of a recently captured Romulan vessel. Data compares these to the sensor records of the Federation ship Intrepid, which was nearby at the time, and discovers a discrepancy in the time codes. Someone has tampered with the Romulan records.

Picard and Riker accompany Worf and his brother to the Klingon home world. Worf's brother is ambushed but survives. Picard steps in as Worf's "second." The Council sessions seem to offer little hope for Worf's cause until Data also learns that another Klingon— Worf's nurse— survived the massacre as well. Picard ventures into the heart of the ancient Klingon capitol to find her, only to have her refuse her aid. On his way back he is attacked by assassins, dispatching one only to nearly lose his life. He is saved only by the old woman's change of heart, for she stabs the assassin in the back when she catches up with

Picard. Her appearance at the Council throws things into an uproar. The head of the Council calls everyone into his private chambers. The truth is revealed: the father of Worf's accuser was the real traitor. When the Romulan records were seized, this information threatened the entire power structure of the Empire, for the traitor was a member of a very ancient and powerful family. Since Worf, apparently the sole survivor of his line, was away serving in Starfleet, a decision was made to cast the blame on his father. No one believed that he would ever challenge the charges. According to Klingon ideals, the honor of the Empire outweighs that of any single family, a point that even Worf must agree upon. It seems that he and his brother must die, until he proposes another alternative. He agrees to undergo discommendation, in effect "de-Klingonizing" himself, accepting the blight on his family name and exiling himself from the Empire.

Although this is humiliating, it shows true Klingon honor, for it demonstrates loyalty to the Empire and also leaves open the margin, however slight, of someday gaining revenge.

EPISODE SIXTY-SIX: "ALLEGIANCE"

Written by Richard Manning and Hans Beimler

Directed by Winrich Kolbe

Guest Cast: Steven Markle, Reiner Schone, Joycelyn O'Brien, Jerry Rector, Jeff Rector

En route to an important rendezvous with another Starfleet vessel, Picard is abducted by a mysterious force. An energy fluctuation is detected in his quarters, but when a security team investigates, they find a duplicate Captain. While this impostor runs the Enterprise, the real Picard finds himself held captive in a small space with two other humanoids. One is a first year Starfleet cadet, while the other is a Mizarian, one of a peaceful race that is known for its passivity— it has surrendered its planet without a fight more times than history can recall. The purpose for their captivity is unknown, and their captors maintain complete silence.

The false Picard inquires about the nearest pulsar, sets course for it, and forbids all communication. He slowly begins to lose the confidence of his crew by acting oddly. He tries to pick up Doctor Crusher, joins the officers in their poker game, orders ale for everyone in Ten Forward, and leads a rousing drinking song. To make matters worse, he seems intent on taking the ship dangerously close to the pulsar.

As these events develop, the real Picard has problems of his own. A fourth captive materializes, a large, vicious feline creature from a wild, anarchic planet. The food provided by their captors is unpalatable to this new arrival, who admits, however, that there is a good deal of food available to him; he expresses considerable interest in the Mizarian, but relieves everyone by telling them that he can go three or four days before his hunger becomes dangerous. Attempts to escape are punished by a green stun ray. Once these fail, the captives begin to suspect each other, and tensions mount.

They begin to question each others' identities: could one of them be an agent of their captors? When Picard's identity is questioned, the Starfleet cadet is quick to confirm it, citing a number of Picard's accomplishments. At last, Picard restores an uneasy balance, and all four of them— including the previously aloof Mizarian— cooperate in a new escape attempt. This time, the door opens, only to reveal another barrier behind it.

On the Enterprise, the officers finally turn against the false Picard when he insists on staying near the pulsar even as the shields begin to fail. Riker takes command and leaves the area.

The real Picard finally realizes that the entire situation is an experiment of some sort, and he is certain that the young cadet can confirm this. He is correct— the "cadet" is really an alien. One of the missions cited by the "cadet" had been classified by Starfleet, and the knowledge of it could only have been lifted directly from Picard's mind. The alien assumes its true form, and is joined by an identical member of its species. Their kind, being identical, have no concept of leadership, authority or power, and have been experimenting by mixing up beings with different attitudes to authority.

The experiment over, they return their captives to their rightful places.

Picard comes face to face with "himself" on the bridge of the Enterprise, just before it assumes its true form. Picard covertly signals Riker, and the aliens find themselves trapped in a force field— just long enough for Picard to teach them how unpleasant captivity can be.

EPISODE SIXTY-SEVEN: "CAPTAIN'S HOLIDAY"

Written by Ira Steven Behr

Directed by Chip Chalmers

Guest Cast: Jennifer Hetrick, Karen Landry, Michael Champion, Max Grodenchik

Two Vorgons, creatures from the twenty-seventh century, seek Picard on the resort planet of Risa— but they are too early. Picard is still on board the Enterprise, where he is under a great deal of stress after an important negotiation. His officers try to talk him into a vacation on Risa— he resists, insisting that he will wait until an upcoming maintenance stop, until Deanna mentions that her mother will be joining her there, and he relents. He packs some books— James Joyce's *Ulysses* among them— and beams down, promising to bring Riker a certain souvenir he's asked for.

On Risa, his reading is constantly interrupted by a stream of beautiful women. He is baffled until one explains that his gift for Riker is a symbol of sexual availability. Annoyed at Riker for trying to spice up his vacation, he hides the artifact under a pillow and resumes his reading, only to be bothered by a Ferengi, who seems to think that Picard has something that he wants. Picard chases him away, only to be bothered by Vash, a young woman who had kissed him upon his arrival. He had thought this to be a ritual greeting, but in fact she had slipped him a disc, the very thing the Ferengi is after. Picard gets involved in their intrigues, especially when the Vorgons appear and tell him that he is destined to find the Tax Utat, a powerful device stolen from their future and hidden on Risa. Picard joins Vash on her expedition to the site described on the disc, despite constant problems with the annoying Ferengi. Along the way, romance develops, even though he doesn't really trust Vash.

When they reach the site, the Vorgons appear to watch, as does the Ferengi, who forces the humans to dig at gunpoint. When at last it becomes clear that the Utat is not there, the Vorgons vanish, and the Ferengi, unwilling to accept failure, picks up a shovel and begins to dig for himself.

Back at the resort, Picard finds Vash preparing to leave, and confronts her, having deduced that their expedition was merely a ploy to shake off the Ferengi; Vash had already found it! She reveals it to him, only to have the two Vorgons appear and demand it at gunpoint. Picard questions them, since they, too, might be thieves, perhaps the ones that stole it from the future in the first place. They demand it anyway.

He sets it down on the floor and backs away quicky, signalling Riker, who has already been instructed to implement "Transporter Code Fourteen." The device is destroyed. The Vorgons withdraw, after revealing that Picard had been recorded in history as the destroyer of the Utat; their efforts to thwart him had failed.

Picard returns to the ship; somehow, all this adventure has relaxed him, although he still has one minor point to discuss with Riker.

EPISODE SIXTY-EIGHT: "TIN MAN"

Written by Putman Bailey and David Bischoff

Directed by Robert Scheerer

Guest Cast: Harry Groener as Tam, Michael Cavanaugh, Peter Vogt, Colm Meaney

The Enterprise receives new orders, and takes on Betazoid Tam Elbrun, a specialist in first contact. A possibly sentient space ship, nicknamed "Tin Man," is circling a near-nova star, and Tam is to try to contact it. Deanna studied Tam at University— unlike most Betazoids, his mental powers did not develop at adolescence, but were functional at birth, leaving Tam a brilliant but tortured telepath. He is best known for his involvement in a disastrous first contact where forty-seven Federation lives were lost. Uncomfortable around other humanoids, he seeks out exotic life forms. He becomes intrigued with Data, who he cannot read telepathically.

The Romulans have a claim on the space involved, and have two ships en route to Tin Man. One of them catches up with the Enterprise, at great cost to its engines, and attacks, damaging the shields. The Enterprise stops for repairs while the Romulan proceeds. Tam is outraged that the Romulans should make first contact. When he sense that the Romulans mean to destroy the entity, he warns it, and it destroys the warship in an amazing display of power. Tam is forced to reveal that he has been in contact with the being for quite some time; his powers are greater than ever suspected. "Tin Man" is thousands of years old, the last of its kind; once it lived symbiotically with a crew of some unknown race, but that crew was destroyed long ago, leaving it alone. It is circling the doomed star in order to end its life.

Picard does not trust Tam's desire to beam aboard the entity, but relents when Data volunteers to go along. Once aboard, Tam decides to stay, far away from humanity but with "Tin Man" for company. A second Romulan vessel attacks, but both it and the Enterprise are thrown 3.8 billion kilometers away by the sentient ship, just as the star goes nova. Data is unharmed, having been returned to his ship, but the whereabouts of Tam and "Tin Man" are unknown.

EPISODE SIXTY-NINE: "HOLLOW PURSUITS"

Written by Sally Caves

Directed by Cliff Boles

Guest Cast: Dwight Schultz as Barclay, Charley Lang, Colm Meaney

Diagnostic engineer Reginald Barclay swaggers into Ten Forward, where he shoves Geordi around and decks Riker before turning his attentions to a fawning Deanna. This holodeck fantasy ends when Barclay is called to duty— he's late again— and he stands revealed as a reclusive, insecure man. He makes others nervous: Wesley has nicknamed him "Broccoli", while Ryker wants him transferred. Picard, however, insists that Geordi try to draw him out. When an anti-gravity unit carrying medical samples from a nearby planet malfunctions, Geordi assigns Barclay to investigate. This attention only serves to make Barclay more nervous.

When Barclay is late again, Geordi finds him on the holodeck, battling three musketeers who resemble Geordi, Data and Picard. Geordi realizes that Barclay has a problem. More engineering problems arise as transporters

begin to malfunction. A food replicator reverses the molecular structure of another engineering officer's glass; there seems to be no explanation for these phenomena.

Later, when Barclay is late again, Riker storms to the holodeck, and is outraged to encounter a foolish caricature of himself. Deanna tries to see it as harmless diversion until she meets Barclay's sexy version of her. Barclay is in more trouble, but a new crisis has arisen: the Enterprise has begun to increase its speed and cannot be stopped. As the ship approaches maximum warp, Barclay proposes that all the problems might be linked. Investigation proves him right. When the antigravity unit dropped the medical supplies, two officers were contaminated with a rare substance used in medical containment units on the planet in question. They have been contaminating the Enterprise themselves. The problem is resolved, and Barclay finally has done something worthwhile outside of his fantasies. He says farewell to the cast of his holodeck programs, and orders the computer to erase them all—

but at the last minute, he saves one program.

EPISODE SEVENTY: "THE MOST TOYS"

Written by Shari Goodhartz

Directed by Timothy Bond

Guest Cast: Jane Daly, Nehemiah Persoff, Saul Rubinek

The Enterprise obtains a rare, volatile substance from space trader Kivas Fajo, which will be used to remedy major water contamination on a distant planet. The transport shuttle explodes on its last run, but the crew's vital mission gives them little time to mourn the shuttle's pilot, Data. His death is a hoax, commited by Fajo; all of the android's component elements were placed on the shuttle, in their proper proportions, to assure a proper scan.

Data has become the latest addition to Fajo's collection of unique objects, which includes a 20th century Roger Maris trading card, Dali's "Persistence of Memory", and the "Mona Lisa." Fajo, protected with a personal force field, insists that Data sit in a chair, on display, and that he get rid of his Starfleet uniform. Data refuses. He and Fajo engage in debate about their situation, and Data admits that he can use deadly force in self defense, although he never has. Fajo throws a corrosive on Data's uniform, giving him the option of donning another costume or going nude.

When Fajo brings a rival collector to see Data, the android (who has dressed) assumes an inert position. He appears to be no more than a mannikin. Fajo becomes furious, and later threatens to kill one of his own associates if Data does not sit in the chair. Data complies. The woman, who had accompanied Fajo for fourteen years, turns against him because of this, and helps Data escape.

The Enterprise crew decontaminates the water table, only to find that it was sabotaged— with a chemical that could only be countered with the substance obtained from Fajo. This, combined with unresolved questions about the explosion, sends them after the collector.

Data's escape plans are foiled when Fajo and his crew interrupt them.

The crew is incapacitated, but Fajo kills the woman helping Data. Data turns a disruptor on Fajo, but Fajo is certain that the android will not harm him. He promises to kill others if Data does not follow his wishes. The Enterprise arrives and beams up Data, but must deactivate the disruptor before bringing it aboard; it seems to have discharged in transit. Fajo is brought to justice without ever knowing if Data had intentionally fired the weapon.

EPISODE SEVENTY-ONE: "SAREK"

Television story and teleplay by Peter S. Beagle

From an unpublished story by Mark Cushman and Jake Jacobs

Directed by Les Landau

Guest Cast: Mark Lenard, Joanna Miles, William Denis, Rocco Sisto

The Federation is finally about to enter negotiations with the reclusive Legarians. The Enterprise has been chosen to host the meeting, and the Federation's emissary is none other than the 202-year old Vulcan Ambassador Sarek. Picard is pleased to have him aboard; they had met years earlier, when Picard was a lieutenant, at Sarek's son's wedding, and Picard hopes to get to know him. Sarek is preceded by two assistants, one human, the other the Vulcan Sakath, who insist that the Ambassador must rest. Picard invites the Vulcan's second wife (also human) to a Mozart recital that evening; surprisingly, Sarek also attends, only to leave suddenly when the music moves him to shed a tear.

Strange tensions develop among the crew, culminating in a huge brawl in Ten Forward. Even Riker is hit in the melee. Deanna reports that she sensed Sarek had lost emotional control at the recital, while Dr. Crusher mentions Ben Dai Syndrome, a disease affecting Vulcans of advanced age. If this is causing him to lose control, his Vulcan telepathy may be the cause of the strange disruptions among the crew. Sarek's human assistant will admit to nothing, but Sakath tells Data that he has been using his telepathy to help Sarek maintain control.

Sarek dismisses Sakath when he learns of this, but consents to be tested for the disease. He will not postpone the negotiations until the results are in, however, which leads to an argument with Picard. Sarek loses his temper. Once he calms down, he and Picard agree to a mind meld: Sarek will take Picard's self-control, while Picard will hold the emotional side of the Vulcan. The negotiations are successful, but Picard must endure the weight of Sarek's regrets and his long unvoiced love for his first wife Amanda and his son Spock. He endures it, and the two men reverse the meld in time. Sarek retires to Vulcan, his long career capped by one final success, while Picard has gotten to know him better than he's ever hoped to.

EPISODE SEVENTY-TWO: "MÉNAGE À TROI"

Written by Fred Bronson and Susan Sackett

Directed by Robert Legato

Guest Cast: Majel Barrett, Frank Corsentino, Ethan Phillips, Peter Slutsken, Rudolph Willrich, Carel Struycken

A diplomatic reception on board the Enterprise, in orbit over Betazed, is underway, with Lwaxana Troi in attendance. Riker beats a Ferengi at 3-D chess, who complains that he was distracted by the Algolian ceremonial rhythms being played as musical accompaniment. The Ferengi brain cannot comprehend sound patterns as music. The main Ferengi in attendance, Taug, is taken with Lwaxana, and is even more determined to have her once she loudly rejects him. His interest is enhanced by the fact that her telepathy might help him gain an edge in negotiations.

Picard insists that Riker take some shore leave on Betazed, so the First Officer and Deanna visit their old haunts, only to run into Lwaxana and her manservant. When the servant goes off to collect some berries, Taug beams down with dried flowers for Lwaxana. When she tosses them aside, he beams back to his ship— abducting her, Deanna and Riker.

While Taug tries to woo Lwaxana, Riker and Deanna try to find some way out of the Ferengi brig. Riker kibbitzes a chess game two Ferengi— including the one he beat— are playing, and winds up playing a game, from a distance, with the constant loser. After a while, he gives up, since he can't really see the board. The Ferengi, desperate to win, lets Riker out to continue the match— only to be KO'd.

While Lwaxana tries to play up to the Ferengi captain, Riker tries to access the ship's computer, but can't make any transmission without Taug's security code. Deanna contacts her mother telepathically, and Lwaxana, who has Taug wrapped around her finger by this point, tries to get the code. She almost succeeds, but the Feregi ship's Doctor intrudes at the wrong moment. Taug, embarassed, allows the Doctor to perform neural scans on Lwaxana's telepathic brain, a procedure which could kill her.

An Away Team investigating the abduction of the two Enterprise officers finds the ugly flowers, which do not grow on Betazed but thrive on the Ferengi homeworld. Picard and crew head off in search of Taug's ship.

Riker cannot crack the security code, but comes up with an alternative plan. The Ferengi ship has a warp field phase adjuster, which controls the warp drive's tendency to interfere with subspace transmissions. Riker uses this to set up a repeating pattern in the Ferengi subspace channels.

As the torture of Lwaxana commences, Wesley delays his departure for Starfleet Academy in order to help locate Riker, and misses the ship that would have taken him there. He recognizes the pattern in the static from the Ferengi transmissions— Riker has reproduced the Algolian ceremonial rhythms, which the nonmusical Ferengi will only perceive as part of the general static.

Riker manages to stop the testing of Lwaxana but is disarmed.

The Enterprise locates them, and Lwaxana offers to stay behind if Riker and Deanna are returned to the Enterprise. Taug agrees. Lwaxana then sets up a scenario in which Picard is one of her former lovers. Picard is slow to catch on, but when he does he acts out the role, swearing that he would rather destroy the Ferengi ship than have Lwaxana belong to another. Taug is unprepared for this and hastily beams Lwaxana back to Picard, who, as usual, would be more than happy to do without her gratitude.

EPISODE SEVENTY-THREE: "TRANSFIGURATIONS"

Written by Rene Echevarria

Directed by Tom Benko

Guest Cast: Mark Lamura, Charles Dennis, Julie Warner

The Enterprise investigates the wreckage of an escape pod and discovers a severely injured humanoid. When Geordi helps regulate the alien's nervous system via tricorder linkage, a strange light enters his head, but seem to do him no harm. On the Enterprise, the alien, called John Doe, regains consciousness but has no memory. He heals from his injuries at an amazing rate, but seems to be undergoing additional mutations that are unrelated to his healing process.

Meanwhile, Geordi has gained new confidence in dealing with women. Data investigates an unknown variety of information storage device found in the wreckage; it seems to use chemical configurations, but resists decoding. Doe is subject to periodic energy bursts, which cause him great pain and make his body glow. When O'Brien comes into sickbay with a dislocated shoulder, Doe instinctively heals him with a touch of his hand. Doctor Crusher is very impressed with Doe, and is attracted to him, but his mystery continues until Geordi and Data discover that the information matrix uses memory RNA to store its data. This reveals a navigational chart which enables them to extrapolate Doe's point of origin. Doe is alarmed at this, for despite his amnesia he knows he must not return to his home. A ship from that area is speeding at high warp to intercept the Enterprise; Doe senses that he is endangering his rescuers, and attempts to steal a shuttle. When Worf tries to stop him, he accidentally falls from a great height and breaks his neck, only to be brought back to life by Doe's healing touch.

The other ship arrives, manned by Zalkonians. They claim Doe as a dangerous disruptive influence, but Picard refuses to hand him over to face a death sentence; for some reason, the Zalkonians fear him greatly. At last the truth is revealed: the Zalkonians are evolving to another level of existense, but destroy anyone who, like Doe, comes close to the breakthrough point.

Doe has bought sufficient time to reach the point of departure, and becomes a luminous being, no longer bound by his body. He returns to Zalkon to reveal the truth to his people, and the Enterprise resumes its travels, having witnessed the birth of a new species.

EPISODE SEVENTY-FOUR: "THE BEST OF BOTH WORLDS

(Part One)"

Written by Michael Piller

Directed by Cliff Bole

Guest Cast: Elizabeth Dennehy, George Murdock

The Enterprise responds to a distress signal from the outermost reaches of Federation space, only to find the colony and its nine hundred inhabitants missing, a vast crater where the settlement once stood. Admiral Hansen and a Commander Shelby join the Enterprise; they fear that the Borg are responsible. The Federation is not ready for the Borg.

Shelby, an ambitious woman, is gunning for Riker's first officer chair. Riker has been offered his own command for the third time, but wants to remain on the Enterprise. Friction develops between him and Shelby.

The Borg enter Federation space and destroy a ship. When the Enterprise intercepts them, they hail Picard by name, and try to pull the Enterprise in with a tractor beam. They manage to break free with difficulty, for the Borg adapt quickly to any change in phaser frequency or shield harmonics. Picard steers the ship into a nebula cloud, but the Borg bombard it and drive him back out. Another attack ensues, during which several Borg appear on the bridge and kidnap Picard. Once they have him, they ignore the Enterprise and head towards the heart of the Federation— Earth.

Riker becomes acting commander of the Enterprise. He plans to attack the Borg ship with a concentrated phaser burst through the deflector shield.

An away team led by Shelby beams onto the Borg ship, where they disrupt systems and cause the ship to drop out of warp. They also discover that Picard has become a Borg before they beam back to the Enterprise.

Picard, now a Borg called Locutus, has been chosen to speak for the Borg. He demands that the Enterprise surrender. Riker, faced with what his former captain has become, gives Worf the order to fire on the Borg ship.

SEASON FOUR

INTRODUCTION

The cliffhanger continues and concludes, with a high level of excitement all around. Picard seems to be restored a bit too easily at the end, but the next episode, "Family," focuses on his recuperation at his family estate on Earth. This episode is very good, and is interesting without any threat to the ship or crew, proving that a mere character study can carry an entire episode. (Even so, a fourteen-second shot of the Enterprise in drydock over Earth cost over ten thousand dollars to create. This episode was not a cheater by any means.)

The third episode, "Brothers," is a sequel to "Datalore" but transcends that "evil twin" potboiler and brings Data face to face with his own creator—and his evil twin, too. Brent Spiner plays all three roles, and probably deserves some sort of award for this episode. His more routine problems are examined in the episode "Data's Day," but even these include deducing that a transporter accident was staged by the Romulans to cover the fact that a Vulcan ambassador was really one of their spies.

Klingon affairs are also given due consideration, as Worf learns he has a son, loses his mate, and exacts a Klingon revenge on the killer, all in "Reunion. "In "The Drumhead," his family's dishonor is used against him in a Federation court, and in that same episode it is learned that some Klingons are working with the Romulans, which certainly leads to interesting developments in the episode "The Mind's Eye."

In "The Final Mission," countless prayers are answered, as Wesley finally bids farewell to the Enterprise. On the other hand, the character had achieved better handling under other writers and better stability in the series as a whole, although he had admittedly become almost a background character by this time, the episode "The Bonding" in the third season being almost the sole exception.

"First Contact" is an intriguing look at another Federation mission gone awry, and does not shy away from questioning some of Starfleet's ethical positions regarding "helping" other cultures.

Reginald Barclay finally gets his act together in "The Nth Degree"—a little too together for the Enterprise, and Lwaxana Troi finally acts like a relatively normal humanoid being in "Half A Life," a dramatic episode which acts difficult questions without providing any easy answers, but merely equally difficult choices. It forever removes LwAxana from her role as a clown. The episode "Suddenly Human" is another which raises difficult questions without taking the easy, or obvious, way out.

On the other hand, there are a few weak stories such as "Identity Crisis," in which it is painfully obvious that Geordi will be saved at the end of the episode no matter how bad things get for him, and "QPid," in which Picard and crew boldly go into the public domain and must act out the Robin Hood story, courtesy of Q. The best thing that can be said for this one is that the cast obviously had a lot of fun swashing their buckles. Using public domain characters worked in "Elementary, Dear Data," but here it seems like plot padding—which is what it is.

Although the script quality wavered a bit in the fourth season, the majority of the episodes maintained the level of intelligence we've come to expect from this series.

EPISODE SEVENTY-FIVE: "THE BEST OF BOTH WORLDS

(Part Two)"

Written by Michael Piller

Directed by Cliff Bole

Guest Cast: Elizabeth Dennehy, George Murdock

The attack on the Borg ship fails, causing extensive systems damage to the Enterprise. The Borg, having absorbed Picard into their group mind, now possess all his knowledge and experience, and resume their course to Earth.

Admiral Hansen communicates with the Enterprise: the Federation has assembled an armada of forty of their own ships, in addition to the Klingons. They are even considering contacting the Romulans. Riker receives a field commission, and promises to join the Federation forces as soon as the Enterprise is functional again. Shelby becomes First Officer.

Hansen communicates again: the Federation has engaged the Borg, and the battle is not going well. His transmission is cut off abruptly. When the Enterprise reaches the battle site, they find a scene of complete devastation.

Riker plans to separate the saucer section of the Enterprise for a diversion. Picard knew of this plan, but Riker has altered it considerably, hoping to outwit the memories of his former mentor.

The Borg ship's magnetic field now blocks transporter beams, so Worf and Data take a shuttle into range and use its escape transport to beam onto the Borg ship and recapture Picard/Locutus. They return to the shuttle, clear the Borg field, and beam back to the Enterprise just before the shuttle is destroyed. The two ship sections reconnect.

Picard/Locutus is still linked by subspace signal with the Borg mind.

Data creates a neural link with Picard/Locutus, and eventually reaches the Borg command system. It is divided into various command sub-units, but he cannot access any of the vital areas. The Borg halt their advance on Earth and attack the Enterprise; Riker orders a last-ditch, warp-speed collision with the Borg ship. Picard's personality emerges, and repeats the word "sleep." Crusher takes this as an expression of fatigue, but Data realizes that Picard is telling him what to do: the Borg regenerative system is of low priority, easily accessed, and Data uses it to convince the Borg that it is time for a regenerative cycle, effectively putting them all to sleep. The Borg attack stops. A power feedback caused by this induced malfunction causes the Borg ship to self-destruct, freeing Picard from their sub-space link. The Borg machinery is removed from his body. The Enterprise docks for repair, and Shelby leaves to head the task force rebuilding the fleet.

EPISODE SEVENTY-SIX: "FAMILY"

Written by Ronald D. Moore

Directed by Les Landau

Guest Cast: Jeremy Kemp, Samantha Eggar, Theodore Bikel, Georgia Brown, Dennis Creaghan

The Enterprise, still docked for repairs, remains in orbit over Earth. Picard returns to his home in France for the first time in twenty years, where unresolved conflicts with his brother still remain. His older brother Robert, a farmer keeping the family traditions alive, has always regarded Jean-Luc as arrogant and ambitious. While Picard gets along well with Robert's young wife and their son, Robert himself remains distant and critical. Picard's old friend Louis visits him; Louis is involved in a project to raise a section of the sea floor, and thinks that Picard would be the ideal man to direct the project. The project directors are more than eager to have Picard lead them. Picard is tempted, but uncertain. On one hand, he is dedicated to Starfleet; on the other, his experience with the Borg has left him uncertain of his ability to go on in any leadership position.

Worf's adopted human parents, of Russian descent, visit him on the Enterprise. He is at first embarrassed by them, for they are very emotional and forward. He refuses to discuss his discommendation with them, so they ask other crew members about him. Finally, they tell him that they are very proud of him, and know that his honor has not truly been broken; he overcomes his discomfort, and realizes how important they are to him.

Wesley Crusher finally meets his father, when he receives a holographic message recorded by Jack Crusher when Wesley was a baby. This helps him resolve many of his feelings about his father's death.

Tensions mount between the Picard brothers until Jean-Luc punches Robert. They fight until they are covered in mud, at which point they break out laughing. Jean-Luc's laughter soon gives way to tears, for he has been unable until now to face the self-doubt raised by the Borg's use of him. Now that his emotions have broken through, he can begin to deal with them, and he decides to return to command the Enterprise.

EPISODE SEVENTY-SEVEN: "BROTHERS"

Written by Rick Berman

Directed by Rob Bowman

While escorting the brother of a sick boy away from sickbay, Data suddenly begins to act strange, as if he is being controlled by an outside force. He changes the course of the Enterprise, assumes maximum warp speed, and shuts down the life support systems on the bridge; all the other members of the bridge crew must evacuate, and they don't realize Data's responsibility until there is nothing they can do about it. The bridge is sealed off with force fields. Simulating Picard's voice, Data localizes all command functions on the main bridge. The crew is unable to undo any of this,, but they do succeed in shutting off site-to-site transporter function. This does not stop Data from transporting to his destination: he programs the computer to create a shifting series of force-fields, which allow him to reach a transporter room and beam down.

Once there, he is restored to normalcy by an old man who reveals himself to be Dr. Soong, the creator of Data. Soong, presumed dead, had escaped the crystalline entity and taken refuge on a distant planet, where he has brought Data by means of a homing signal. Meanwhile, Picard and his crew have regained the bridge, only to find that Data (with Picard's voice) has entered a lengthy numerical security code. The Enterprise cannot move, and the sick boy needs Starfleet medical facilities very badly. Sensors pick up a single life form on the planet below, as well as a space vehicle, with no life signs, approaching.

The space vehicle turns out to contain Lore, who drifted in space for two years before being re-assembled by traders. The homing beacon also brought him to Soong. Many of the things Lore told Data about their past prove to be lies: Data was built without emotions because that was the one program that went awry with Lore. Data was brought to the planet because the dying Dr. Soong has finally developed a component that will give him basic feelings. He puts off the installation to rest; later, he implants the emotional chip into Lore, who has overpowered his brother in a fit of jealousy and dressed in his uniform. This causes the already unstable Lore to become completely unbalanced; he assaults Soong, then leaves. Riker arrives with an away team in time to revive Data, who watches his creator, and his last chance to gain emotions, die. The Enterprise resumes its course in time to save the dying boy.

EPISODE SEVENTY-EIGHT: "SUDDENLY HUMAN"

Teleplay by John Whelpley and Jeri Taylor

Story by Ralph Phillips

Directed by Gabrielle Beaumont

Guest Cast: Sherman Howard, Chad Allen, Barbara Townsend

The Enterprise responds to distress signals from a disabled Tellerian training ship. Its crew of five contains five teenaged crew members, one of whom is human. A genetic trace reveals him to be Jeremiah Rosa, whose parents were killed in a Tellerian border war. His grandmother is a Starfleet admiral. However, Jonathan calls himself Jono, for he has been fully assimilated into his new culture. Scornful of women, he refuses to remove his gloves to avoid contamination by aliens: the crew of the Enterprise.

Captain Picard finds himself cast in the unwanted role of surrogate father, since he, as the ranking male figure on board, is the only human Jono will respond to. He tries to reintroduce Jono to his former culture. This is complicated by the arrival of Jono's adoptive Tellerian father, Captain Endar.

Traces of healed injuries suggest that Jono was abused by the brutal Tellerian society, and Picard refuses to turn him over, which leads to the danger of renewed conflict with the alien race. Jono is troubled as memories of his real parent's death begin to haunt him. He attempts to kill Picard with a Klingon dagger, expecting to be killed for the transgression; death seems the only resolution for his growing dilemma. The knife glances off of Picard's sternum and he survives. Realizing that Jono is, in essence, no longer a human but a real Tellerian, he returns him to his father, Endar. The old injuries were merely the results of childhood foolhardiness. Impressed by Picard, the boy removes his gloves, and honors the Captain with a Tellerian farewell.

EPISODE SEVENTY-NINE: "REMEMBER ME"

Written by Lee Sheldon

Directed by Cliff Bole

Guest Cast: Eric Menyuk, Bill Erwin

At Starbase 133, Doctor Crusher greets a Doctor Quaice, her old teacher and mentor, who is taking passage aboard the Enterprise. Quaice is retiring after the death of his wife, and their conversation turns to the subject of loss.

Crusher then drops into engineering to see Wesley, who is conducting an experiment with a static warp field. The warp field collapses, and a momentary flash of light appears. Doctor Crusher then goes to Quaice's quarters to check on him, only to find no trace of him or his belongings. He is not on the Enterprise, and there is no record of him having ever come aboard. Further investigation reveals no record of him anywhere in the Federation. Could the static warp field have had something to do with this?

Slowly, more and more members of the medical team vanish without a trace, until Crusher is the only medical staff on board. This seems perfectly normal to the bridge crew, for one doctor should be sufficient for a crew of 230. Crusher protests that the crew should exceed one thousand; by this time, people are starting to wonder about her. The crew keeps shrinking, but only she registers this as change. A strange vortex threatens her in sick bay, but she resists it.

Worf, Wesley, and ultimately the entire crew vanish, leaving her and Picard alone on the bridge. She is about to tell him something important, but he vanishes too. The vortex returns, but she fights it, and it vanishes.

The scene shifts to Wesley and Geordi, who are trying to rescue Crusher from the warp field. The Traveller (from Episode Five, "Where No One Has Gone Before") appears to help them establish a stable gateway into the field; Crusher has created the reality within it with her own mind, and must realize her situation and choose to go through the portal. The vortexes she fought were actually Wesley's attempts to rescue her. The Traveller and Wesley try to create another portal; both of them begin to phase out in the process.

Inside the bubble, Crusher discovers that her universe consists of a sphere 705 meters in diameter. It begins to collapse, taking sections of the ship with it. She realizes her situation and tries to get to the original site of the mishap, racing for engineering as her reality vanishes around her. At last she makes it to the vortex and jumps clear just as the field collapses, and she is reunited with Wesley on the real Enterprise, where everything is perfectly normal.

EPISODE EIGHTY: "LEGACY"

Written by Joe Menosky

Directed by Robert Scheerer

Guest Cast: Beth Toussaint, Don Mirault

The Enterprise answers a distress signal from a Federation freighter orbiting the planet where the late Tasha Yar was born. A world with a violent history, it promises death to any outsiders who land on its surface. The freighter explodes; its two crew members make it to an escape pod, which crashes on the planet. An away team beams down after them but cannot locate them. Instead, they encounter a group called the Coalition, which tells them that the crewmen are being held by their enemies, the Alliance. These two groups have divided the capital city since the government fell, the inhabitants having moved deeper and deeper underground during the lengthy civil conflict. A stalemate of sorts exists between the two groups, for all their members have implants which trigger the opposing side's proximity detectors. Conflict is limited to supply raids and minor skirmishes.

The Alliance holds the crewmen as hostages and demand Federation assistance; the Coalition learns of Tasha Yar, and produces her sister Ishara, along with an offer to help the Enterprise rescue the crewmen from their enemies. Ishara feels that Tasha abandoned the struggle on their homeworld, but learns of her valor from the Enterprise crew, especially Data, who establishes a tentative friendship with Ishara. Ishara even seems interested in following in her sister's footsteps, but her first, secret obligation is to the Coalition.

A foray deep into Alliance territory is necessary to rescue the hostages. Doctor Crusher removes Ishara's implant so she can guide the away team. The rescue is a success, but Ishara breaks away on a mission of her own: to destroy the Alliance's defense system, thus enabling her side to attack without detection. Data discovers her and discerns her plan; he must stop her, or the resulting deaths will be on the Federation's hands. After a brief standoff, he stuns her and stops the destruction. Her phaser was set to kill.

Data struggles to understand the human concept of trust, which entails risk but is necessary for understanding, while Picard realizes that they were all misled by their desire for Ishara to be just like their much-missed comrade, Tasha Yar.

EPISODE EIGHTY-ONE: "REUNION"

Teleplay by Thomas Perry and Jo Perry &

Ronald D. Moore and Brandon Braga

Story by Drew Deighan and Thomas Perry and Jo Perry

Directed by Jonathan Frakes

A Klingon cruiser hails the Enterprise. Worf's old flame K'Ehleyr

beams over with a message for Picard: the leader of the Klingon High Council is dying, and wants Picard to discover which of the contenders for his position has been poisoning. K'Ehleyr also has a surprise for Worf: their last encounter produced a son, Alexander. K'Ehleyr is now willing to make the marriage vows she earlier declined, but Worf resists because of his discommendation.

The two Klingon contenders arrive, and discover that Picard has been chosen by the late Klingon leader as the arbitrator, who determines the challenger's right to battle for the ascension. At the preliminary ritual, a bomb goes off, killing two Klingon aides. Picard delays further ceremonies by insisting on an archaic ritual which demands a long recitation of the challengers' accomplishments, a ritual which could take hours or days.

The Enterprise crew determines that the bomb was a sort used only by the Romulans, and that it was implanted in the forearm of the aide of one of the challengers: Worf's old enemy, the Klingon responsible for Worf's family dishonor. It seems that he, like his father, is a traitor, doing business with the Romulans.

As this goes on, K'Ehleyr tries to discover the reasons for Worf's discommendation, which neither Worf nor Captain Picard will reveal to her. She manages to put together the truth, but she is discovered and killed by the traitor. Worf discovers her body and beams over to the Klingon's ship, claiming right of revenge. His claim is questioned until he reveals that K'Ehleyr was his mate; he fights his enemy to the death, triumphing over him seconds before a security teams arrives to escort him back to the Enterprise. (Apparently, right of vengeance outweighs dishonor in Klingon ethics.)

The Klingon High Council approves Worf's action, since the Klingon he killed was revealed as a traitor. Picard takes him to task, but all he will receive in punishment is a reprimand on his record. Although his enemy is dead, Worf must keep the truth behind his dishonor a secret until the time is right for him and his brother to set matters right.

EPISODE EIGHTY-TWO: "FUTURE IMPERFECT"

Written by J. Larry Carroll and David Bennett Carren

Directed by Les Landau

Guest Cast: Andreas Katsulas, Chris Demetral, Carolyn McCormick

Riker's birthday party—where he tries, unsuccessfully, to play "Misty" on the trombone—is interrupted when the Enterprise investigates subspace fluctuations on a nearby planet. Riker leads an Away Team, only to pass out when poison gasses overcome him. He regains consciousness in sick bay, where Doctor Crusher addresses him as "Captain." It seems that he

was infected by a virus when he beamed down, a virus that lay dormant for sixteen years and then wiped out all of his memories dating to the the time of the original infection. A bearded Admiral Picard boards the Enterprise; Riker is the key man in peace negotiations with the Romulans, and must proceed in that capacity despite his memory loss. The Romulan ambassador beams aboard the Enterprise. Other changes surprise him: Ferengi have joined the crew, Geordi has cloned eye implants instead of his visor, and Riker has a son named Jean-Luc! Riker is uneasy in these circumstances. The computer seems to be operating slowly, Riker still can't play "Misty" and something always distracts him when he tries to find out who his wife was. At last, he manages to access visual records, and finds that his wife was Minuet, who only existed as a hologram program. He confronts Picard and the Romulan ambassador on the bridge. In the face of his realization, the Romulan reveals that it was all a holodeck-type simulation using neural scanners to read Riker's mind. The Romulans are surprised to learn the truth about Minuet, for Riker's emotions regarding her seemed so real.

The Romulans then throw Riker into a cell with a captured Earth boy, Ethan, who they'd used as Riker's "son." Ethan helps Riker get away, but strange discrepancies begin to creep into this reality. Ethan refers to the Romulan commander as an ambassador; when Riker questions this slip, the Romulans recapture him, but he ignores them, having realized that the boy is the one responsible for the illusions he's experienced. The Romulans and their base disappear, revealing a barren cavern. The boy is actually an alien whose mother concealed him when their race was about to be destroyed by enemies. Neural scanners in the cavern walls have provided him with everything he needed, but he tricked Riker so that he could have some real company to ease his loneliness. When this truth is revealed, Riker takes the alien child back to the Enterprise with him.

EPISODE EIGHTY-THREE: "FINAL MISSION"

Teleplay by Kacey Arnold-Ince and Jeri Taylor

Story by Kacey Arnold-Ince

Directed by Corey Allen

Wesley is finally accepted to Starfleet Academy. Picard takes him along when he goes to negotiate a dispute on a mining colony. The Enterprise receives a distress call from the planet Gamelan V, which seems to be under some sort of radiation attack. Riker takes command of the ship to investigate this, while Picard and Wesley board a mining shuttle and head toward their destination. The ramshackle vessel loses a thruster and goes out of control, crashlanding on a moon of the mining planet. Picard and Wesley are stranded with the shuttle pilot on a barren desert world with no food or water. Tricorder readings indicate magnetic field fluctuations in a nearby mountain range, so they head toward it, leaving an arrow ti indicate their direction.

The Enterprise discovers that Gamelan V's gravitational field has captured a 300-year-old space barge filled with radioactive wastes which threaten the population of the planet. Geordi uses remote construction modules to attach thrusters to the barge in order to steer it into the system's sun, but the barge begins to break up, and the Enterprise must tow it with a tractor beam, through an asteroid belt, while radiation levels on the ship approach lethal levels.

After a long trudge through the desert, the castaways reach the mountains, and discover a cave with a fountain of water inside.

Unfortunately, a force field prevents them from reaching it. When the shuttle pilot fires on the force field with his phaser, he triggers a cave-in which seriously injures Picard. Further attempts to break through the field unleash an electromagnetic "sentry" which kills the pilot. Wesley eventually jury-rigs his phaser, tricorder and communicator to cancel out the two protective devices, thus reaching the water. An away team shows up soon after, Riker having resolved the problem at Gamelan V.

EPISODE EIGHTY-FOUR: "THE LOSS"

Teleplay by Hilary J. Bader and Alan J. Adler and Vanessa Greene

Story by Hilary J. Bader

Directed by Chip Chalmers

Guest Cast: Kim Braden, Mary Kohnert

Deanna's therapy with a woman who has lost her husband reveals that the patient is lying to herself about her recovery. Shortly after the session, the Enterprise seems to suffer some sort of sensor malfunction; at the same time, Deanna is struck with a powerful headache. The ship cannot change course, and is being pulled slowly along by an unknown force. Deanna realizes that she has lost her empathic powers, which for a Betazoid is much like going blind. As she goes through the stress induced by this, Data attempts to analyze the ship's problem. He discovers that they are caught in a field of two-dimensional particles, which may be sentient, although there seems no way to determine this. An attempted overload jump to warp speed fails to free the Enterprise. They, and the particle cluster, are headed inexorably toward the gravitational field of a cosmic string fragment.

After another session with her patient, Deanna resigns as ship's counsellor. Riker and others try to talk her into staying, but she feels injured and inadequate. She re-evaluates these feelings when her patient turns out to have made an important breakthrough in her last session: Deanna's intelligence and experience worked even without her empathic ability.

She reasons that if the cluster is sentient, it might actually be going toward the string fragment by choice, unaware that it is pulling the Enterprise along with it. Photon torpedos have already failed. Data uses the deflector dish to create a vibrational echo of the string fragment behind the Enterprise. This succeeds in confusing the cluster long enough for the Enterprise to break free. Deanna's powers return, having been dampened by the cluster, and she senses that the cluster is heading into the gravitational field because that is where it belongs.

EPISODE EIGHTY-FIVE: "DATA'S DAY"

Teleplay by Harold Apter and Ronald D. Moore

Story by Harold Apter

Directed by Robert Wiemer

Guest Cast: Rosalind Chao, Sierra Pecheur, Alan Scharfe

In order to help Commander Maddox better understand him, Data sends him a communication describing a "typical" day in the life of the android. On the day in question, Data is to act as father of the bride in the wedding of Keiko to Chief O'Brien. When Keiko calls the wedding off, Data misgauges the effect that the news will have on O'Brien. He also has a long way to go in learning the use of friendly jibes and insults, although he does not offend Geordi when he calls him 'a lunkhead.' When Geordi assures him that Keiko will change her mind again, Data resumes his preparations for the wedding, and arranges for Doctor Crusher to give him dancing lessons, since her records indicate that she won a dance competition many years earlier. It is also revealed that Data keeps a pet cat in his quarters.

Vulcan Ambassador T'Pel beams aboard to meet Picard; she is on a mission of utmost secrecy, one which will take them into the Neutral Zone.

The Ambassador queries Data about the Enterprise's security. Although she has the correct clearance codes, he tells her he must inform Picard; she withdraws the question, claiming that is was merely a test of his own security precautions.

T'Pel's mission brings the Enterprise face-to-face with a Romulan warbird. She beams over to begin secret negotiations, but a transporter accident kills her, leaving only minute organic traces on the transporter pad. The Enterprise leaves, but investigations reveal that the traces do not correspond with the records from when T'Pel beamed aboard. The Romulans somehow managed to alter their own transporters to fake T'Pel's death.

Picard pursues them and demands the Ambassador's return, only to the discover that she was not a Vulcan after all, but a well-placed Romulan spy.

The Enterprise heads back to Federation space.

The wedding goes on as planned, in a traditional Japanese ceremony officiated by Captain Picard. Data has learned a little more about humans, although he has also gained more questions to be answered about them as well.

EPISODE EIGHTY-SIX: "THE WOUNDED"

Teleplay by Jeri Taylor

Story by Stuart Charno, Sara Charno and Cy Chernak

Directed by Chip Chalmers

Guest Cast: Bob Gunton, Rosalind Chao, Mark Alaimo, Marco Rodriguez, Time Winters, John Hancock

While surveying a sector near the space of Federation enemies-turned-allies, the Kardassians, the Enterprise is fired on by a Kardassian ship. After a brief exchange of fire, Picard discovers that the peace has been broken by the Federation ship Phoenix, commanded by Ben Maxwell. Maxwell has been out of communication for some time, and is apparently acting on his own initiative: the Phoenix has destroyed a Kardassian science station without provocation. The Federation orders Picard to investigate, and to take a Kardassian team aboard as observers.

This brings up memories for chief O'Brien, who served with Maxwell in the conflict with the Kardassians. Maxwell lost his family in a border skirmish, which may account for his actions, while O'Brien recalls a battle in which he killed a Kardassian to save his own life. He has trouble dealing with Kardassians on board, not because he hates them, but because they remind him of his only act of aggression against another living being.

The Enterprise's sensors locate the Phoenix in time to watch it destroy a Kardassian warship and freighter. Pursuing at high speed, they catch up, and discover that Maxwell believes the Kardassians to be re-arming. He agrees to return to Federation space, and Picard allows him to keep command of the Phoenix. Maxwell soon breaks away and heads toward another Kardassian freighter. If Picard will not board the freighter and see that Maxwell is right, then Maxwell will fire upon it. Picard in turn threatens to use force against the Phoenix. O'Brien uses his expertise to beam over through a cyclic break in the Phoenix's shields, and talks to the unhinged Maxwell, reviewing their past together and helping Maxwell back down from his dangerous position. Maxwell surrenders. When the Kardassian captain thanks Picard, Picard reveals that he believes Maxwell's claims, but acted as he did to preserve the peace. In parting, he warns the Kardassian that the Federation will be keeping an eye on them.

EPISODE EIGHTY-SEVEN: "DEVIL'S DUE"

Teleplay by Philip Lazebenik

Story by Philip Lazebenik and William Douglas Lansford

Directed by Tom Benko

Guest Cast: Marta Dubois, Paul Lambert, Marcelo Tubert

The Enterprise arrives to evacuate a science station crew from the planet Ventax, which is undergoing drastic social upheavals. The people of this world believe that an impending apocalypse is about to occur; earthquakes and other signs, as predicted in the Legend of Ardra, a thousand-year-old document which seems to be a contract promising a thousand years of peace in exchange for the ownership of the planet and its peoples. Oddly enough, this world has enjoyed an idyllic millennium, which was preceded by a period of great strife. Ardra, their equivalent of the Devil, is a legendary figure credited with bringing this change about— but now the contract is up.

Picard doesn't believe this, and discounts the earthquakes as coincidence. He beams down to negotiate the release of the science team, who are being held hostage, but the government is is hysterics. When a beautiful woman appears in a burst of energy and claims to be Ardra, Picard is not impressed, but she does demonstrate remarkable powers. She can alter her shape at will, becoming various creatures, including a Klingon demon and Earth's Devil.

The Away Team beams up, leaving Data behind to study the ancient contract, as well as Geordi. Picard wonders if Ardra could be another renegade Q from the Continuum, only to find Ardra on the bridge. She cannot be removed, even by transporter beam; she keeps returning. Data informs the Captain that the contract is in complete accordance with the Ventaxian law, and cedes to Ardra everything on land, sea, air— or in orbit. Ardra claims the Enterprise is hers under the contract, and vanishes.

Picard is certain that Ardra is some sort of cosmic con artist, and vows to outsmart her. Data tries to find a loophole in the contract. When Ardra appears in Picard's chambers and tries to seduce him, he resists her, and she relocates him to the world below— in his pajamas. He heads back to the Enterprise by shuttle, only to have it vanish before him. He returns to Ventax, where Geordi has detected a jump in the level of Z-particles, which indicates a hidden power source.

Picard arranges for arbitration, and Ardra, confident, agrees, with Data as the arbitrator. If Picard cannot disprove Ardra's claim, she wins him.

The case seems to go against Picard, as Ardra demonstrates her various powers. Picard cannot explain them, until Geordi informs him that he's found the coordinates of Ardra's power source.

Picard argues that the social changes on Ventax took place gradually, which is proven by the historical record. After the contract was signed, the legendary Ardra left, and did not oversee any of the reforms that took generations to heal Ventax's ecology and social problems. Even this pressing argument seems to fail, until Picard learns that Geordi has located a ship, cloaked with a copy of a Romulan device; the Enterprise was merely concealed by a shield extension, and is right where it should be.

Picard counters Ardra's claim by "stealing" her powers. He induces minor quakes, changes shape, and makes Ardra vanish. She cannot undo anything he does. Picard reveals that "Ardra" is, as he suspected, a con artist. An Away Team has taken over her ship, thus giving Picard her powers, which used transporters, tractor beams and other existing technologies to trick the Ventaxians. This resolved, the Ventaxians thank Picard, and the Enterprise takes the crooked impostor into custody.

EPISODE EIGHTY-EIGHT: "CLUES"

Teleplay by Bruce D. Arthurs and Joe Menosky

Story by Bruce D. Arthurs

Directed by Les Landau

Guest Cast: Pamela Winslow, Rhonda Aldrich

Picard takes Guinan along on a "Dixon Hill" holodeck excursion, but she fails to see the entertainment value of Hill's violent 20th Century world. Data intrudes shortly after a holodeck thug is gunned down in Hill's office, but he does it by patching through to the antique phone in Hill's office. The Enterprise has detected a Class-M planet, and is about to investigate a wormhole-like energy fluctuation nearby. Picard goes to the bridge, just as the ship enters the wormhole, and everyone on board but Data falls to the floor unconscious.

The crew regains consciousness. The wormhole seems to have brought them to a point one day's distance from their previous location in a matter of seconds. Still, peculiar things have happened. Moss cultures begun by Dr. Crusher have undergone 24 hours worth of growth. Could the wormhole have had some strange effect on them? Picard sends a probe back to the planet, but it is no longer a Class-M world. It is now completely inhospitable.

Picard wonders if 24 hours have actually elapsed. If so, then Data is lying— but why? Did they really go through the wormhole? Bio-scans, compared with transporter traces, reveal that the crew's cellular functions do not correspond with a lapse of a thirty seconds, but make perfect sense if 24 hours have passed. On the other hand, no one has any beard growth. The computer chronometer seems to have been tampered with. Only Geordi and Data could have changed it, and only Data was functional during the lost time. Examinations reveal nothing wrong with the android officer, but Picard is suspicious of him. Perhaps Data even rigged the probe to send back a false image.

Deanna feels dizzy for a moment, and is disoriented by her own mirror reflection. She seemed to sense an alien presence in it. Worf turns out to have broken his arm and to have had it reset, all in the past 24 hours, but he has no memory of it. Geordi discovers that the probe was programmed to send back a library image of another world. When confronted, Data says he can neither confirm or deny anything. He cannot say what happened, but does not deny that he did anything.

A new probe confirms the original sighting of a Class-M planet, and no evidence of a wormhole. Data will not reveal anything, so Picard heads back to the planet, armed and ready.

Upon arrival, a green energy field enters the Enterprise and possesses Deanna. In an alien voice, she tells Data that the plan failed. Data tells Picard that they must leave immediately, but the captain refuses. He demands that Data reveal who ordered him to cover up the events of the missing day.

Data reveals that the order was given by Picard himself.

The truth comes out: the planet is occupied by a reclusive, xenophobic race that wishes to keep its existence secret. The "wormhole" was a trap which induces a biochemical stasis and diverts any ships from discovering the secretive beings. Data, not being biological, instituted emergency automatic defense procedures and revived the crew. The alien presence occupied Deanna, and broke Worf's arm when he tried to intervene. Dr. Crusher reset the injury. When the alien explained its wishes, Picard suggested that it suppress their memories, and ordered Data to reset the chronometer, and to never reveal the truth to anyone.

Since this has failed, the alien has no choice but to destroy the ship and crew. Picard explains that their curiosity was aroused by the various clues left behind, and suggests that the aliens remove all traces and reminders of their passing. The aliens agree, and the entire process is repeated; the Enterprise crew wakes up on the other side of a small wormhole, and no one but Data will ever know that anything unusual ever occurred.

EPISODE EIGHTY-NINE: "FIRST CONTACT"

Teleplay by Russell Bailey, David Bischoff, Joe Menosky,

Ronald D. Moore and Michael Piller

Story by Marc Scott Zicree

Directed by Cliff Bole

Guest Cast: George Coe, Carolyn Seymour, George Hearn, Michael Ensign, Steven Anderson, Sachi Parker with Bebe Neuwirth as Lanel

The Federation is secretly studying Malkorian society, which is on the verge of achieving interstellar flight. Riker, altered to resemble a Malkorian, is injured and taken to a hospital, where it soon becomes apparent that he is not what he appears to be: his organs are in the wrong places, and certain features are surgical implants. He claims that they are hereditary defects, and that his phaser is a toy for a neighbor's child, but the doctor treating him is not convinced. To make matters worse, Riker's communicator is lost.

Picard takes a chance and beams down with Deanna to reveal himself to the Malkorian Science Minister, Mirasta, a forward-looking woman who is largely responsible for her world's great leaps towards warp technology. She is open minded, and visits the Enterprise, but points out that her culture is very conservative and ethnocentric, believing themselves to be the center of the universe. The planetary Chancellor is fair-minded if cautious, but the Security Minister, Krolar, is a fanatic about his traditional way of life.

The doctor treating Riker is dedicated to helping him recover, but his efforts at keeping the strange facts of Riker's case quiet fail, and word of the alien soon spreads through the hospital.

Mirasta and Picard beam down to the Chancellor's office. The Chancellor is skeptical of the Federation's aims, but Picard wins his respect. On Mirasta's advice, however, he does not mention the covert survey teams.

The Chancellor tours the Enterprise, where he and Picard share a toast with the wine given Picard by his brother on his last visit to Earth. Still, the Chancellor is uncertain what to do.

Riker is visited by a nurse, Lanel, who is fascinated by the idea of aliens. Since this seems to be the key to getting her help, Riker, somewhat humorously, admits that he's an alien. Lanel offers to help him escape if he will make love to her— making love with an alien has long been her fantasy!

Later, when Riker tries to slip out of the hospital, he is detected, and mobbed by a frightened crowd. He suffers kidney damage and internal bleeding, and is taken into intensive care, where the doctor struggles to help him.

The Chancellor discusses the situation with his ministers. Krolar is not only the most resistant to the idea, he also has word of a spy, presently in the hospital. The Chancellor is disturbed to learn of the covert operation.

Krolar takes matters into his own hands, and goes to the hospital to interrogate Riker, whom he believes represents an invading force. Krolar orders the doctor to awaken Riker, but the doctor refuses, because the stimulants could prove fatal. Krolar uses his influence to have the doctor removed as head of the hospital, and his ambitious replacement is all too anxious to follow Krolars orders.

Once Riker regains consciousness, Krolar arranges to be alone with him. He has discovered how to operate the phaser, and places it in Riker's hand, intending to kill himself while making it look like murder. His death will put an end to any notion of contact with aliens. Riker struggles to keep the phaser from firing, but Krolar succeds in triggering it, and is blasted across the room.

The phaser discharge gives the Enterprise a fix on Riker, and Crusher and a medical team beam down to the hospital in time to save both Riker and Krolar, who did not realize that the phaser was set on stun.

Krolar survives, and awakens in the Enterprise's sick bay. His plan is easily deduced, and the Chancellor chides him for such a foolhardy undertaking. Still, it has become apparent that his world is not yet ready to make contact with other worlds, and he asks Picard to leave. The entire affair will be hushed up, and funds will be diverted from technology to education in order to help eradicate ancient prejudices. Mirasta, who has long dreamed of space travel, asks to be taken with the Enterprise, and Picard and the Chancellor agree, since she would now be subject to to many restrictions on her home world. All that will remain of this first contact will be rumors, which, the Chancellor imagines, will fade in time.

EPISODE NINETY: "GALAXY'S CHILD"

Teleplay by Maurice Hurley

Story by Thomas Kartozian

Directed by Winrich Kolbe

Guest Cast: Susan Gibney, Lanei Chapman, Jana Marie Hupp

When the Enterprise stops at Starbase 313 to pick up science equipment for the Guernica system, Geordi is delighted to learn that they are taking on an important passenger: Dr. Leah Brahms, who Geordi "met" as a holographic projection in "Booby Trap" (Episode 52). His expectations are dashed by the real article, however, for Brahms seems angry about Geodi's altered specifications. They don't get along too well, and Geordi finds himself on the defensive as Brahms examines his work. She is alarmed to find some design changes already planned for the next class of starship, not realizing that Geordi had devised them by collaborating with "her." Geordi tries to start over by inviting her to dinner. She relaxes somewhat, but is put off by Geordi's attentiveness. He is surpised to learn that she is married.

Meanwhile, the Enterprise has been investigating odd readings in the uncharted Alpha Omicron system, where they find a creature that actually lives in the vacuum of space. When the Enterprise probes it, it responds with a probe of its own, and then attacks the Enterprise. A low-level phaser blast, intended in self-defense, kills the creature. Soon, however, new energy readings are detected in the body: apparently, it was about to give birth, and the baby is still alive. With Crusher's guidance, the Enterprise uses a phaser beam to help the creature get out of its parent's body. When the Enterprise leaves, the baby follows, having imprinted on the ship. It thinks that the Enterprise is its mother. Even worse, it feeds on energy, and attaches itself to the hull and begins to drain power. Since it is over a shuttlebay door, it might be possible to shake it off by depressurising the shuttlebay. Data extrapolates the parent creature's course, which leads them to an asteroid belt inhabited by more of the creatures, but the attempt to dislodge "Junior" fails.

Leah Brahms, intrigued by Geordi's work, examines his records— including the holodeck program. Geordi rushes to the holodeck to find a furious Dr. Brahms face to face with her own holographic image.

She feels as if her privacy has been violated, and, despite Geordi's protestations, wonders just how far he went with her simulation.

Eventually, however, matters cool down, and Leah and Geordi come up with a means of "weaning" the space infant. They manage to alter the vibrations of the ships power, in essence "souring the milk," until the creature detaches and joins the adults of its species, which were on the verge of attacking the Enterprise.

Geordie and Leah Brahms become friends after all, and Geordi learns not to project his expectations on people, but to try and see them for who they really are.

EPISODE NINETY-ONE: "NIGHT TERRORS"

Teleplay by Pamela Douglas and Jeri Taylor

Story by Shari Goodhartz

Directed by Les Landau

Guest Cast: Rosalind Chao, John Vickery, Duke Moosekian, Craig Hurley, Brian Tochi, Lanei Chapman

The Enterprise locates the missing Federation science ship Brittain adrift in an uncharted binary star system, and finds all of the crew dead except for one Betazoid, who is practically catatonic. Deanna tries to contact the Betazoid, but his thoughts are jumbled and make no sense. Records indicate that the crew became unhinged and descended into extreme paranoia, eventually killing each other off with extreme violence. There seems to be no chemical or biological cause for this, and there seems to be no solution to the mystery.

Deanna begins to have strange dreams in which she is adrift in a dark cloudy vortex. The lights shine in the distance, and the phrase "eyes in the dark" is repeated. The rest of the crew begins to have odd experiences. Chief O'Brien becomes convinced that Keiko is cheating on him, for no good reason. Picard hears his door signal chime repeatedly, only to find no one at the door. Crusher and Deanna visit him, but must knock on his door before he realizes that they're there. Crusher fears that the Enterprise is starting to experience the same problems that beset the Brittain. Picard orders the ship to clear the area, only to find that they cannot. They are adrift.

Eventually, they learn that they are trapped in a space rift which drain the ships energy. This type of rift has been encountered once before, and was escaped from by use of a large explosion: the earlier ship was carrying a cargo of an extremely volatile cargo. Unfortunately, the Enterprise is not, and cannot use its replicators at all. The earlier space rift was not accompanied by the peculiar mental phenomena affecting the crew, however.

No one on board has had any dreams for the past ten days, except for Deanna, who is afflicted by the same nightmares over and over. Data, who does not sleep, is the only one unaffected. Hallucinations begin to crop up: Picard is assaulted by a renegade turbolift, Riker finds snakes in his bed, and Crusher is menaced by the corpses of the Brittain's crew in the autopsy room. The lack of REM sleep is causing a chemical imbalance which threatens to drive everyone insane. Worf, unable to cope with an invisible enemy he cannot attack, attempts Klingon ritual suicide, but is stopped by Deanna.

At Picard's request, Data takes command of the ship. Deanna realizes that the dream she's having is a telepathic message, perhaps from a ship on the other side of the space rift. The transmission is what is blocking everyone else's ability to dream; her Betazoid brain works on a different frequency. "Eyes in the dark" seems to indicate the nearby binary star. Data realizes that the binary star resembles a model of the hydrogen atom. Hydrogen can trigger a violent explosion with a rare element, but does the other ship have hydrogen, or do they need it? And, can Deanna signal them back at the right time? The crew is going crazy, and a brawl in Ten Forward is averted only when Guinan pulls a vicious looking weapon from behind the bar and fires a warning shot.

Deanna enters electrically induced REM sleep a,d signals "now" to the other craft, as the Enterprise releases hydrogen gas into the rift. A huge explosion sets free the Enterprise and the unknown ship, enabling both to go on their separate ways.

EPISODE NINETY-TWO: "IDENTITY CRISIS"

Teleplay by Brannon Braga

Based on an unpublished story by Timothy De Haas

Directed by Winrich Kolbe

Guest Cast: Maryann Plunkett, Patti Yasutake, Amick Byram, Dennis Madalone, Mona Grudt

Before serving on the Enterprise, Geordi LaForge was assigned to the USS Victory, and served on an Away Team which inveastigated the still-unsolved disappearance of a Federation outpost's staff. Now, five years later, the members of that Away Team are mysteriously abandoning their posts and stealing shuttlecraft. Geordi is joined by his friend Susannah, the only other Away Team member not to have vanished. They begin to study the records of their investigation.

The Enterprise locates and tracks one of the stolen shuttles, which is heading to the outpost world where the mystery began. The shuttle hits the atmosphere at too great a speed and explodes. Two more shuttles are located at the outpost site, but they are empty. Tattered Starfleet uniforms and strange alien footprints are the only clues to be found. Worf senses that they are being watched, but their instruments cannot sense any life forms on the planet. Geordi stops Susannah from wandering off; she is acting strangely, and insists that their former companions are alive, and nearby.

Back in sick bay, tests reveal that her blood chemistry has gone completely haywire, and she seems obsessed with returning to the planet.

Tests reveal alien skin cells on the torn up uniforms, but the footprints match no known species. Geordi and Susannah review the Victory tapes, but the light from the viewscreen hurts her eyes, and she collapses. Her hands seem to be fusing, and her skin develops blue veins: the changes match the alien cells. She is taken to sick bay, and it seems that she is actually changing into another species. The cause eludes Dr. Crusher.

Geordi has the computer recreate the Away Team visual records on the holodeck, and isolates a shadow that doesn't belong to anyone from the Victory team. Extrapolating its source, he discovers that some sort of humanoid was nearby all along.

Susannah's changes continue. Her skin can simulate light, and her body seems to generate s disruptive field interferes with instrument readings. Crusher finally locates a parasite in Susannah's thymus gland, a parasite which uses the immune system to spread genetic instructions. The parasite is removed surgically, but it is up to Susannah's own system to heal itself.

Meanwhile, Geordi has changed, and goes transports down to the planet. Data rigs an emergency beacon to the Ultra-violet range, which might be able to "see" the aliens. An Away Team beams down to Geordi's transporter coordinates, taking the recovering Susannah along at her own insistence.

The UV light reveals the humanoid forms as glowing blue outlines. The others are too far gone for help, but Geordi is still partially human, but afraid to come back. Susanna coaxes him into trusting her, and he is saved in time.

The parasite seems to have been an alien means of reproduction, which lay dormant for years; Geordi returns to normal after the operation removes it.

EPISODE NINETY-THREE: "THE Nth DEGREE"

Written by Joe Menosky

Directed by Robert Legato

Guest Cast: Dwight Schultz, Jim Norton, Kay E. Kuter, Saxon Trainor, Page Leong, David Coburn

Reginald Barclay has made great strides in confidence. Although still shy and unsure of himself, he is taking part in Dr. Crusher's acting classes, and takes the part of Cyrano de Bergerac in an amateur production. Data is perplexed when the others applaud the awkward performance, and Riker explains the concept of politeness to the android officer.

The Enterprise is investigating the breakdown of an unmanned space telescope array. Its fusion reactors— eighteen in all— are unstable, and the controlling computer is down. An alien probe is hovering over the array.

Geordi takes Barclay along in a shuttlecraft to investigate the probe. It resists all scans until they try a positron beam, which triggers a blast of light from the device. The shuttle computers are disabled, and Barclay is knocked out, while Geordi's visor protects him from the blast. Geordi returns to the ship, and the probe begins to follow.

Barclay seems to be all right, but begins to suggest new medical techniques to Crusher. The probe has assumed a collision course with the Enterprise, and is emitting an unknown but threatening field. It also matches the ship's speed, resists phasers, and stays too close to the ship to make a photon attack feasible. Back in engineering, Barclay suddenly takes charge. The ship drops to impulse power when he uses the warp field generator to boost shield power 300 per cent, which makes it safe to hit the probe with photon torpedos despite its close range. The threat is destroyed.

Barclay is full of surprises, and his confidence begins to approach arrogant proportions. When Geordi plans to repair the telescope reactors one by one, with a projected repair time of two to three weeks, Barclay steps forward claiming that he can program a new control system for the reactors and repair them all simultaneously. Data points out that this would take twice as long as Geordi's plan, but Barclay claims that he can do it in two days. Deanna is perturbed, for she senses that something has changed Barclay.

The once-shy engineer's acting improves remarkably, and he even makes a pass at Deanna in Ten Forward, inviting her for a walk in the arboretum. She declines for professional reasons, since she was once his counsellor. The next day, Barclay is late for a meeting. This seems more like the old Barclay, especially when the computer locates him on a holodeck, but when Geordi goes to fetch him he finds that he's been up all night working on advanced theoretical problems with a holo-sim of Albert Einstein! Einstein even seems grateful to Barclay for explaining things to him.

A medivcal scan reveals that Barclay's brain has increased its production of neurotransmitters by 500 per cent, and that the two hemispheres of his brain seem to be acting as one unit. With an IQ between 1200 and 1450, he may be the smartest human who ever lived.

This bothers the Captain, but Barclay has done nothing wrong, so all Picard can do is keep an eye on him.

One of the telescope reactors begins to go critical, threatening a chain reaction with the othe reactors. Barclay takes charge again, but finds that the Enterprise computer is too slow for him, so he goes to the holodeck and creates a neural scan interface. When Picard tries to get his ship out of the blast range, he finds that the bridge computer will not respond. When the computer comes back on line, the reactors have all shut down. Picard asks the computer to explain what happened, and is astounded when it answers with Barclay's voice.

Barclay has become the center of the computer. Most of his higher brain functions and memories has expanded into the computer core. Any attempt to return these functions to his physical brain would be fatal.

Barclay begins to see the universe as a single, simple equation, and sees how its speed can go far beyond warp. His intentions are completely in line with the Enterprise's mission, but Picard doesn't like the idea much. Worf and a security team cannot reach Barclay, however, and Barclay begins to create a subspace distortion which pulls the ship into it. The distortion is intense, but eventually ends, and the Enterprise winds up in the center of the galaxy, some thirty-thousand light years from where it started.

Suddenly, the computer returns to normal, and the huge image of an old man's head appears on the bridge, looking over the crew with a quizzical expression. Barclay returns to the bridge and explains. The Cytherians have the same basic mission as the Enterprise, except that they stay at home and bring other entities to them for an exchange of information. Their probes were meant to instruct other beings how to reach them, and Barclay wound up as their instrument, and was returned to normal once he'd brought the ship to them.

The Enterprise remains in Cytherian space for data exchange, and is eventually returned to familiar space. Barclay muses on the experience, and Deanna takes him up on his offer of a walk through the trees.

EPISODE NINETY-FOUR: "QPID"

Teleplay by Ira Steven Behr

Story by Randee Russell and Ira Steven Behr

Directed by Cliff Bole

Guest Cast: Jennifer Hetrick, Clive Revill, John deLancie

The Enterprise plays host to a Federation archaeology symposium in orbit above Tagus 3. He is nervous about his keynote speech, which is about the ruins below, which have been sealed off from further exploration by the Tagians, but Deanna assures him that the speech will go well. When he returns to his quarters, he finds Vash, with whom he shared an adventure on Rhysa ("Captain's Holiday," episode 65). They pick up their romance where it left off.

The next morning, Dr. Crusher drops in for morning tea with Picard, only to find Vash there. Although Picard has told Vash all about his crew, he didn't tell his crew about her. Crusher takes her on a tour of the ship. She recognizes Riker from Picard's impression of him, when the First Officer tries his charm on her, but once again learns that Picard has not talked about her to his friends. By the time of the official reception, she is very upset, and accuses Picard of being embarassed by her. (Worf notes that she has nice legs— "for a human.")

Picard goes to his office, and finds Q at his desk. Q is keen on helping Picard in some way, since he owes him a favor from their last encounter and wants to free himself of the obligation as soon as he can. Picard tells him to forget it, but the mischievous Q won't take no for an answer, and vanishes.

Picard tries to explain to Vash why he keeps his personal life personal, but is distracted when he discovers that Vash is planning to violate the ban on excavations on Tagus 3. Q watches their argument, and intrudes into Picard's quarters later with an offer to help Picard with the troublesome woman. Again, Picard declines, and Q leaves in an even greater state of annoyance.

When Picard begins his speech, Q disrupts it by changing the costumes of the executive staff, culminating in Picard's refurbishment in a Robin Hood outfit complete with mustache and goatee. They all vanish, to reappear in an Earthlike forest. Clearly, they are meant to be Robin and his band, even though Worf is adamant that he is "not a merry man!" Riker is Little John, Data is Friar Tuck complete with tonsure, and Geordi is minstrel Alan A-Dale.

They are attacked by Sir Guy of Gisbourne, and Worf is injured with an arrow before they flee into the woods. Q appears on horseback, having taken the role of the Sheriff of Nottingham, and explains that he has set in motion a scenario that will last until the next afternoon, at which point the Enterprise crew will be returned to their proper places. Q is merely an observer until then. Picard is content to sit and wait until the time is up, until Q points out that Maid Marian is being held by Sir Guy, who will kill her if she doesn't marry him. Picard is not impressed until he realizes that Maid Marian is actually Vash, and orders his crew to stay behind while he rescues her.

Q, meanwhile, is astounded to learn that Vash has agreed to marry Sir Guy. When Picard tries to save her, she grabs his sword and turns him over to Sir Guy. Q is more and more impressed by Vash's shiftiness, but catches her trying to send Riker a message, and reveals her trickery to Sir Guy.

The next day, their execution is interrupted when the Enterprise bridge crew, disguised as monks, come to rescue the Captain. An old-fashioned swashbuckling melee ensues, and Picard vanquishes Sir Guy.

Q is disappointed that everyone survived, but keeps his word and restores things to normal.

Vash, however, has a surprise for Picard. Q is so impressed with her that he offers to take her anywhere she wants to go in the universe, and she accepts. The two of them take off on an interstellar treasure hunt, leaving Picard perplexed by the wiles of the opportunistic archaeologist.

EPISODE NINETY-FIVE: "THE DRUMHEAD"

Written by Jeri Taylor

Directed by Jonathan Frakes

Guest Cast: Jean Simmons as Admiral Satie, Bruce French, Spence Garrett, Henry Woronicz, Earl Billings, Anne Shea

A Klingon exchange officer, J'Dan, has been caught accessing security codes, and is believed to be a spy when the Romulans obtain secret information concerning the dilithium chambers. One of the chambers explodes, raising the possibility of sabotage, but J'Dan denies all charges. Deanna senses that he is lying. J'Dan offers to help clear Worf's family name in exchange for a shuttle craft, but Whrof turns down the offer with a few Klingon body blows.

Starfleet calls retired Admiral Satie in to investigate the situation.

The daughter of an important Federation lawmaker, she brings along two aides, including a full Betazoid, Sabin. The damaged area can't be examined until radiation levels drop, so they can only interrogate J'Dan again. The Klingon allegedly needed injections for a certain disease, but Worf discovers that his hypo has been converted so that it can read isolinear chips. Convering the information into amino acid sequences, the device can be used to inject the information into someone's blood. Faced with this, J'Dan admits his spying, but denies having sabotaged the dilithium chambers. Sabin believes this to be true. But how did the information leave the ship? Satie suspects a conspiracy.

She soon focuses her attention on a medical crewman, Simon Tarses, who helped J'Dan with his injections. Born on the Mars colony, Tarses is mostly human but says that his paternal grandfather was a Vulcan, a claim which would explain his elongated ears. Sabin senses that Tarses is lying about something, and suspicion begins to build.

When the radiation levels drop, Geordi discovers that there was no sabotage. The explosion was just the result of subatomic material fatigue.

This does not slow Satie's investigations, which begin to develop a life of their own. A hearing convenes, with Riker as defense, and Tarses is hammered with questions. Satie demands the names of anyone J'Dan talked to in Ten Forward. Sabin falsely suggests that the explosion was caused by a corrosive chemical. Tarse is completely off guard when he is accused of lying about his grandfather, who was really a Romulan. On Riker's advice, Tarses refuses to answer under the Seventh Guarantee, the Federation equivalent of the Fifth Amendment.

Picard warns Worf, whi is an enthusiastic supporter of Satie, that things may be getting out of hand. He tells him about the drumhead trials of the 19th Century, when military officers in the field would sit on an inverted drumhead and dispense summary justice, with no right of appeal.

The Captain then talks to Tarses, who admits that he lied about his ancestry for fear of prejudice. Now his career seems to be completely ruined.

Picard confronts Satie, who defends the lie about the explosion as a useful tactic. She reveals herself as a self-important chauvinsit for the Federation, and accuses Picard of blocking her investigation. She has already gone over Picard's head, and called more hearings. Admiral Henry of Starfleet Security will be taking part as well. Picard vows to fight her all the way.

Later, Picard receives a command from Satie to report for questioning at the next hearing.

At the hearing, Picard requests to make an opening statement. Satie refuses him this request, but he is ready for her, and invokes the specific regulation that guarantees this. He questions the entire proceeding, and asks that it end before it hurts anyone else.

Satie attacks him, noting that he has violated the Prime Directive nine times while commanding the Enterprise. She suggests that his involvement in the affair of the Romulan spy T'Pel ("Data's Day," episode 83) was less than innocent. When Worf rises to his captain's defense, his father's alleged treacher— a rumor that has reached the Federation— is raised against him.

Satie returns to her attack on Picard and brings up his capture and use by the Borg, and all but accuses him of being reponsible for the loss of 39 ships in that conflict.

Picard keeps himself in control and quotes from writings about freedom, which regard as evil the very practices Satie is using. Satie tries to shut him up, but not before he reveals that these words were written by her father. Satie rises to her feet and demands that Picard not sully her father's name. She loses control completely, and threatens to destroy Picard, accusing him of being in on her imagined conspiracy. Admiral Henry rises without a word and walks out of the room. Sabin calls a recess. Everyone leaves the room, including Sabin, leaving Admiral Satie standing alone.

The hearings are terminated, and Satie leaves the ship, having revealed her obsessed and unstable nature. In the end, the only reputation she ruined was her own.

EPISODE NINETY-SIX: "HALF A LIFE"

Teleplay by Peter Allen Fields

Story by Ted Roberts and Peter Allen Fields

Directed by Les Landau

Guest Cast: David Ogden Stiers as Timicin, Majel Barrett, Michelle Froes, Terrence M. McNally, Carel Struycken

Captain Picard is treading lightly: Lwaxana Troi is on board. She tags along when he goes to greet Dr. Timicin, a scientist from Kaylon-2, and attaches herself to the unwary guest.

This is the first Federation involvement with Kaylon-2, an insular world with a dying sun. Timicin's life work is in solar helium fusion enhancement, which will use modified photon torpedos to revitalize his sun. The Enterprise is taking him to test his technique on a star identical to his own.

Lwaxan keeps barging in on Timicin and the engineering crew, but Timicin, a widower, actually finds her attractive.

The test almost works, and holds at the proper temperature for a while, but then exceeds the limit. The Enterprise flees the resulting nova, and Timicin is despondent that his life's work is over.

Lwaxana tries to comfort him. After all, he can always try again. Timicin reveals that, on his planet, 60 is the age of The Resolution, a ceremony celebrating the life of a person— and culminating in his or her ritual suicide. Lwaxana is outraged at what seems to her to be a waste. Timicin has his doubts, for he feels he could find what went wrong with the test if only he had enough time. Otherwise, his work will be continued by others, and his planet's sun only has a few more generations to go before it fails. His involvement with Lwaxana deepens, and he decides to continue his work, and asks Picard for asylum. Picard grants it.

When Timicin turns against his home's traditions, the planetary government refuses to communicate with him or receive any of his findings.

Two ships from the surface prepare to attack the Enterprise, and Timicin's daughter beams over to plead with him. Finally, he realizes that he cannot go against the beliefs he has always upheld, and decides to undergo Resolution after all. Lwaxana is hurt by this, and refuses to speak to him, but finally decides to take part in the ceremony as a finally gesture of her love for Timicin. Lwaxana has finally got her man, only to have to learn to let go of him.

EPISODE NINETY-SEVEN: "THE HOST"

Written by Michel Horvat

Directed by Marvin V. Rush

Guest Cast: Franc Luz as Odan, Barabara Tarbuck, Nicole Orth-Pallavicini, William Newman, Patti Tasutake

Beverly Crusher is caught up in a whirlwind romance with thr alien emissary Odan, who is on his way to negotiate a dispute between two moon

colonies. Odan's father had helped bring peace between the two moons a generation before, and now the Governor of the parent world has called Odan in to avert a war, which would cause the planetary population to choose sides and disrupt their society as well.

Odan declines to transport to the conference site, so Riker pilots the shuttle that will take him there. An unidentified ship from the Beta moon attacks the shuttle, wounding Odan. Riker is about to tranbsport back, but Odan says that this would kill him, so Riker brings the shuttle back manually.

Crusher is distraught, but does her best to save Odan. There seems to be some sort of parasitic growth in his abdomen. Odan reveals a truth that shocks her: Odan *is* the parasite, and the humanoid body is merely a host, a sybiotic life style that has been the norm on his planet for all time. The body can die, but the parasite must not.

When the body dies, Crusher can keep Odan alive in stasis for a few hours, but will need a temporary host for it until a replacement arrives in forty hours. Odan's "father" had actually been Odan in a different host body.

Riker agrees to the risky operation, which succeeds with only one complication— Riker's personality is submerged beneath that of Odan, who proclaims his continued love for Beverly. This places her in an unusual position. Everything she loved about Odan still exists, but in Riker's body, and Riker has been like a brother to her. She cannot bring herself to face Odan again.

Representatives from the Alpha and Beta moons beam over, but are sceptical about the claim that Riker is Odan. One of them is an old man who negotiated with Odan's "father," and is convinced when Odan describes an assassination plot that was hushed up years earlier.

Riker's body threatens to reject Odan, who persists in pursuing Beverly. Finally, she gives in to her confused passion.

The negotiations proceed without much progress, but Odan insists that he be removed from Riker in 24 hours, no matter what happens, as he cannot risk Riker's life for his own. The host body is delayed.

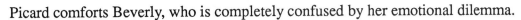

Picard comforts Beverly, who is completely confused by her emotional dilemma.

After six hours of talks, Odan emerges successful, but Riker's body collapses. The Enterprise rushes at Warp 9 to intercept the host body, while Odan is removed from Riker and put in stasis.

To further Crusher's perplexity, the host body turns out to be female. The operation is a success, and Odan resumes its pursuit of Beverly, but the doctor explains that it is just too difficult for her to have a relationship with all these changes. They both love each other, but it just won't work, and Odan leaves after kissing Beverly on the wrist.

EPISODE NINETY-EIGHT: "THE MIND'S EYE"

Teleplay by Rene Echevarria

Story by Ken Schafer and Rene Echevarria

Directed by David Livingstone

Guest Cast: Larry Dobkin, John Fleck, Edward Wiley, (Majel Barrett receives screen credit as the Voice of the Computer for the first time in the history of the series.)

Geordi LaForge is on his way via shuttlecraft to a conference on Risa when a Romulan ship decloaks directly in his path. The shuttle shields fail, and Geordi is beamed away; the shuttle is held by a tractor beam.

The Enterprise, meanwhile, is taking a Klingon ambassador to K'reos, a Klingon colony where a fight for independence is underway. The Ambassador and Picard are headed there to investigate the Governor's claim that the Federation is supplying the rebels.

On the Romulan ship, Geordi is strapped into a chair and deprived of his visor. An impostor is sent to Risa in his place. A Romulan officer subjects him to direct stimulation of the visual cortex, which causes him to see whatever the Romulans program. As this is demonstrated, a female Romulan commander observes from the shadows. (Although her face is never seen, she speaks once, and sounds remarkably like Denise Crosby!) The officer explains to the commander that Geordi's pre-existing implants will make it all but impossible to trace the alterations they plan to implement. Later, they test Geordi in a simulated 10 Forward, and order him to kill Chief O'Brien; he does so, but hesitates, and they take him away for more brainwashing sessions.

Geordi returns to the Enterprise as it arrives at K'Reos. He seems happy and relaxed, and recounts details of his vacation. Deanna detects nothing wrong; in fact, she is pleased that he seems so happy.

Data detects a blip on the E-band wavelength but cannot determine the cause.

Picard and the Ambassador beam down to see the Governor of K'reos.

He reveals that Federation medical supplies have been found in rebel camps, but Picard counters by saying that the Federation does not restrict access to such supplies. The Governor counters by producing what appears to be a Federation phaser rifle. He insults Picard with a choice Klingon epithet, and is surprised when Picard leans forward and curses him in fluent Klingon. The Governor is so impressed he compliments Picard, saying that he must have some Klingon blood.

Later, Geordi and Data test the phaser rifle. Physically it matches Federation specs, but it is actually much more efficient in its power output than the real thing; it is a Romulan replication, perfect in every way except that it was charged with a Romulan power source. Clearly, the Romulans are trying to crack the Klingon/Federation alliance, but the Governor is still not impressed.

Data detects more E-band emissions.

Geordi overrides the computer and routes a cargo bay transporter's power to the auxiliary replicator system, beams weapons down to the planet, and erases all memory of the event.

The Governor intercepts this "delivery" and accuses Picard of complicity; the Enterprise is hemmed in by Klingon ships. The Ambassador convinces the Governor not to act until he contacts the Klingon High Command.

Yet another E-band transmission: Data considers that it might be some sort of Romulan transmission.

Geordi goes to the quarters of the Ambassador, who is revealed as the spy. He intends to have the Governor beam up to see how the investigation on board the Enterprise is being carried out. When the Governor is on board, Geordi is to kill him among witnesses, and to claim that he was acting on behalf of the Federation.

Another E-band blip prompts Data to compare it with all known phenomena, and learns that it is similar to a human brainwave pattern. He also determines that the E-band could be used to affect human brainwaves if processed through a system set up to process the electro-magnetic spectrum.

This, of course, is exactly what Geordi's visor does. Data goes to check out Geordi's shuttle, not knowing that Geordi has already taken a phaser and headed for the cargo bay where the Klingons are observing procedures.

Data finds traces of tractor beam stress on the shuttlecraft. Close examination of the memory chips in the shuttle reveal that they have been replicated— using Romulan technology. When Geordi will not respond to Data's communication, Data contacts Worf and orders him to arrest LaForge.

The other Klingons are between Worf and Geordi, however, and will not let the dishonored Klingon pass. Worf's shout alerts Picard, who deflects Geordi's aim upwards just as he fires. Worf then removes LaForge from the area.

Data arrives and explains his deductions. Geordi had been abducted, brainwashed and controlled with E-band transmissions— which originated on the Enterprise. The only two people with Geordi at the time of the transmissions were Picard and the Ambassador.

Picard suggests a search of them both, but the Ambassador refuses, as a diplomat and a Klingon, to be searched by the Federation. The Governor seems to agree: he will take the Ambassador back to K'Reos and let him be searched by his fellow Klingons. The Ambassador suddenly asks Picard for asylum.

The Captain tells him that he will gladly grant it— after the search has been conducted. The Klingons all beam back down.

Geordi and Deanna begin the slow and painful process of restoring Geordi's true memories, which have been concealed beneath false ones of his pleasant vacation.

EPISODE NINETY-NINE: "IN THEORY"

Written by Joe Menosky and Ronald D. Moore

Directed by Patrick Stewart

Guest Cast: Michele Scarabelli, Rosalind Chao , Pamela Winslow

As the Enterprise nears the Mar Obscura Nebula, an area marked by a large amount of dark matter, Data works on adapting photon torpedos for use as a means of intense illumination. He is helped by another officer, Jenna, who has recently ended an unsatisfactory relationship. Data has promised to remind her of her reasons for the breakup, and does so when she begins to doubt the change. He has accessed the history of human romance in order to be supportive of his friend.

The altered photon torpedos light up the nebula for a few moments, providing the Enterprise with a visual glimpse. Sensors detect a Class-M planet close within the nebula; Picard opts to investigate, since there may be new life-forms in the area.

In Medical, Dr. Crusher picks up an instrument which seems to have fallen off a shelf by itself, but gives it no second thought.

Jenna, meanwhile, tells Data about her childhood. His various logical comments make her laugh, and she wonders aloud why she's never met a man as supportive as he is. She becomes embarrassed and turns to go, but returns to kiss Data on the cheek. She tell him that he is very handsome and gives him a more passionate kiss, then leaves.

Data begins to seek advice about his new relationship. Guinan just tells him that the next move belongs to him, and that he'll have to figure things out himself.

When Data returns to his quarters, Geordi joins him and returns his cat Spot, whom Geordi had found outside. Data wonders how the doors opened for the cat to escape, since the doors are keyed only to humanoids. The computer tells him that there have been no intruders. Geordi advises Data to ask someone else for romantic advice.

Deanna Troi advises caution, and Data reveals that he has studied history carefully and has many appropriate role models.

Worf points out that Klingons conquer what they desire, and goes on to suggest that Data had better not hurt Jenna, who is under Worf's command.

Riker is bemused by the affair, and advises Data to pursue it despite the risks, since the experience will be wonderful— if it works out.

Data takes flowers to Jenna and tries to woo her. He is successful, even though he tells her that he has developed a "romance" program to help him out.

Picard discovers everything knocked off the desk in his ready room, but there is no apparent explanation.

Jenna visits Data to give him a gift, but must point out the appropriate responses to her android suitor.

The Class-M planet seems not to be at the proper co-ordinates, but soon reappears. The computer reports depressurization in the main observation lounge; when they investigate, everything is all right, but the room is a shambles.

Data tries to act natural with Jenna but his routine is a matter of derived behaviors: when he arrives, he calls out "Honey, I'm home!"

He is very solicitous and romantic, but he is drawing on a database rather than real feelings, and Jenna is bothered by his behavior. Thinking that a lover's quarrel might improve matters, Data acts angry, but this only adds to the confusion. When he explains that he is drawing on extensive cultural and literary sources, Jenna tells him to stop, and just to kiss her. When she asks him of his thoughts during the kiss he tells her: he was working on a warp drive problem, reviewing the works of Dickens, calculating the safest pressure for the kiss, and other matters. Jenna is distressed by this, but at least she was in his thoughts somewhere.

More problems develop as the Enterprise moves through the nebula cloud. Various systems malfunction, and decompression occurs between two decks. When Geordi and an engineering team go to investigate for structural damage, one of them dies, caught between two levels in a grisly accident.

Data concludes that the preponderance of dark matter in this region of space is causing gaps in normal space. When the ship encounters one of these, parts of the ship phase out, hence the decompression and the strange death of the crewperson. These "holes" are moving through space, but can, with adaptations, be detected. A shuttle some distance ahead of the ship could detect them early and, with navigational linkage, guide the Enterprise through the nebula to safety. Picard insists on piloting the shuttle.

Picard guides the ship most of the way through, but the gaps in space become more numerous, and the shuttle is damaged and goes out of control. Picard is beamed out just as the shuttle explodes; the Enterprise makes a break the rest of the way, and passes through the nebula intact.

As the ship heads for the nearest Starbase, Jenna tells Data that she's realized that it won't work between them. Even though Data is attentive and concerned, he cannot provide everything a relationship needs, since he lacks real emotions. He agrees with this assessment, and she goes, leaving him alone with his cat Spot.

EPISODE ONE HUNDRED: "REDEMPTION"

Written by Ronald D. Moore

Directed by Cliff Bole

Guest Cast: Robert O'Reilly, Tony Todd, Barbara March, Gwynyth Walsh, Ben Slack, Nicholas Kepros, J.D. Cullum, Denise Crosby

The Enterprise is en route to the Klingon home world, where Gowron is about to become the leader of the High Council. Picard asks Worf if it isn't about time he did something about his discommendation, but Worf still feels that he must wait. Gowron's ship appears, and the Klingon confers with Picard: he needs help to avert a Klingon civil war. The family of Duras, who Worf killed, is still very powerful. Two sisters survive Duras, and although they cannot take part in the Council, it is likely that they have something ip their sleeves, and have at least three fleet commanders on their side. Picard says that he will act out his final obligations as the arbiter of succession, but cannot promise aid in any civil conflict.

Worf escorts Gowron to the transporter room, where he tells him the truth about his dishonor and asks for his help in restoring it. Gowron refuses, since he would alienate the Council by revealing Duras' treachery, but he is impressed by Worf.

Worf asks Picard for a leave of absence, which is granted. Worf meets with his brother Kurn, who feels that the Klingon leadership has betrayed the Empire and must be swept away. He is certain that Gowron will be killed by Duras' family, but promises to do it himself if not. Kurn has four squadron commanders sworn to help him. Worf, as the elder brother, changes these plans: they will support Gowron. . . but not until he is backed into a corner by his many enemies, and agrees to restore Worf's honor. Kurn agrees, and talks all but one of his allies into going along with this new plan.

At the Klingon High Council, Picard asks if there are any challengers to Gowron's claim. Lursa, Duras' sister, appears with her other sister and a Klingon boy who they say is Duras' son. Under Klingon law, Picard must consider this claim as well.

At Lursa's home, it is revealed that she is in collusion with the Romulans, including the shadowy commander first encountered in "The Mind's Eye." She is more patient than the Klingons, and it seems that her long-term plans may have something specifically to do with one particular human— Jean-Luc Picard.

Lursa invites Picard to her home. He beams down, and she and her sister offer him tea— Earl Grey, of course. They attempt to sway him to their way of thinking. He sees through them. If he backs their claim, Gowron will certainly be killed. If he doesn't back them, they'll claim Federation interference, and start a war against Gowron. They agree with his opinion, but point out another factor— if they must fight to topple Gowron, the Federation alliance will certainly fall when they come into power. Picard leaves.

The next day, Picard rejects the boy's claim, because he has no experience, and backs Gowron. As predicted, the boy accuses Picard of serving Federation interests. The rest of the Council backs the Duras family, leaving Gowron alone.

Later, Worf visits Gowron's ship and offers him aid, in return for his honor. Gowron scoffs, but when the ship is attacked by two other Klingon vessels, Worf takes the weapons station and destroys one of the attackers after tricking it to lower its shields. Gowron's ship is at the mercy of the other attacker until Kurn's ship appears and drives them off. The Enterprise, meanwhile, has withdrawn from the battle area, as Picard realizes that he cannot get involved any more deeply than he already is.

Back in the nearly-empty Council hall, Gowron is sworn in as Council leader, and his first act is the restore Worf's family honor. Worf grasps the naked blade of a Klingon dagger in the ceremony, but does not flinch.

Back on the Enterprise, Gowron again asks for Picard's help. Worf also asks, but Picard cannot risk drawing the Federation into a civil war. He then orders Worf to return to duty. Worf refuses and resigns his commission in Starfleet in order to join with Gowron.

As Worf is about to leave the Enterprise, Picard goes to his quarters to see him off. The entire crew lines the hallway to the transporter room, and they all stand at attention as he passes. Little is said (Klingons hate long goodbyes) but it is obviously a moving experience for Worf.

After Worf beams off, the Enterprise leaves orbit. Down on the planet, the Duras family and their Romulan friends receive the news with some happiness. Only the boy is angry, since he is impetuous and wants to kill Picard! The Romulan commander again counsels patience; she's certain that Picard will be back soon enough. It almost seems that she has something in for the good Captain. As the episode ends, she steps into the light, revealing her face. She is blond, rare for a Romulan, but the most striking thing about her is this: she is the spitting image of Tasha Yar. Denise Crosby is back— but who is she, really?

Boring, But Necessary Ordering Information!

Payment:

All orders must be prepaid by check or money order. Do not send cash. All payments must be made in US funds only.

Shipping:

We offer several methods of shipment for our product. Sometimes a book can be delayed if we are temporarily out of stock. You should note on your order whether you prefer us to ship the book as soon as available or send you a merchandise credit good for other goodies or send you your money back immediately.

Postage is as follows:

Normal Post Office: For books priced under $10.00—for the first book add $2.50. For each additional book under $10.00 add $1.00. (This is per indidividual book priced under $10.00. Not the order total.) For books priced over $10.00—for the first book add $3.25. For each additional book over $10.00 add $2.00.(This is per individual book priced over $10.00, not the order total.) These orders are filled as quickly as possible. Shipments normally take 2 or 3 weeks, but allow up to 12 weeks for delivery.

Special UPS 2 Day Blue Label Rush Service or Priority Mail(Our Choice). Special service is available for desperate Couch Potatoes. These books are shipped within 24 hours of when we receive the order and should normally take 2 to 3 days to get from us to you.

For the first RUSH SERVICE book under $10.00 add $5.00. For each additional 1 book under $10.00 add $1.75. (This is per individual book priced under $10.00, not the order total.) For the first RUSH SERVICE book over $10.00 add $7.00 For each additional book over $10.00 add $4.00 per book.(This is per individual book priced over $10.00, not the order total.)

Canadian shipping rates add 20% to the postage total.
Foreign shipping rates add 50% to the postage total.

All Canadian and foreign orders are shipped either book or printed matter.

Rush Service is not available.

DISCOUNTS!DISCOUNTS!

Because your orders keep us in business we offer a discount to people that buy a lot of our books as our way of saying thanks. On orders over $25.00 we give a 5% discount. On orders over $50.00 we give a 10% discount. On orders over $100.00 we give a 15% discount. On orders over over $150.00 we giver a 20 % discount.

Please list alternates when possible.

Please state if you wish a refund or for us to backorder an item if it is not in stock.

100% satisfaction guaranteed.

We value your support. You will receive a full refund as long as the copy of the book you are not happy with is received back by us in reasonable condition. No questions asked, except we would like to know how we failed you. Refunds and credits are given as soon as we receive back the item you do not want.

Please have mercy on Phyllis and carefully fill out this form in the neatest way you can. Remember, she has to read a lot of them every day and she wants to get it right and keep you happy! You may use a duplicate of this order blank as long as it is clear. Please don't forget to include payment! And remember, we love repeat friends.

COUPON PAGE

_____Secret File: The Unofficial Making Of A Wiseguy $14.95 ISBN # 1-55698-256-9

_____Number Six: The Prisoner Book $14.95   ISBN# 1-55698-158-9

_____Gerry Anderson: Supermarionation $14.95

_____Calling Tracy $14.95 ISBN# 1-55698-241-0

_____How To Draw Art For Comicbooks: Lessons From The Masters

ISBN# 1-55698-254-2

_____The 25th Anniversary Odd Couple Companion $12.95   ISBN# 1-55698-224-0

_____Growing up in The Sixties: The wonder Years $14.95   ISBN #1-55698-258-5

_____Batmania $14.95   ISBN# 1-55698-252-6

_____The Year Of The Bat $14.95

_____The King Comic Heroes $14.95

_____Its A Bird, Its A Plane $14.95   ISBN# 1-55698-201-1

_____The Green Hornet Book $14.95

_____The Green Hornet Book $16.95 Edition

_____The Unofficial Tale Of Beauty And The Beast $14.95   ISBN# 1-55698-261-5

_____Monsterland Fear Book $14.95

_____Nightmare On Elm Street: The Freddy Krueger Story $14.95

_____Robocop $16.95

_____The Aliens Story $14.95

_____The Dark Shadows Tribute Book $14.95   ISBN#1-55698-234-8

_____Stephen King & Clive Barker: An Illustrated Guide $14.95 ISBN#1-55698-253-4

_____Drug Wars: America fights Back $9.95 ISBN#1-55698-259-3

_____The Films Of Elvis: The Magic Lives On $14.95   ISBN#1-55698-223-2

_____Paul McCartney: 20 Years On His Own $9.95   ISBN#1-55698-263-1

_____Fists Of Fury: The Films Of Bruce Lee $14.95   ISBN# 1-55698-233-X

_____The Secret Of Michael F Fox $14.95   ISBN# 1-55698-232-1

_____The Films Of Eddie Murphy $14.95   ISBN# 1-55698-230-5

_____The Lost In Space Tribute Book $14.95   ISBN# 1-55698-226-7

_____The Lost In Space Technical Manual $14.95

_____Doctor Who: The Pertwee Years $19.95   ISBN#1-55698-212-7

_____Doctor Who: The Baker Years $19.95   ISBN# 1-55698-147-3

_____The Doctor Who Encyclopedia: The Baker Years $19.95   ISBN# 1-55698-160-0

_____The Doctor And The Enterprise $9.95   ISBN# 1-55698-218-6

_____The Phantom Serials $16.95

_____Batman Serials $16.95

MORE COUPON PAGE

_____Batman And Robin Serials $16.95

_____The Complete Batman And Robin Serials $19.95

_____The Green Hornet Serials $16.95

_____The Flash Gordon Serials Part 1 $16.95

_____The Flash Gordon Serials Part 2 $16.95

_____The Shadow Serials $16.95

_____Blackhawk Serials $16.95

_____Serial Adventures $14.95   ISBN#1-55698-236-4

_____Trek: The Lost Years $12.95   ISBN#1-55698-220-8

_____The Trek Encyclopedia $19.95   ISBN#1-55698-205-4

_____The Trek Crew Book $9.95   ISBN#1-55698-257-7

_____The Making Of The Next Generation $14.95   ISBN# 1-55698-219-4

_____The Complete Guide To The Next Generation $19.95

_____The Best Of Enterprise Incidents: The Magazine For Star Trek Fans $9.95
                                                    ISBN# 1-55698-231-3

_____The Gunsmoke Years $14.95   ISBN# 1-55698-221-6

_____The Wild Wild West Book $14.95   ISBN# 1-55698-162-7

_____Who Was That Masked Man $14.95   ISBN#1-55698-227-5

NAME:_____

STREET:_____

CITY:_____

STATE:_____

ZIP:_____

TOTAL:_____ SHIPPING_____

SEND TO: Couch Potato, Inc. 5715 N. Balsam Rd., Las Vegas, NV 89130

"The first and only book of it's kind! The story of a new generation of adventures aboard the starship Enterprise. Star Trek fans and film students won't want to miss this one."
—Enterprise Incidents

THE MAKING OF THE NEXT GENERATION
BY EDWARD GROSS

THE COMPLETE GUIDE TO THE NEXT GENERATION
By James Van Hise

As the title suggests, this volume is a comprehensive guide to the first season of STAR TREK: THE NEXT GENERATION, providing a synopsis, critical commentary and credits for every episode, from "Encounter at Farpoint" to "The Neutral Zone". In addition, the text profiles each of the show's characters and actors that portray them: Captain Jean Luc Picard/Patrick Stewart, Commander William Riker/Jonathan Frakes, Doctor Beverly Crusher/Gates McFadden, Counselor Deanna Troi/Marina Sirtis, Lt. Commander Data/Brent Spiner, Lt. Geordi LaForge/Levar Burton, Security Chief Natasha Yar/Denise Crosby, Lt. Worf/Michael Dorn, Acting-Ensign Wesley Crusher/Wil Wheaton and the starship Enterprise itself.

THE COMPLETE GUIDE TO THE NEXT GENERATION serves as the perfect book for your reference library. $19.95

The Making Of The Next Generation
Written by Edward Gross
Pioneer Books and the author of TREK: THE LOST YEARS, team up again to explore another untapped aspect of the STAR TREK universe, with THE MAKING OF THE NEXT GENERATION.

THE MAKING OF THE NEXT GENERATION provides a behind the scenes look at the first season of STAR TREK: THE NEXT GENERATION, featuring interviews with cast members Patrick Stewart, Jonathan Frakes, Brent Spiner, Levar Burton, Denise Crosby, Gates McFadden, Michael Dorn and Wil Wheaton, a set visit, interviews with such crewmembers as directors Paul Lynch and Joseph Scanlan and writers Dorothy Fontana, Richard Krzemien and Tracy Torme, as well as an examination of the metamorphosis that each script passed through on its journey from concept to aired episode.
$14.95.............132 pages
ISBN#1-55698-219-4

A SPECIAL ISSUE OF
FILES MAGAZINE.

Next Generation

THE COMPLETE GUIDE

A GUIDE TO EVERY EPISODE

PROFILES OF EVERY CHARACTER

BIOGRAPHIES OF THE STARS

$19.95/$27.95 CANADA

BY JAMES VAN HISE

The Trek Crew Book Written by James Van Hise
The crewmembers of the starship Enterprise as presented in the original STAR TREK television series and feature film spin-offs. These fascinating characters, beloved by millions of fans, are the primary reason for the phenomenal on-going success of this Gene Roddenberry created concept.
Never before has a book so completely revealed this ensemble of fine actors, focusing on their careers, examining their unique portrayals of their most famous on-screen alter egos, profiling the characters themselves and presenting in-depth interviews with William Shatner, Leonard Nimoy, DeForest Kelley, James Doohan, George Takei, Walter Koenig and Nichelle Nichols.
Before there was a NEXT GENERATION, there was the original crew and now their story is finally told.
$9.95............108 pages
Painted Cover
ISBN #1-55698-257-7

Couch Potato Inc.   5715 N. Balsam   Las Vegas, NV 89130   (702)658-2090

DOCTOR WHO: THE COMPLETE BAKER YEARS
Written by John Peel

The most popular actor ever to play Doctor Who is Tom Baker. Tom Baker has terrific charisma in the role. He brought the series to America, added millions of new viewers and enchanted audiences.

DOCTOR WHO: THE COMPLETE BAKER YEARS provides summaries and critiques of every Baker episode of the series, profiles Tom Baker as well as the Doctor and the rest of his team; interviews cast members Lalla Ward, Liz Sladen and Louise Jameson, as well as producer Philip Hinchcliffe and writer Bob Baker. Additionally, a special archives section re-presents articles on the Baker Years as they appeared in the British press of the time and a unique index provides easy access to information in the volume.

Fans of Tom Baker, this one's for you! $19.95 ISBN#1-55698-147-3

THE DOCTOR WHO ENCYCLOPEDIA: THE BAKER YEARS
Written by John Peel

This volume contains references for *all* the characters who appeared during the Baker Years, and then examines all of the monsters that have come up against the good doctor in a special section. Want to know who the Trakenites are? Or where the Synge hails from? The answers are all here. THE DOCTOR WHO ENCYCLOPEDIA: THE BAKER YEARS is the perfect companion piece to John Peel's THE TREK ENCYCLOPEDIA.

$19.95 ISBN#1-55698-160-0

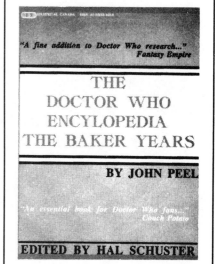

"A fine addition to Doctor Who research..."
Fantasy Empire

THE
DOCTOR WHO
ENCYLOPEDIA
THE BAKER YEARS

BY JOHN PEEL

"An essential book for Doctor Who fans..."
Couch Potato

EDITED BY HAL SCHUSTER

THE DOCTOR AND THE ENTERPRISE
Written by Jean Airey

THE DOCTOR AND THE ENTERPRISE is an outrageous satire that combines elements of the aforementioned Traveller of Time and Space with the also aforementioned crew of a certain starship known as Enter....well, you know. Thrown in for good measure is a Wizard of the aforementioned O.Z., a pair of ruby slippers (which just don't shine like they used to), vicious Tin-Woodsmen and more warp outs, beam downs and crack ups than can be described here. Get ready for thrills, excitement and, most of all, plenty of laughs, as famous characters are brought to their most ridiculous extremes.

So kick off your shoes (but watch out for the cat), sit back (still watching out for the cat), put your feet up (but not too high, or you'll screw up your circulation) and enjoy the wild antics of THE DOCTOR AND THE ENTERPRISE. You'll never be the same.

$9.95...........136 pages ISBN#1-55698-218-6 Heavily illustrated

The Lost In Space Tribute Book Written by James Van Hise
LOST IN SPACE remains television's second most popular science fiction series, only falling behind the legendary STAR TREK. The show began in 1965 and ran for five seasons, but has continued to live on in syndication ever since, with legions of fans clamoring for a reunion film.
Now, for the first time ever, Pioneer presents THE LOST IN SPACE TRIBUTE BOOK, the ultimate guide to this unique television series.
Author James Van Hise presents a guide to every episode aired during the series' run, plus exclusive interviews with the late Guy Williams, June Lockhart, Marta Kristen, Mark Goddard, Angela Cartwright, Bill Mumy, the Robot and, of course, Jonathan Harris, as well as various behind-the-scenes personnel.
As a special bonus, the book features blueprint reproductions and a guide to the Jupiter 2 spacecraft.
$14.95.........164 pages
Color Cover, Black and White Interior Photographs, Blueprints and Charts
ISBN# 1-55698-226-7

Couch Potato Inc.   5715 N. Balsam   Las Vegas, NV 89130   (702)658-2090